THE KOREANS

THE KOREANS

WHO THEY ARE, WHAT THEY WANT, WHERE THEIR FUTURE LIES

Michael Breen

Thomas Dunne Books
St. Martin's Griffin
New York

THOMAS DUNNE BOOKS
An imprint of St. Martin's Press.

ISBN 0-312-24211-5 (hc)
ISBN 0-312-32609-2 (pbk)

First published in Great Britain by Orion Business

First St. Martin's Griffin Edition: January 2004

10 9 8 7 6 5 4 3 2 1

For Mum and Dad

Contents

Preface

A relative of mine once asked me, 'Korea? That's part of Vietnam, isn't it?'
The question startled me because, after several years in the country, I had
started to feel that it was the centre of the world.

Korea has that effect on you. Its people are so dramatic, so passionate, and
the twentieth-century issues they have thrashed around with – colonialism,
communism, political violence, war, industrial development, democracy,
human rights – seem to be so important, that it is easy to forget that the
Koreans are not well known.

Although theirs is a middle-size country – north and south Korea are
roughly the same size as Britain and have a combined population of almost
70 million – Koreans feel small, because they live amid giants. Their
geopolitical neighbours are China, Japan, Russia and America, who between
them have done to Korea just about every nasty thing that can be done to a
smaller country. The Koreans learned to roll up into a ball and let
themselves be kicked in order to survive. It is no wonder that they conceive
of themselves as small.

Although only recently arrived to our attention, they are in fact an
ancient and complex people, whose rise out of poverty into democratic
capitalism is one of the inspirational themes of our age. Their authentic
history stretches back to the year AD 668, which makes them one of the
world's oldest nations, and the records of earlier history go back almost two
thousand years before that. This history has some notable peaks. The
Koreans had a civilising influence on ancient Japan. They were the first in
the world to use metal movable type for printing books.[1] They produced
some of the world's finest ceramic art. But Koreans themselves do not talk

so much about these achievements. They are in their own view a people made anew, reborn from a past they would sooner forget.

They are a vigorous and expressive people. But they also bear a terrible sadness and anger because of their history, which they can neither express nor completely shake off, and which many outsiders fail to understand. Foreigners who have entered that world of the Korean heart, through marriage or long exposure to the culture, find themselves in love and in hate with the people, plunging to great depths when touched by their passions, and released to the surface again in paroxysms of rage when expelled. For Koreans are a closed shop. There is probably no more homogeneous a country on earth. You feel that you are forever the guest, never the family member.

Guests are not supposed to give advice, but Korea is one of those countries that people always seem to be lecturing about how to behave and manage themselves. Close up, Koreans seem to always be making mistakes. The incredible thing is that they have created the world's 11th largest economy, and are becoming democrats, without having taken any of our advice.

At the time of writing, the North is suffering from extreme food shortages and the South is recovering from the near-collapse of its financial system. My experience of previous Korean crises suggests to me that the South will overcome its problems. It may eventually have no choice but to help the North to deal with its difficulties. The Koreans seem to possess a vigour so strong that it will probably propel them even more to the global centre stage in the next generation.

If this assessment is half accurate, it reinforces our need to know more about them. Who are these people who are entering our lives, as our employers and business partners, who study in our colleges and who make our cars and toys? What makes them different from the Chinese and the Japanese? Where have they come from and where are they heading? This book is an attempt to address our ignorance of the Koreans and answer these questions. It represents an effort to understand a passionate nation that is barging into a crowded world with its elbows out, demanding membership in the once-exclusive whites-only club of major powers.

The emphasis of this book is on the nature and values of Koreans and on the recent history which underlies their national development. It begins with an outline of Korean values and highlights some features of the national character. Part Two deals with the country's long and difficult history and the more recent traumas of colonisation by Japan and division into communist North and pro-Western South. Parts Three and Four are about how the south Koreans emerged from hopelessness and wrought miracles of change. After being written off as backward and incapable of development, they moved out of the paddy fields and into Silicon Valley in one generation. This growth, through the 1960s and 1970s, led in the 1980s to a historic shift from dictatorship to democracy. These processes continue and are laying the groundwork for possibly another miracle, reunification of the divided nation.

I have not especially studied, nor have any particular theories of, national psychology, or economic and political development which form the basis for these chapters. I write from a personal view about the character and achievements of the Koreans. It is mostly about the south Koreans, not the north Koreans, because they have been the miracle-makers and also because they are the people who are impacting our lives. The reader should assume that, unless otherwise stated in endnotes, quotations are from interviews conducted between 1982 and 1998.

The Koreans are not easy to understand. I lived for fifteen years in Seoul, for most of that time as a journalist and later as a business consultant, and have relied during that time on the expertise of others. They are too numerous to mention here. But for their specific input on this book, I would like to thank: Peter Bartholomew, Brian Barry, Steve Bradner, John Burton, Craig Campbell, Cho Gab-je, Jim Coles, Daniel Davies, Martina Deuchler, Aidan Foster-Carter, James Freda, Steve Glain, John Gustaveson, Jim Harting, Hong Suhn-kyong, Thae S. Khwarg, Ken Kaliher, Kil Jeong-woo, Kim Dae-jung, Kim Jung-eun, Kim Sang-hyun, Lynne Kim, Catherine Lee, Lee Han-woo, Lee Jung-hee, Lee Kyu-uck, Lee Na-mi, Lee Yoon-sang, Lee Young-ho, Mallory Leece, Bryan Matthews, Clare McVey, Moon Jin-ho, Moon Seung-yong, Moon Tahn IL, Laxmi Nakarmi, Noh Tae-hoon, Pai Hyung-il, Paik Sang-chang, Park Yong-soo, Park Young-sook, Paul Rogers, Roh Jae-won, Roh Sungil, Bill Rylance, Mark Setton, Michael Schuman, Shim Jae-hoon, Suh Joon-sik, Colin Turfus and Stephen Wright.

I should especially like to express my gratitude to John Burton, who, with Charles Scanlon, initially encouraged this project, and who spent a considerable amount of time going through the manuscript and offering ideas to improve it. I am also grateful to William Chasseaud, Aidan Foster-Carter, Steve Glain and Catherine Lee, who all read the whole or parts of the manuscript and pointed out mistakes and weaknesses. As they are all experts, I can confidently blame them for any that remain.

For additional help, thanks to Paul Barker, Richard Barlow, Choo Youn-kong and Kim Chin-wha. Harvey Reynolds of the US 8th Army library at Yongsan, Seoul, and Woo Jae-bok of the Korea Herald library were also very gracious with their time.

At Orion, credit goes to Martin Liu, the publishing director of business books, who identified the need for a book on Korea. I would also like to express my appreciation to Chelsey Fox, my agent, for representing me and guiding me through the mysteries of the publishing world. Finally, I owe a debt to my family. It is time I emerged from my bunker and spent some time with them.

Seoul, May 1998

Note on Korean spelling

Our alphabet does not have sufficient symbols to cover our own sound system, let alone the Korean. So it is not possible to convey precise Korean pronunciation via the English alphabet. Western authors on things Korean (other than linguists who prefer the unambiguous precision of what is called the Martin system) have always used the McCune-Reischauer system. In general, I have kept to this system. In a few cases, for the informal purposes of this book, I've taken a few liberties and made spellings simpler.

The reader should note that with Korean names, the surname comes first. This often creates confusion. Even a paper as scrupulous as *The New York Times* once referred in a news story to President Roh Tae-woo (1988–93) as 'Mr Woo'. To avoid this kind of embarrassment, many Koreans invert their names for the benefit of Westerners. I have kept to the Korean way, but have made two exceptions. The first is with Syngman Rhee, the south Korean president from 1948 to 1960. He should be Rhee Syngman. But he is so widely known by the westernised version that it might cause further confusion to switch it back. The other exception is that some endnotes refer to books in which a Korean author has published under the westernised version of his or her name.

Korean surnames generally have one syllable. There are some rare two-syllable surnames. The only one that appears here is that of Sakong Il, a presidential economic adviser, whose book on the Korean economy is listed in the bibliography. First names have either one or two syllables. When there are two syllables, one is a generational name shared by same-sex siblings and cousins. Usually they are separated by a hyphen, but some Koreans like to combine them into one word. Again, Syngman Rhee provides an example.

PART ONE

Society and Values

Chapter One

THE THREE MIRACLES

Most foreign journalists I know, at the end of a three-, four-, or five-year stretch in Seoul, will admit as they leave, 'I can't figure this place out.' This is not false modesty, but, for a journalist, admission of a serious professional problem.

There are many contradictions and obstacles to understanding. The Koreans are forthright and obscure at the same time. It is difficult to know when they are telling you what they think, what they think you want to hear, or what they want to happen. This last one is especially irksome for the information-gatherer. For example, a government specialist on north Korea might not discuss a collapse-and-absorption scenario for reunification with you, even off the record, because the government is afraid of it. He will predict gradual reunification as if willing it to happen.

This kind of communication failure manifests a lot in business. The foreign manager of the luxury Samsung-owned Shilla Hotel in Seoul once commissioned a marketing study by a consultancy. After some months, he wondered what had happened to it. The staff member who was handling the report had moved to another Samsung Group affiliate. The finished study was sitting on the man's desk, but his replacement had no idea what it was. The outgoing person had simply not mentioned it. This manager found that staff would never report bad news to him, because they saw it as ammunition that could be used against them, not as a means to improve customer service. He arranged for customer-survey sheets to come to his desk. By bypassing his own bureaucracy, he could get a sense of how the hotel was doing.

The local media can be extremely misleading as a source of information. They generally do not see their role as a check on government and business,

3

with the result that government intentions are frequently reported as facts. A huge proportion of news stories, when you follow them up, turn out to be speculation, trial balloons, rumour and deliberate distortion.

Opponents engage in a high degree of melodrama and posturing of the hold-me-back-or-I'll-hit-him variety. This creates another serious problem for journalists. Given that media thrive on words and images, it is easy to assume that posturing is the real thing. Given the absence of information and lack of understanding about north Korea, this can lead to very dangerous escalation. In the 1990s, the United States became very alarmed by north Korea's refusal to permit international inspection of its nuclear power sites. On two occasions in the 1990s, international TV reported that war was imminent on the peninsula and flew in correspondents to report on the 'mounting tensions' caused by north Korea. One of these moments developed in 1994, after a north Korea negotiator had lost his temper with a south Korean counterpart and threatened to turn the South into a 'lake of fire'. I was in a group that flew into Pyongyang around this time. We found the north Koreans almost oblivious to the excitement in the outside world. The mounting tensions were in Washington.[2]

For the person trying to nail down information and make sense of it, these difficulties make Korea one of the harder places to deal with. As one foreign journalist put it, 'You need a high-level bullshit indicator to figure out what's going on.'

Korea may be hard to read day to day. But viewed over the long term, its issues have been quite simple and definable. In the 1950s, the two halves of the country went to war. The question was, would the southern side, which the West was supporting, win and survive after the terrible slaughter was over? In the 1960s, the weaker South began to develop economically and the question was, would it succeed? By the 1980s, the question was, would democracy ever come? In the 1990s, the question is whether the powerful South could switch from a centrally directed, or dirigiste economy, to a truly free-market economy. Another current question is, what will become of north Korea? Will this communist nation reform or collapse and be absorbed into south Korea?

Underlying these simple issues has been a deeper question. The story of Korea is about the recovery of a lost national identity that equally affects 47 million people in south Korea, 23 million in north Korea and several millions in America, Japan, China and elsewhere who, although naturalised, may still consider themselves to be Koreans. After the Second World War, the Koreans came out of a half-century of Japanese domination with such a profound sense of worthlessness that they seemed to have lost any notion of who they were or where they came from. One foreign scholar recalls daily conversations with Korean students in the 1980s: 'There weren't many foreigners on campus and people always asked me where I was from and what I was studying. I'd say, "I'm studying Korean Thought" and they'd give me a puzzled look and say, "But we have no Thought." They didn't know the wealth of their intellectual history.'

Not only did the Koreans feel worthless and powerless. They were also a divided people. The barbed wire was rolled out along the 38th parallel in 1945. After much violence, it separated out left and right. This North-South border cut right through families, creating ideological enemies under the same roof, and eventually forcing millions of non-ideological Koreans to live in permanent involuntary separation from their close family.

In a cruel sense, the division of Korea after the Second World War served as a way out of worthlessness. Broadly, it seemed to offer two options, two alternative ways to be Korean. The underlying question for four decades was not how the two Koreas might be unified but, which alternative would win? Korea will be whole only when this choice is made, when one of the options is adopted by all Koreans.

The Koreans were forced apart by major powers. But, despite all the propaganda on both sides to the contrary, they have not struggled to come together again. Each side has struggled for ascendancy. That struggle is now over and the south Korean option has won. The south Koreans are the ones who are creating for all Koreans a sense of worth and a place in the world, and it is they who will set the tone for the future unified Korea. The question now is, will they manage it peacefully?

The reunification of the Koreas would certainly be an interesting event. But, beyond that, is it relevant to the West?

One of the big concerns since the end of the Korean War in 1953 has been a renewed warfare. Technically, north Korea's opponent is the United Nations. Practically, it is south Korea, the United States and several other countries, including Britain, who fought in the first war under the UN flag. South Korea has become important to us in other ways. International reaction to the financial crisis in 1997 was an indication of how important Korea had become. Most developed nations have some of Korea's foreign debt and there were fears that a default would trigger a monumental crisis in Japan, where there was already a banking crisis. The International Monetary Fund came in with its biggest ever bailout, lending the Koreans $58 billion to pay off short-term loans and avert bankruptcy.

We find ourselves increasingly drawn into a relationship with Korea. Once known as the Hermit Kingdom, the country was sealed tight against the outside world until this century. Although still obscure and inaccessible to the western perception, the Koreans are probably destined for leadership in the next century.

South Korea has provided an important development model for China and the developing eastern European states. Koreans also provide a crucial argument for the universality of democracy. Millions of Asians are convinced by the arguments in defence of authoritarianism and collective rights made by Asian intellectuals and politicians. They point to western social ills and blame democracy for what they see as western decadence. They say that they need a different type of democracy, one more relevant to their family-based heritage, a democracy with Confucian characteristics. The Koreans are disputing this position by virtue of their example, and demonstrating that democracy is universal. As Kim Dae-jung, the south Korean president, has put it: 'Culture is not necessarily our destiny. Democracy is.'[3]

Another reason that Korea will be important is because it has the will to be. No nation has been great without its own sense of manifest destiny. The south Koreans have been lifted up by a nationalistic self-assurance. In another time and in other circumstances, such sentiments may have led to imperialism or some kind of aggressive expansion. But the realities of the global village are likely to make the Koreans graduate into a confident internationalism. This is the paradigm change that Koreans are currently being pressured by the needs of their economy to make. If they are successful, as I believe they will be, their nationalistic energy will be transformed into a creative force behind a new generation of entrepreneurs, teachers and artists.

The Korean growth of the past decades has been led by small groups of powerful men in politics, business and in the military. The downside of their success has been the stifling of the creativity of the broader population. Many Koreans have emigrated, notably to the United States, where they have excelled in business and in education. The change is now coming that will allow for a flourishing of more individual economic and intellectual creativity within Korea itself.

Once they have our attention, we find there is so much that can be learned from the Koreans. Ironically, they are the last to acknowledge that they have something to teach the world. Although in public they assert a confidence, privately Koreans are extremely critical of themselves.

In many of the contradictory aspects of Koreans, I have found the most interesting lessons. They combine great flaming emotion with an extremely fine sense of etiquette. They devote themselves to work and they devote themselves to family. They often appear incompetent and yet they achieve. They ascribe to collective values and yet are probably the most individualistic of all east Asians. As Confucianists, they have an instinct for relationships. They can be quite aggressive, but extremely hospitable. They can be very sacrificial, yet realistic about their own needs. They are materialists. They pursue status and titles and yet these often just function as a guide for their behaviour, not as a source of ultimate worth. People of high status can be very sombre and serious and self-important. But then with their mates they're as free as little boys and girls. Grandmothers hire coaches with their pals and get drunk on outings. They can be puritanical about sexual relations and yet more uninhibited than lap-dancers. They are naturally conservative and yet have an ability to absorb differences. The stereotypical Korean is a materialistic shaman-Confucian-Buddhist-Christian. They are fascinating for an outsider to observe and work alongside for they have telescoped development which took several generations in western countries into the span of a working lifetime.

This passionate mix of contradictions can be difficult for the more ordered western mind to handle. As I have suggested, foreigners often find themselves responding in contradictory ways. They criticise Koreans a lot and yet they cannot tear themselves away from them. They might declare there is nothing good in the country, except of course their Korean spouse, who is the most important person in their life.

This contradiction is nicely symbolised for me by the way in which I grew to like Korean cuisine. The first time I was confronted by a soup in a Korean restaurant, I found it was too salty and too spicy, and full of murky items which for all I knew had been dropped in it by mistake. I was glad my host did not reveal the contents. It came surrounded with small plates on which there were leaves and twigs which we were plainly expected to eat. I picked up a bulging green pepper and bit into it. It was so hot it almost blew my face off. 'You're supposed to dip it in here,' another foreigner said. That's the Koreans, they dip peppers in a salty paste to spice up the taste. The proud master of these side dishes was a tight roll of what could have passed for used bandages. 'Have some kimchi,' my host said. So this was kimchi. I'd heard of this. It was strips of cabbage parts which had been drenched in red pepper juice. This was what smelled on people's breath in the underground. The courses kept coming. The side dishes were all shared. Everyone poked at them with their chopsticks. In the end, it was difficult to measure how much you had eaten, especially as half the food was left. This food was all washed down with beer.

But now I have grown to love this food so much and the socialising that goes with it that in Britain I have withdrawal symptoms. This cuisine is not the kind you admire visually. It's a kind of assault on the mouth, spice and salt, and so tied up in my mind with long nights with friends and sources and fascinating conversations and arguments that I can't be objective about it. For me, it's the best food in the world, after fish and chips. So, too, with the Koreans. They assault you with their fury and nonsense. I reckon if you were stuck on Mount Everest in a prolonged storm, there would be no more reliable and courageous companion than a Korean. The trouble is, he would be a smoker. If the cold didn't get you, the smoke would.

The Koreans are a very artistic people. It is a pity that much of their literature is inaccessible internationally because of language. Although the young generation prefers western music and films, there are some excellent local film-makers and musicians. One of their most powerful traditions is *pansori* singing. This art originated as a kind of blues. Ballads performed as a one-man or one-woman show over several hours to outdoor audiences. The *pansori* artist speaks, shouts, sings and mumbles her way through a tale. The mixture of forms was partly designed as a way to talk about the upper classes and let off steam in way that only the lower classes could fully understand. This old form was introduced to the younger generation in 1993 by the film director, Imm Kwon-taek, whose movie *Supyonje* told the story of a wandering performer who blinded his daughter so that she would stay with him and discover the soul of her art. Imm waited for years before he found the singer who he felt was right for the part. Seoul itself is packed with shops selling traditional folk craft. Antique chests and furniture, paintings and ceramics and pottery. Ancient stoneware and pots are still being dug up, usually illegally, and sold, at rising prices, mostly to Japanese tourists.

Someone several years ago described the Koreans as the 'Irish of the East'. You could pick other comparisons. They have suffered in this century as horribly as the Poles, their nation severed in two and millions of their people slaughtered. They are as vigorous in their character and the defence of their identity as the Israelis, and as chaotically attractive as the Italians. But the Irish label will do best, for it allows us most fully to highlight the broad themes of both the national character and their relationship with their neighbours. Because they are a divided people, like the Irish, they strike the casual outsider as being their own worst enemy. Their hatred has turned inward as a consequence of terrible violence. Of all the national divisions of modern times, that between north and south Korea has been the most vicious and extreme. However, like the Irish, the Koreans are also a lyrical people, inclined to the spiritual, and exhibiting

8

a warmth and hospitality that belies their violent image. They can be unrestrained in their passions, quick to cry and to laugh. One of the nicest aspects of Koreans is that they are not raised to feel that displays of emotion are a weakness. They push themselves to study and succeed. At the same time they can be embarrassingly earthy and blunt. If you have an ugly spot on your nose, the English and the Japanese will politely pretend it's not there. The Korean will stick his finger in your face and inform you, 'Hey, you've got a spot.' As if he couldn't tell from the deep fingernail grooves around it that you already knew.

There are, of course, constraints on Koreans, as there are on any other people. Law does not play such as central a role in controlling behaviour as it does in western society, but the need to be accepted by peers is more crucial for survival. There are aspects of Korean society that westerners would recognise in their own. (I've been surprised a few times after describing the authoritarian culture of a company to a westerner to be told, 'Yes that reminds me of this British company I worked for ...'). Most differences are explained by legal, political or economic factors. But there is a fundamental divergence between Confucian and Christian ideals, which underscores many of the differences between east Asian and western society. In our society, our lingering class structure notwithstanding, we basically take each person to be of equal value. Society is ordered by an idea of justice. Law is therefore crucial in restraining and guiding behaviour. Noble feelings do not beat in the heart of each member, but there is a general ideal of equality. In east Asia, proper relationships are the ideal. These relationships are mostly understood as variations on family relations. Koreans actually call strangers by familial terms – *ajossi* (uncle) for an older man, *eggie oma* (baby's mum) for a young mother, *halmoni* (grandmother) for an elderly lady, and so on. There is an active effort to cultivate affectionate relationships with people in society whom you see as your 'family members'.

Egalitarian westerners note that family relationships are essentially unequal and do not see a society as a super-extended family. In fact, we consider such an idea of society to be conducive to corruption. Although we recognise that some have greater authority or experience, we feel uncomfortable with the inherent inequality in a world-view which requires people to conceive of themselves vertically. Again, not all Korean hearts beat to the rhythm of Confucian virtue, but society has been built around such ideals. Given the vertical nature of Korean relationships, we may pose an image of the Koreans as being in a more or less ordered pile, concentrated in their capital, and scrambling upwards. In such an environment in which society is ranged vertically up the power pile, status is the key to everything and is sought by all. Koreans are careful not to indulge in behaviour that will damage theirs.

In such a society, everyone is a politician. You find that the Koreans are extremely skilled at etiquette and strategic behaviour. At the same time, the harsh fact of strong central authority has created a passivity, an acceptance of the realities of power. Although this is beginning to change in politics, it is still apparent in organisations and companies where people often feel it is best to keep quiet, rather than offer suggestions and speak out. Authoritarian structures act as a brake on behaviour and self-expression, and were probably at work in the minds of those passive, staring people that early western travellers and imperialists came across in east Asia and whom they considered to be 'inscrutable orientals'.

Although they come from the same Confucian-influenced part of the world, Koreans are different from the Chinese and Japanese. They strike a foreign observer as much more individualistic, free and expressive than their neighbours. Women's dress illustrates the differences. The traditional Korean *chima* flattens down the breasts, but splays out and allows sufficient flexibility for you to run about and kick a ball in one. The Japanese *kimono*, by contrast, wraps the legs up so tight that a woman is forced to shuffle along with subservient small steps. I'm not sure what to make of the Chinese tradition of foot-binding.

Ancestry is of common importance in east Asia. My own paternal ancestors came from Ireland to Scotland during the potato famines of the mid-nineteenth century. An Irishman in Seoul once rebuffed my attempt at finding common ground with a snort that my ancestors were probably 'bloody soupers'. These, I was aware, were Catholic peasants whom the British fed during the famine on condition that they convert to Protestantism. (The evidence, he said, was that my forbears went to Presbyterian Scotland, not to America.) This was an untypical exchange, but it led me to ponder over my luck at coming from a country where ancestry doesn't matter to most people. If I were a Japanese of Korean descent, I may have to conceal the fact from both Japanese and Koreans to be seen as pure.

In many ways, the Japanese are rather like the middle- and upper-class British, restrained and polite and rather condescending. The Japanese find their neighbours coarse, hurtful and sullen, about what they don't quite know, except it has something to do with historical whining. They fail to grasp, because they've not been taught, that they have been a source of immense suffering. The Japanese occupation of Korea from 1905–45 was not just a historical experience. It was the brutal capping of hundreds of years of abuse by foreign powers. The Chinese dominated Korea for centuries, but this period is recalled as more of a Confucian older brother–younger brother relationship than as political abuse. The Chinese also suffered under the Japanese.

You will see on the map that Korea hangs out of north-east China at the eastern end of the Asian massif. It lies gripped in the fist of China, touched by a fingernail of Russia, over the foot-shaped islands of Japan, which sit fluid in the sea and fractured as if from the endless kicking of the poor Koreans. The hapless peninsula is even squashed in a bit from this drumming. To continue this cartographical theme, I will note that the shapes of Korea and Britain are very similar, but upside down, as if they were made for each other. I used to point this out to Koreans as a lead-in to the undiplomatic suggestion that their experience may have been more fortunate if the British and not the Japanese had taken over as colonial masters at the beginning of the twentieth century. It's a suggestion that doesn't go down well. The history is still too close and painful to consider such airy options. Their question is by what calculation should they ever have been dominated at all? It is more of a primal scream than a question. Indeed, in a way, the extraordinary rise of the Koreans out of their poverty and subjection can be seen as one prolonged primal, raging yell of 'Never again'.

It is too insulting to suggest that an entire people are barking into the pillow any more than we are, but there is a complex psychological factor behind Korean growth, which I will try to address in later chapters. The important aspect about it to note here is that Korean growth is not a manifestation of negative motivation. Rather it is a manifestation of a determination not to remain in the grip of self-doubt and poverty. It is frequently assessed as a rapid sequence, that at each stage proved all the experts wrong and stunned even the Koreans themselves. In short, miracles. These are a people who are making miracles. In fact, one travel writer, who ignored warnings of violence and wretchedness to visit the country, ended up writing a book on this theme of Korean miracles.[4] The word was first employed by foreign experts as a neat way to deflect the status-threatening question of why they hadn't seen the economic development coming. The clever thing to do had been to write the Koreans off at each stage along the way. So the growth was, er, miraculous. Although it has since become rather overworked in reference to the economic rise, it is an appropriate way to describe this case of escape from the past, because even in an era when the entire world is moving out of poverty and injustice, the Korean case is notable because it was so unlikely.

The Koreans had survived over the centuries as a separate people because of their fierce sense of identity, honed by a distinct language and the adoption of Chinese Confucianism in a more extreme application than the Chinese themselves. What is extraordinary is that they managed this with very little protective state power. Their leaders were scholarly, in contrast to the warlike Japanese. Rather than exhaust themselves fighting and get obliterated, they employed an instinctive tendency to roll over when faced with superior power. They survived, sullenly and fractiously, but intact.

However, in the modern period, the conditions that allowed for this survival worked against economic growth. Passive and scholarly people do not run factories so well. It took a revolution in the 1960s by what used to be considered an underclass, the military, before the Koreans began to work hard and purposefully. Now, in the last fifteen years of this century, we have been seeing these people thrown out and cleaned up, for theirs was a very corrupt relationship, by the new society that they created.

The ejection of the first miracle-makers was the defining aspect of the second miracle, the one which is bringing democracy. I was in Korea through the 1980s to see this one begin. At the time, it seemed so unlikely. People were worried that the dictatorship of Chun Doo-hwan (1980–8) was getting more entrenched. But the wave of economic growth was affecting all, dictators and dictated. Still, when this wave broke and Chun conceded in 1987 and democracy rolled in, it did so with all the characteristics of a miracle. In later chapters, we will look more closely at these events.

In terms of the national healing and the miracles, the Koreans are in midflow. There is another miracle to come. The third and final part of the Korean healing will be the reunification of its bitterly divided halves. There are various scenarios for how it may happen. But when it does, I wonder if the Koreans will not be so locked into the patterns of growth that they will, by habit, look around for a new goal. They may even try to overtake Japan. A lot of ancestral fists will be punching air should that come to pass.

The worst of Korean memories all seem in one way or another wrapped up with Japan. As part of Japan, colonial Korea was on the losing side of the Second World War and, in 1945, was divided into two zones and occupied by the armies of the Soviet Union and the United States. This led three years later to the establishment of two separate and independent states. The North was pro-Soviet, and the South was pro-American. The Koreans that the West is coming to know are the south Koreans. They are the miracle-makers. The story here is one of healing and the north Koreans, unfortunately, took bad medicine, and are, as we write, in many ways worse off than they were thirty years ago. But one way or another, they will be grafted on to the new Korea that the South has created, either by a collapse and absorption or by a more friendly process.

Despite the involvement of 87,000 British troops in the United Nations' forces fighting for the South during the 1950–3 Korean War, Korea has never figured significantly in the British imagination. Partly because of the war, it has always been considered a distant and rather grim place. The old perceptions are rapidly changing. We now find south Korean students in our towns studying at language institutes and preparing for entry into British public schools. Thousands of British companies deal with Koreans. We are buying Korean cars, Hyundais, Daewoos and Kias, and electronics equipment, not just shoes and teddy bears. We are reminded of the time we couldn't quite pinpoint a couple of decades or more ago when 'made in Japan' was quietly upgraded from a pejorative. Britain has now become the investment location of choice for Korean companies looking at Europe, with the big groups such as Samsung, Daewoo, LG and Hyundai now familiar names. Incredibly, the children of those ragged refugees who, in 1950, stood politely to the side of the dirt track and clapped as our uncles in the British regiments moved to the front, run some of the biggest conglomerates in the world. When we recall that over 1000 British troops were killed in the Korean War, it is surprising that we have not tracked the Korean performance more closely as a measurement of the value of that sacrifice of British men. The Koreans remember.

There is a moving tale of a blind American war veteran who visited Korea with his family in the 1970s as part of a veterans programme organised by the Korean government. The man had lost his sight on a Korean battlefield and was extremely resentful that he had been sent to fight in their irrelevant civil conflict. He had sent an anti-Korean letter to a newspaper, which was spotted in the States by the programme organiser, a Korean, who responded by challenging the man to visit. He accepted and spent a week in the group, touring the country with his wife and twelve-year-old son acting as his eyes. They created in his mind's eye new images of the rebuilt country to replace the Nissen huts and ruins of twenty-five years earlier. At the end of their visit, the veterans had an audience with Park Chung-hee, the dictator who started the country's economic development. Paris went down the line, shaking hands with the visitors, and when he reached the blind man, he shook his hand warmly and his wife's, and then he took their son's hand and leaned over and said to him, 'I have heard about your father. He lost his eyes so that our country could be free.' The man broke down and cried.[5]

One of the recent consequences of the rapid change has meant an end to the predominant presence of Americans on the Korean landscape – so

13

dominant was it in fact that the Korean word for them, *mee-guk saram*, was used for any non-Asian – and a fast-rising awareness of other nations. The British are among the most popular, for the Koreans know a bit about our history and literature. They are taught in school that we are 'gentlemen', one of those nice bubbles of prejudice in our favour that it would be unkind to pop.

So, as the relationship deepens, we will find that the Koreans are going increasingly to be our friends, our students, our teachers, our partners, our employers and employees. And it's nice that they talk of us as gentlemen. It's much nicer than the way we have been talking about them.

Chapter Two

IMAGE AND IDENTITY

As a boy, I used to collect picture-card flags of the world and stick them in a scrapbook. I remember, when I was about eight, making a list of all the nations, their capitals and the rivers that flowed through them. Seoul was the capital of the South because they both began with 'S'. I got the north Korean capital, Pyongyang, mixed up with Phnom Penh, the Cambodian capital. That's my first memory of Korea.

A Korean friend once taught me the first two lines of a folk song called 'Arirang'. In a street in Chester once, I found myself in a brief conversation with a young oriental man. When he said he was Korean, I sang the lines of the song to impress him. He looked at me in an electric way, as if I were a long-lost brother, and his eyes filled with tears. This experience came back to me many years later when I was on a crowded underground train in Seoul and a student asked me if he could practise his English on me, a common proposition on the underground. Assuming I was an American, he launched into a loud, heavily accented rendition of John F. Kennedy's inauguration speech, which he had learned by heart: 'Ask not what your country can do for you. Ask what you can do for your country.' I tried to suppress him with quiet conversation, feeling all the time I had been accosted by a maniac, until, mercifully, we arrived at his stop. I realised that even if he had been quoting Churchill, I would have found the encounter embarrassing. I wondered then why I had felt assaulted by a mad native politician, while my lonely Chester friend saw in me a touch of home.

The answer lies in the relative awareness and images of our countries that we encounter abroad. When Koreans go abroad, what knowledge and feelings about their country can they expect to run into?

Until very recently, if you asked anyone the first half-dozen words that

15

came into their mind when you said the word 'Korea', they would probably have selected from among: divided, violent, riots, police, military, grim, war, corruption, tariffs, Olympics, World Cup, freezing, MASH, cars, ships, computer chips, financial crisis. And they would be the people who read broadsheet newspapers. For them, those economic words are creeping up the charts. But people who read tabloids will still say: communist, starving, dog-eating, football, cars, sex industry, Mao Tse-tung, south-east Asia, tropical, grass skirts. You can see near the end that they start to lose it. Not much is known about Korea, and what is, is overwhelmingly negative. This appraisal is by no means new.

Beatrice Webb, the socialist, thought the Japanese were OK, good potential socialists, but found the Koreans 'horrid'.[6] The writer, James Kirkup didn't seem to regard the Koreans very highly either, and considered the Irish of the East epithet an 'insult to the Irish'.[7] His baptism was in Seoul in the bitterly freezing winter.

> Lying between chill sheets that night in my icy room, I tried to organize my first impressions of Seoul. In the back of my mind I felt that the place reminded me of somewhere I had been before. The impression of gloom and darkness and wildness could not be dispelled ... and everywhere there was the curiously clanging, grumbling tone of Korean speech. From time to time I was reminded of northern Japanese towns in winter time – Akita, Aomori, Niigata or Sapporo. But then it flashed into my mind that what Seoul really reminded me of was the Arctic: the bare, freezing desolations on the outskirts of Kiruna and Narvik.[8]

The stifling summer can also put off authors. In the mid-1960s, the British journalist James Cameron took the train from the southern port of Pusan up to Seoul and penned this unforgettable description:

> The sun seemed abruptly to leap into the sky and the heat came pouring down. And with the heat, the smell; it rose off the fields almost visibly as the morning grew. Although as one's experience of Korea lengthened the first revulsion dulled, the smell remained as a background for all other sensations. This characteristic of Korea – the hand-fertilizing of the paddies with domestic ordure – was of course by no means unique in the East, but it is a fact that here it reached an especial concentration of evidence. I have never known a country where there was a more lively and thriving commerce in human excrement, even throughout the continent of Asia, which always seems to Europeans excessively reluctant to part with its sewage.[9]

What a smell! What a style! Cameron is of course describing what he sees and, out of journalistic integrity, should not be expected to air-freshen his experience to avoid hurt feelings. But imagine the identity crisis for our Korean abroad when he meets people, who he knows are thinking, 'Oh, yes, Koreans, the sewage people.' He might well feel that, were he to complain, they would simply retort, 'Well, old boy, if you funny chaps put your poo-poo where it belonged, you wouldn't have these problems. Ha ha.' So, in the face of superior power, he suppresses his hurt, and waits.

I came across these descriptions many years ago in a book of excerpts of travel writings about different countries over the centuries, in the British Council library in Seoul. Korea got only one page and the tone was all negative. Japan, by contrast, had several pages of quotes by foreign visitors going on about lotus ponds and stone gardens. Japan! Psychopathic domination of Asia? No-panties coffee shops? No. Mainly landscape gardening.

The faecal peasant has receded into history, but this attitude of western disdain by Cameron still remains. The favourite of Seoul-based correspondents, and one which is widely accepted in that community as the greatest opening paragraph on Korea in the history of the universe, is by the American humourist P.J. O'Rourke, who visited in 1987 and saw a political rally. 'When the young man bit off the end of his finger and wrote the name of Kim Dae-jung in blood on his white anorak, then I knew for the first time what it meant to be a foreign correspondent – I mean, here was something that was really f****** foreign.'[10]

Admittedly, this is a selective edit on my part in order to make the point that negative views of Korea seem to prevail. I confess I find this puzzling because, even when Korea was extremely impoverished, the impressions of visitors changed with exposure to the people. One of the first travellers to write on the country was Isabella Bird Bishop, who arrived in Pusan about a century ago and found it to be 'a decayed and miserable town' full of 'mangy dogs and bleary-eyed children'.[11] Her description of 'low hovels built of mud-smeared wattle' and reeking ditches carrying off domestic refuse sounds medieval. And yet: 'The distaste I felt for the country at first passed into an interest which is almost affection, and on no previous journey have I made dearer and kinder friends, or those from whom I parted more regretfully.'[12]

Although the causes of 'distaste' have changed, this passage matches my own experience. I have found this to be common among expatriates. The Koreans have a way of upsetting you and getting into your heart at the same time. The first time I realised that other people felt this way was during the opening ceremony of the Seoul Olympics in 1988. I was sitting high up in the stands in a row of about twenty foreign correspondents. We were not sports writers, but reporters based in Seoul and Tokyo who covered business and politics. We had experienced numerous run-ins with government spokesmen over our relentless coverage of protests and government abuses. But here we were not working, just enjoying the fact that the Olympic organisers had given us free tickets. The ceremony began with the parade of nations. Our own teams came in and we felt bursts of patriotism. Some teams marched in ranks, and others, especially the Americans, treated it like a party. There were various types of uniforms and costumes and some famous faces. It was exciting and we were noisy. Right at the end, the large Korean team entered the stadium in formal step. When we spotted them, our line spontaneously rose to its feet, something we had not done for our own teams. There was a chain reaction and within a few seconds the entire media and VIP section was standing up and applauding the Koreans. Perhaps the VIPs would have stood anyway, out of respect, but they were beaten to it by the people who were probably the country's biggest critics. I saw then that Korea had got to other journalists, too. I think what we had in common was not simply exposure to the country. More importantly, these were people who were making the effort to understand Koreans.

I have found the single biggest obstacle to understanding Koreans has been their nationalism. The first problem with nationalism is that it can be so parochial that it discourages you from wanting to make the effort with people. The Koreans use the image of the frog in the well to explain their own parochialism. All the frog knows of the outside world is the distant patch of sky at the top of the well. The only reality is what happens in the well where it lives. North Koreans offer an extreme example of existence in a narrow band of experience. I've been told by very sincere young north Koreans that Kim Il-sung is the most famous political leader in the history of the world. Even young south Korean intellectuals develop theories which suggest that the history of the twentieth century is a deliberate plot against Korea.

The frog is, by definition, a racist. Arriving at the airport once, I was waiting in line and watching an immigration official deal with a man who looked Indian or Nepalese. I guessed he was coming to Korea for labouring work. Something was not in order and the visitor had to fill in another form. As he was doing this the official must have decided that it should be handled by someone else. He leaned over the counter and slapped the man on the head with a sheaf of papers and jerked his thumb over to the left as if to say, 'Over there.' This scene was met with some incredulous exchanges between westerners in the queue. Although westerners do not get abused in this way, every foreigner is seen as a different species who dropped into the well by mistake.

I figure that the way to deal with nationalism in people, who aren't sticking a gun in your face, is to recognise that it is necessary, almost like a phase they have to go through. This education came by way of westerners in international marriages. One American friend, married to a Korean, had two bilingual daughters in the Seoul International School, where classes were in English and many teachers were foreigners. The older child, who was twelve, started to declare that she was American. My friend's wife became extremely agitated when the daughter announced she did not want to go to church with her mother any more because it was a Korean church.

'I persuaded my wife that it was just a phase,' he said. 'A child has to be able to identify with the larger group, to know where she comes from. She wasn't really rejecting her Korean identity. My wife saw it in terms of ethnicity and I saw it in terms of values. My daughter was just reflecting that she was working out this process.' If this process is smooth and healthy, the potential for disturbance passes. I appreciated then that I had been British and OK with it for such a long time that I never thought about it. In a similar way, Korean nationalism is a working out of something that has not gone so smoothly.

This may be a strategy to understand people, but it does not, of course, mean that you are required to accept their behaviour. I asked a foreign banker who has worked closely with the leading conglomerates in Seoul what he felt about all this and, once I agreed not to mention his name, he went into this tirade:

'I make it a point never to buy any Korean products on principle. Why? I will not support such a rabidly nationalistic, xenophobic and mercantilist economy. Koreans are so predatory and nationalistic. They have a closed economy and a zero-sum attitude to trade. Protectionism in the early stages of an economy is not unreasonable. But in the case of Korea it is almost a religious doctrine to keep foreign things out. If you buy a foreign car, you're seen as a traitor. They pick narrow industrial sectors and all jump in like copycats. If I see a Korean sports team, I root for the other side. Why? Because they're so full of themselves that they leave no room for other parties to participate and enjoy themselves. The 1988 Olympics was worse than the Hitler Games of 1936. Dealing with Koreans is like dealing with bright adolescents. They're full of energy and want to do everything yesterday. But they throw tantrums and are prone to dangerous and erratic behaviour if their whims are not indulged. In most countries, intellectuals

19

become universal. You learn that great ideas and values have no national boundaries. What is profoundly disturbing is that Korean intellectuals become more xenophobic and nationalistic, and perpetrate the idea that all of Korea's problems are the result of wilfulness by foreigners. This is the mark of a scoundrel.'

'But,' he said after a pause, 'I love many aspects of Korea.'

Such views are not confined to foreigners. Koreans themselves are their own worst critics. The retired chairman of one of the large conglomerates, who also asked not to be identified slagging off his own country, had this to say on the same theme:

'Koreans are very ambitious but, unlike the Japanese, we don't know how to get along with each other. The Japanese individually are not as forceful as we are, but collectively they are very powerful. I'm an engineer so I don't know the reasons, but I think our problem is the backwardness of our minds. Perhaps because we had so many invasions. In war, people try to survive and you can't trust others easily. Distrust developed throughout our history. I think we distrust each other out of a kind of survival instinct. If I don't trust others, I have a better chance of surviving. We are a small country. Outwardly we are obedient to big powers and to our bosses, but inwardly we rebel. It is so difficult for us to change this. We like to show off and pretend we have more than we do. Heaven has a plan and gives each nation a destiny. Somehow we feel our time is coming. But people sense this and get overambitious and greedy. Koreans are greedy for more than God has given us. You see this mentality in business all the time. In your country, democracy didn't just drop from heaven. You had a certain history and there were problems along the way and you could advance by solving them. There are steps to go through. But we Koreans want to avoid the steps. We are a greedy, backward and selfish people.'

Koreans have a bad image of themselves. It's no wonder, then, that their image overseas needs some improving.

It's a constant frustration that the few opportunities they get to promote their international image run such a strong risk of getting sabotaged. Once, when a Korean President, Roh Tae-woo, was visiting Britain, animal-rights activists chose that event to publicise their efforts to expose dog-eating by Koreans. The activists, quite rightly, were not objecting to the fact of eating dog – after, all, we eat rabbits, which grosses a lot of people out – but the cruel method of killing them. Dogs are hung up and beaten to death, the idea being that the terror drives adrenaline into their muscles, which apparently makes the meat better. When he arrived in Britain, the media bloodhounds hung Roh up for similar treatment. Korean diplomats were extremely offended when British tabloids urgently advised the Queen to lock up her pet corgis.

Of course, the offended is also an offender. In Korea, you see this problem in reverse. There, because most foreign countries are so little known, a single association with them can throw their image off in the Korean mind. Several hotels in Korea, especially those near hot-springs resorts, have Turkish baths (*turkey-tang*). These are places where men are bathed, oiled and sexually massaged in a private room by a young woman. As they're the main association in the Korean awareness with the word 'Turkey', I was always surprised that it took the Turks so long to complain. In Japan they did years ago, and the baths there were renamed 'Soapland'. But in Korea, they didn't complain until 1996. The establishments were ordered by the government to change their name. They agreed and the matter was settled. Now they're called steam baths.

A different kind of insensitivity cropped up in June 1997, when an advertisement which used Adolf Hitler to promote chewing gum appeared on Korean television.[13] Hitler doesn't mean much for Koreans. I was once in a cinema in Seoul where a documentary feature on him was showing and the audience was riveted by the close-up shots and analysis of how he could get a mass audience in his emotional grip. Behind me, two young men kept saying 'waaaah' (Korean for 'wow') in admiration. I looked around the cinema and sensed that Adolf was working his magic there. It was understandable in a political culture where mass mobilisation of people is still a feature of politicking, and the Nazi evils are remote. The ads were withdrawn after formal complaint by the German government.

We cannot let this subject of national image pass without noting that Korean travellers overseas are not helping to improve the country's standing. It is apparent from the volume of stories you hear about Koreans abroad that they are giving their country a name for coarse selfishness. Airline people remark about the difficulties of dealing with Korean passengers and newspaper stories describe how they have been banned from some girlie bars in Thailand and the Philippines. I was interrogating a British stewardess on a flight to Seoul about this once. She was saying that the Korean flight was the worst of the entire global network. I said I couldn't understand what the problem was. As we were talking, a short, stocky Korean man pushed passed me and barked, 'Ya! Whisky!' ('Ya' is the Korean for 'oi'). She served him silently and when he'd gone, she said, 'You see what I mean?' Cross my heart, I had hardly noticed him except that our conversation stopped for a minute. So that was it? It's because they know what they want but haven't been trained to say 'please'?

Chapter Three

KOREAN HEART

Korea is an exquisitely beautiful country. It is three-parts coastline and has a lot of dramatic mountains squeezed up from its shores, just like Scotland. From the air, if you arrive on the right day, the first view can be breathtaking. The peaks stand in mystic ranks, separated by swelling mists, as if posing for an oriental painting. In winter, between snowfalls, a clothing of brown trees pokes out of the lower hills, like the stiff fur of a boar's hide. Spring starts in the south, in Cheju Island, and rolls up the peninsula in a wave of blossom, magnolia, forsythia and azaleas, and full green vegetation breaks out of the glens and crawls high up the slopes, where it collapses in glorious Canadian colours in the autumn. Bears and tigers used to roam the steep forested slopes. There are other dangers. In south Korea, the arrival of spring used to signal the start of the official north Korean infiltrator season when agents were expected to make use of the thick vegetation as cover. The grass on the hills is coarse. A stunning exception is a part of Cheju island, off the south coast, where an Irish Catholic priest has introduced sheep and, after some bureaucratic battles, was allowed to import soft grass from New Zealand for them to graze on.

Given its rugged beauty and variety, it may seem surprising that many foreign residents find rural Korea inaccessible and forbidding, as if they had come to fight a war in it, which of course many recent ones have. American soldiers have to be coaxed by organised tours to venture off base. Many foreigners just forget the countryside is there. Most residents in Seoul, for example, would be hard pressed to name the mountains that stick out in and around the city. It struck me once, as I stared out of my fourteenth-floor office window at a nearby mountain that I'd been idly looking at for five years, that I didn't know what it was called.

In part, Korea's beauty is made less accessible by the local ideas of tourism. This is a country that does not present itself as well as it could. It is not arranged for the cyclist, the hill walker, the history buff. There are plenty of *yogwans* (inns) but staying in them can often be an ordeal because of noise. They cater to drunken groups of all ages more than for individuals. A better option are the Buddhist temples. They are usually located in areas suited for meditation and allow visitors to stay for months if they wish.

The more popular bits of countryside are so assaulted by visitors that one gets dissuaded from taking to them for relaxation. You know when summer's arrived because every year at the right time the newspapers carry pictures of 'half a million' sunbathers sweltering on the sandy crescent of Haeundae Beach, on the edge of the city of Pusan.

But this mobbing of one or two resorts does not explain why the rest of the countryside seems to recede into irrelevance. I used to think it was psychological, that somehow because the peninsula was so militarised and latent with violence, it could not appear embracing and beautiful, as the Scottish Highlands do. I now think in my case it was because I was overtaken by the sheer impact of dealing with the Koreans themselves. Mountains don't come into your office without appointments and expect you to talk all afternoon. Nor do they ring you up at midnight and say, 'It's Kim.' Koreans do, all the time.

South Korea is the fifth most densely populated country in the world. Consider, too, that 70 per cent of its land is uninhabitable mountains, and add the tendency to crowd into cities, where people seem to live on top of each other. Even modern, organised, hygienic Korea still strikes me as a crowded, jumbled mess. Big jars storing kimchi and other food, which used to be buried in plots by the farmhouse, and other junk litter the balconies of modern apartments, rubbish is placed outside on the street where the garbage man comes along daily with his handcart to carry it off. Kitchens and storerooms spill out into the dining areas of restaurants. Workshops and garages tumble across the pavements into the streets. Shopkeepers pile box upon box of produce on to the shelves without regard for merchandising and stack their empty crates in front of their windows on the pavements. Despite the jumble, the streets are clean and free of litter. Economic growth has created an abundance, but neatness and order, like democracy, come hard. How fitting for such a wild, passionate, disordered and intrusive people, who are, despite all this, their country's magnificent resource.

Koreans are very much in the here and now. Although they have a very

23

long and remarkably well-documented history, they take little genuine pride in it. They prefer to take you to a Samsung Electronics plant than to an ancient temple. As one whose eyes also glaze over in castles and temples, it took me a while to figure that the Koreans' attitude to their history was unusual. This revelation came one dark evening in the bar of the Seoul Foreign Correspondens' Club, which is on the eighteenth floor of a building where my office was, bang in the centre of the city. We were talking about tourism.

'What do you see out there?' said a Korean friend, a tourism expert. He was pointing down to the grounds of the historic Doksu Palace. It was pitch black.

'Where?'

'Down there.' He pointed again.

'Well, it's the Doksu Palace, but you can't really make it out,' I said.

'Exactly,' he said.

'What?' I wasn't quite following this Socratic method.

'Can you imagine any other major capital city in the world which hides its most historic sites like this? All the other palaces are the same. You can't see them at night. They should be floodlit for everyone to see.'

This piece of common sense had never occurred to me and I had never heard it mentioned before. You get so used to things. In the centre of this modern city, amid the lights from offices where people were working late, the street lights and cars, were patches of blackness that concealed its most fascinating monuments.

'Is it because they don't know what tourists like to see?' I ventured, instinctively proposing that we criticise the government.

'It's because we Koreans hate our history,' he said. 'We don't want to think about it and we don't want to show it.'

He was only partly right. Koreans have bought into a negative view of their own history in this century. They do not have a regard for their past, not just because it is painful, but more significantly because they do not know how to look at it.[14]

This is a complex issue which starts with how Koreans are trained in school to think. The academic approach to information gathering and learning is not based on the analytical, empirical approach which we use. In the western system, we tend to start with a theory. Upon this foundation, we pile bricks of information. The theories get modified, the significance of the information adjusted. But essentially this is how we analyse, understand and remember things. To give an unrelated example, almost every wildlife programme you can see on TV is based on an evolutionary theory of the survival of the fittest. It is quite simple. Animals live to survive and reproduce. Every piece of information is explained and becomes interesting and relevant because it shows the million ways in which animals defend against predators, find their mates, protect their young. You could look at history in a similar way. How did this society begin? How did it develop? Why did it collapse? We tend to look at human society age by age and figure what we can from artefacts, music, and other evidence of the flowering and changing of culture. But Koreans are not taught political theories, as such. They learn facts.

Historical facts are important from the point of view of a nationalistic, semi-political pride. Questioning and analysing them is not seen as valid. In fact, questioning in class, even at university, is seen as a challenge and an insult to the teacher. In our own history, painful memories and victories are classified, categorised, prioritised, used as supporting evidence, and in this way remembered as a part of history. In Korea, details disappear, and memories are triggered only by anecdotes. As a young American Peace Corps volunteer in the late 1960s, Peter Bartholomew used to teach at a school near the eastern end of the DMZ, the demilitarised border zone which separates the two Koreas. 'In those days, the north Koreans were trying to create a Vietnamese-type uprising,' he said. 'They sent spies and saboteurs. At dusk every day you could hear rifle fire and a couple of times a week south Korean paratroopers were dropped and shore batteries would start up. Every day for about two years, the rifle fire would start around dinner time. In fact, I still get hungry when I hear the sound of rifles. Bodies of infiltrators would be displayed out in front of local police stations to show what happened to north Koreans and collaborators in the villages. If they caught one alive, they'd make the same point by hanging him from a chopper and flying over the villages. But you don't hear these stories. You only hear about the big ones, the few occasions when there was a large group of guerrillas. But these incidents were constant. There was a state of semi-war for years, but it's never mentioned. I don't mean officially. I mean in conversation with the people who experienced it. Why? Because there's nothing to trigger the memory.' The point is that in the western mind, such memories would be classified in a way to give them relevance, so that they would be recalled more readily.

We assume that Koreans deliberately conceal information because until recently they lived in a dictatorship. But this is not necessarily true. The systems, thought process and felt need may not exist to analyse it and store it in the way that we accept.

Bartholomew, now a businessman in Seoul, is an amateur expert in

Korean architecture. He was once invited to give a lecture on architecture and landscaping of the royal palaces to an audience of academics and government officials. 'They knew more about the subject than I did, so I was a bit nervous. I gave a presentation on how the palaces were organised, the economics involved, why they were expanded, abandoned, how aesthetics, royal affairs and politics affected them, and how you could see all this by looking at them. When I'd finished there was silence and then they applauded. People came up and said that they knew all the facts I had mentioned and more, but that they had never thought of drawing parallels and linking them up in this way.'

The Korean way is not to categorise, not to create in the listener's mind, in this example, an overall picture of the buildings, and explain why they were built, in a way that visitors to the palace could relate to. Thus, convincing westerners why they should visit, say, Doksu Palace, does not come naturally. Until I met Bartholomew, the Doksu compound always struck me as a boring collection of buildings with slopey roofs. Why bother to floodlight them? Why, indeed? even Koreans would ask. What they are unaware of is that their fascinating and dramatic history could, if they tried, be brought alive for the visitor.

So much tourism potential is ignored. For example, Sung-kyun-kwan University in Seoul is the oldest university in the world in terms of a set of standing buildings. The classrooms, offices and library built in the fourteenth century are still there.[15] No tour groups ever visit them. There are twelve ancient palaces in Seoul. But there is no map showing where they are and what's in them. Numerous historical sites have been bulldozed. There used to be a stone marking the centre of the old walled city, but it disappeared during construction work in the 1980s. When you do visit places, the interesting things are not explained. At the Tower of London, a guide has visitors going 'ugh' and 'aaah' when he describes a famous execution. Then he will end with a flourish by telling you that the head rolled on the very spot where the Japanese lady there is now standing. Korea's history is full of such drama. But you're more likely to come away from a palace knowing how many tiles are in the roof than hearing any of it.

Korea would appear to have a considerable number of inbound foreign tourists. But the figures of around 3 million tourists a year are misleading. Every business visitor, academic, and overseas Korean with a foreign passport from a country where you don't need a visa gets classified as a tourist. Japanese travel in large numbers for shopping. But not many people actually come to Korea on holiday. The country has everything for tourism – shopping, nightlife, sports, beaches, mountains and history. With more research into what is in the mind of the Japanese, Taiwanese, American and European tourist that they would spend money to pursue, it could be a major tourism destination. Right now, though, compared with other Asian destinations, like Japan, China, Thailand, and the Philippines, it draws blank stares.

The way a people think obviously affects everything, including their own ability to change. Education reform has always been on the cards, but there is still much conservatism. The fact is, though, that the current system fails to meet the needs of modern Korea because it does not train people to think in a sufficiently rational and legalistic way. You can see this in the way that Korean negotiators in international forums make themselves look rather silly and end up making emotional appeals rather than reasoned arguments. A case in point is a current territorial dispute between Korea and Japan. Centuries of mutual dislike seems to have coagulated around the question of who owns a small uninhabited rock between the two, called Tok-do by the Koreans and Takeshima by the Japanese. The Koreans have by far the better case. Japan gave up all sovereignty rights over Korea at the end of the Second World War, but claims that the rock became Japanese just before formal annexation in 1910. This is a piece of legal trickery because Japanese domination of Korean affairs, through 'advisers' in government offices, began in 1905. With a bit of research the Koreans could have found out the name of the Japanese adviser who arranged the transfer of the rock and made a perfectly reasoned case that fell into the category of claims that Japan abandoned in 1945. Instead, they made an emotional, table-thumping response and whipped up a frenzy of nationalistic bluster which featured boatloads of patriotic students, poets, you-name-it, wearing headbands with slogans on them, clambering up on the rock and liberating it for the fatherland.

For long-time foreign residents of Korea, such behaviour, because it is familiar, may be treated with a kind of paternal affection, but it does not induce comprehension. Life on the peninsula for many expatriates is a slow, drawn-out answer to the question of what makes Koreans tick that comes in ever-deepening epiphanies. A twenty-year veteran striding between the car park and his office may still be having daily insights about the Koreans, thrust to the surface of his mind by the irritation of the bruising commute that he's never got used to. He is able to do this because he still feels like an outsider. He is always thinking about 'them' and complaining about 'them' with his expatriate friends.

In this day, there is something a bit pathetically passé about expatriates complaining in generalisations about the natives in a developed country, but even the most generous-spirited among them do it. Foreign managers complain about business partners, their wives complain about the drivers and maids, diplomats and journalists moan about the government, missionaries whinge about their co-religionists and students, and the rare back-packers complain about the people they have run-ins with.

This has always puzzled me because Koreans individually are so sweet and decent. If you're struggling with a map in the centre of the big impersonal city, within seconds someone will stop to help you. But when you refer to them in the collective, you're reaching for negatives. Some foreigners struggle with a great deal of anger against this collective tribe. The more intellectual they are, the more it tends to manifest as an ongoing derogatory verbal PhD thesis. 'Lack of civic consciousness' is a common theme, and you will catch it in these pages, too. It's true, of course, but it misses the basic emotional fact that drives all this thinking in the first place. While many foreigners have very warm experiences with some Koreans, they often feel rejected by Koreans in general. I've asked a lot of people how they've experienced this and why they think it is so and had answers that range from, 'Because they're Korean' to analyses about homogeneity that reach back to prehistory. Foreigners feel used, conditionally accepted, for example, to fight for Korea in wartime and provide free markets and favourable loans in peacetime, and then collectively rejected. They are rejected because Koreans are so nationalistic and have a racist obsession with their blood. But also, foreigners are rejected as a consequence of the east Asian need to label people. This divisive tendency exists in all societies and lies at the root of racism, tribalism, class-consciousness and social engineering. But it appears to be a less examined feature of the mental make-up in east Asia. Perhaps it's something to do with Chinese characters that leads people to think in slogans. I don't know. Perhaps it comes back to education and a way of thinking that is not sufficiently critical and that understands facts in black and white.

When it comes to writing labels about different nationalities, there seems to be a team of rare simpletons at work, who list relevant facts on the back of the label to be drummed into everyone's mind. For example, as we have seen, British equals gentleman. On the back of the foreign label is 'outsider, can't speak Korean, can't understand Koreans, has more power than me, probably wishes us ill, represents his country, maybe has AIDS'.

This labelling of foreigners reached one absurd height at the time of the 1988 Olympic Games in Seoul. A month or so before the Games, I received a phone call from an American sports reporter working on the daily *Korea Herald* who had been asked to proof-read the English translation of the parade-of-nations commentary for the opening ceremony of the Olympics. This was to be the version on the English channel that English speakers in the stadium would tune in to. It would then be translated into eight other languages. The author, a Korean scholar, had written up a few lines about each of the 161 participating nations. Some were diplomatic time bombs. Hondurans, for example, might have paused in mid-applause when their team entered the stadium had they heard themselves described as citizens of a 'well-known Banana Empire'. Zambia was the 'home of the pygmies, people that do not reach a height of higher than 40cm'. My favourite was 'Ireland, also known as Guinnessville, because it is the home of the Guinness Book of Records'.

My giggling colleague had been asked only to check the spelling, not to comment on the text, and was being deviously tempted.

'Should I tell them?' he asked.

He did and the controversial commentary was axed by Park Seh-jik, the chairman of the Olympic organising committee.

Rushing parallel to this stupidity was a gushing torrent of bonhomie characteristic of Koreans in which accuracy is a distant second to feeling. And the feeling was one of Korean pride, not of any interest in other countries. Korea, for example, was equally vaguely described as 'the land of 5000 years of history where the sun rises'. Once, too, there was a time at 'the dawn of human history when all races and peoples lived in harmony'. These bits were left in the Korean-language version.

What tends to happen back, as I have indicated, is that resentful foreigners lump the Koreans together under one label – Korean – and start listing up negatives. Some people get quite possessed by this. One person, who was once in the same Korean language class as I, advised me that I should write a chapter in this book about lying, because, he alleged, 'all Koreans are liars.' On further consideration, he figured that a single chapter wouldn't be enough. It would have to be a theme underlying each chapter. How I would solve this dilemma? Call it, 'The Koreans: Five Thousand Years of Lying'? This man was an extremist. But he represented an unhappiness that foreigners often feel in east Asia, in that they can never really be accepted as anything but an outsider.

Labelling is not altogether a bad habit. So many features of Korea that we can identify are strengths as much as they are weaknesses. Changing labels, such as your job title or rank, can help you reinvent yourself. Ceremony works in a similar way and Koreans love ceremony. As one who abhors ceremony to the extent that I avoided my own graduation, it took me a while to appreciate the deep purpose behind formal ceremony, even if it means dressing up in funny clothes. Ceremony is the means by which you update your software. At a wedding, for example, two people go into a building, go through a ritual, and come out twenty minutes later in some magical way having for ever transformed the way they conceive of themselves. How come? Who knows? People don't care, as long as it works. My failure to attend my graduation ceremony when I was twenty-two probably explained why I was still thinking and behaving like a student at age thirty-two. But Koreans are able to make closures, reinvent themselves, and move forward.

Labels also have substantial value, like ranks in the military, of determining how you are treated in society. In a hierarchical society based on relationships, one's rank is vital. For Koreans at work, the name card is more important than what you actually do, for it is more significant in determining how people feel about you and behave towards you.

As I reject the label put on me by Koreans, particularly the thousands of taxi drivers who have told me I must be a gentleman, the hypocrisy of lumping them as one group, and claiming that they think and behave like this or like that, does not escape me. As intellectually attractive as it is, I fear it makes only limited sense to talk about a national character. Having said that, Koreans are amazingly homogeneous. And in certain ways their behaviour is very predictable. When you meet someone of higher status, say, your old teacher on the street, what do you do? Smile? Shake hands? Hug? Kiss? Or get confused? Koreans never have this problem. They bow deferentially.

So, if we are to distinguish Koreans from the rest of mankind, perhaps we should begin by pointing out how similar they are to us. They are, of course, as human as anyone else. They love and laugh and labour under fears and harbour anger as anyone else does. They bleed when they're cut. They struggle to discipline their children and worry about money. They react defensively like we do, when our feelings are hurt, or our interests threatened, or when we are unwell. They suffer the same illnesses as we do, although in significantly different proportions. They don't have a welfare state, so sick people are not always given the care you would expect. Once I lived next door to a family where the husband, a former maths teacher, was suffering from what I diagnosed as schizophrenia. He'd wander up and down the street in the rain shouting at his demons and point up to my second-floor apartment and shout the name of the newspaper I was writing for at the time. I had never told him this detail and assumed he knew nothing about me. How did he know? Or was it just the demons who knew? (It's easy to get spooked in a foreign country. My British wife lived in Korea, before we were married, on the ninth floor of a fifteen-storey apartment building. She was very startled when she heard a man wandering up and down the corridors of her block chanting 'Satan'. He seemed to come by every two or three days. When she mentioned it to some fellow teachers, they explained that the man was from the local laundry, coming to pick up dry cleaning. What he was calling out was *say-tak*, the Korean word for laundry.)

Koreans are more gregarious than we are. They're so into other people that they don't read books much and they tend to fall asleep when they're by themselves. They are not the sort of people who want to get away from it all, and they don't make a national habit out of rolling their eyes at the prospect of being with their parents. They work hard at their relationships. They don't have fixed bedtimes and will stay up half the night talking with you, flop asleep on the floor and get up early and go to work the next day. They live at close quarters, and so it's a fortunate thing that they like company.

These gregarious people carry a tremendous amount of unresolved pain. This is a society that does not have an industry of personal therapy. They tend to suppress things and get on with life. I would challenge anyone to ask any Koreans that they meet for their recent family history. You will find stories that would make your heart stop.

A Korean friend was in my office once when a Japanese journalist came in for a chat. After the journalist had gone, the Korean man went and stood by the window and stared out. He was staring out at nothing, his fists held stiffly down by his sides. Then he turned to me and said grimly, 'They threw my grandmother down the stairs of our house.'

'Who did?'

'The Japanese,' he said. 'During the occupation. It was his accent when he spoke to me in Korean. I couldn't stop thinking about it.'

The thing was he never knew this grandmother who had been killed by Japanese police. She had died before he was born, but there she was haunting him and calling for revenge. I am sometimes convinced that the Koreans will one day surpass us all. The ghosts will drive them on. There's something different about the way Koreans are haunted. In Britain this is the kind of reaction you find from prisoners of war. These men endured such horrors during the Second World War that the sight of an oriental face can start them shaking. But they could not speak about it and so the memories ended with their generation. The Koreans do not talk about it either, but it is nevertheless passed on because of blood ties and filial piety. These filial children and grandchildren are most profoundly motivated by the perception that their parents were victims, whose dreams in life were smothered by poverty and brutality. Their own success will atone for it and wipe away all the ancestral pain.

Not all this brutality has been caused by foreigners. Another close friend, an American, is married to a woman who comes from a small village near Seoul. During the Korean War, when north Korean soldiers came into the village, her uncle was tied down to the floor of his house and soldiers stoked up the under-floor heating until, slowly, he died in scorching pain. One colleague told me that in the late 1940s, her mother and uncle were denounced by a neighbour in Seoul as being leftist sympathisers and were arrested by police and imprisoned without trial. Their mother went to the prison and bargained to take her children's place. The children were freed and she went into jail. A few days later, the family heard that prisoners were being moved and rushed to see their mother, who was in a line of people tied by ropes and being marched down the street.

'Did you bring any food?' she asked. They had rushed so quickly to see her and forgot to bring any food, not realising the prisoners were surviving only on what relatives brought them. They never saw her again and don't know what happened to her. But my colleague's mother and uncle have lived with this wretched guilt all their lives.

These were just parts of stories I happened to hear from people I had already known a long time. They are all related to the politics of this century. It's touched every family and put Koreans up there with the Poles, the Cambodians and others for sheer enormity of suffering. There are millions more struggles related to the poverty and deprivation that Koreans lived with until this generation. Further, the authoritarian structure of society is a permanent source of more ordinary anguish. Koreans have all been bullied by dictators, teachers, police, army officers, bosses, fathers, big brothers, mothers-in-law and anyone else with more authority.

Women have had a bad time. The first words they may hear is the 'Oh no' of their father and grandparents when they're born. It's not illegal for a husband to beat his wife. I've lived in two places where next door the drunken dad regularly beat up his wife. The mothers' recourse has been to love their children with a passion. Most Koreans would crawl a million miles over broken glass for their mothers, but not for their fathers. God was no comfort because, historically, their shamanistic spiritual world, until the recent arrival of Christianity, was peopled by spirits and ancestors that got angry and wrecked your life if not appeased. There is a self-perpetuating attitude that everyone is a potential bastard, and that you can trust only your family and group. It's here where all the love, sacrifice and support is that helps Koreans avoid loneliness and self-doubt. In the family, the philosophy seems to be that everyone is basically good. This positive attitude is a source of Korean self-assuredness. They approach the world with a personal confidence, but with clenched fists.

Koreans have not become accustomed to foreigners. Therefore the sight of a foreign face still turns heads, even in Seoul. For the first couple of weeks after my arrival in 1982, I found the staring quite embarrassing. Bus stops were the worst. You could get a hundred pairs of eyes blankly sizing you up, thousands if you were walking upstream on a major pavement. All those people noticing your imperfections. Children would turn back and shout 'Hello' in snickering English. For a while, in the late 1980s, it was common for young Koreans to shout 'Hello, Mr Monkey' at westerners, an infuriating taunt that came from a pop song. But it is surprising how soon you stop noticing the stares. In fact, you blend in and yourself stare at foreigners. I've once or twice done a double-take seeing a foreign face in a crowd of local shoppers in the mirrored panel of a department store and realised it was me. What you appreciate is that Koreans in general are not thinking negatively about you. They're just looking. This is very different from the world of the British student that I was used to, where critical appraisal of strangers was the hallmark humour of the insecure.

Although we consider east Asians generally to be conservative and westerners to be liberal, it is my subjective experience that Koreans are much more accepting and embracing of differences. I imagine that this is because, as Confucians, they display an instinct for harmonious relationships with people, whereas the Christian and law-based culture of the West is more concerned with issues of right and wrong and good and evil. We tend to be more critical.

In this regard, the Koreans strike me as being less hung up than we are. A good measure of this assessment is how Koreans carry their emotions very close to the surface. In contrast to the inhibited Japanese, they are not ashamed of their feelings. In any day in Seoul, you will pass arguing drivers, cackling old ladies, a black eye or two, friends of the same sex holding hands, groups of office workers getting drunk together, yelling schoolboys landing *taekwondo* kicks on each other, and schoolgirls going along with their arms around each other's shoulders in giggling conspiracy. All of this happens in an atmosphere of jackhammers and honking horns at a very high decibel level. It's no wonder you forget there are mountains around the city.

Sometimes Koreans get immobilised by their emotions. There are always a few deaths by heart attack reported in the papers after the national team has played in a World Cup match. Men watching the match on TV at home or in coffee shops yell so much and get so worked up that they literally kill themselves.

My wife, who is a ballet teacher, often told me how her students would come to school with streaming colds and flu and still be able to dance, but if one girl wasn't dancing well, it was invariably because her 'heart was hurting', usually after an argument with a friend. And these can happen very often. Koreans are very fractious and argumentative. One reason concerns the importance of status. People can get very angry if they are not treated according to their own idea of their social standing. Disdain can be indicated in subtle ways that we would miss. In Britain, you can get away with slyly rubbing two fingers up the side of your cheek at someone without their even noticing. But Koreans are always ready to pounce on much more minor gestures and inflections in the language. Consider the following cases:

> The National Assembly Trade-Industry Committee had an unexpected adjournment from the very beginning of its session yesterday, due to the 'manner' of Kim Yoon-ho, chairman of the board of the state-run Korea Coal Corporation, at the meeting.
>
> Kim, a retired four-star general who had served as chairman of the Joint Chiefs of Staff, triggered a rage among the panel members by sitting with his legs crossed.
>
> An opposition lawmaker called his colleagues' attention to Kim's 'impolite' manner, and asked him to correct the posture.
>
> The ex-general ignored the request to the astonishment of the participants in the session, saying, 'Why do you take issue with my sitting posture?'[16]

The point here was whether civilian politicians could force a retired general, who represented the political power since the early sixties, to defer to them. They couldn't. Instead of acquiescence, they got the two fingers.

> Seoul police yesterday arrested a 30-year-old student at Korea University graduate school on a charge of beating to death an undergraduate student of the university.
>
> According to the Songbuk Police, Kang Soon-ho, a French literature major in the graduate school, was suspected of hitting and trampling to death Pak Chong-hyon, 24, a junior majoring in law, early Saturday morning in a residential alley near the school over a dispute.
>
> The mishap occurred around 2.30 a.m. when the two, both then drunk, met in the alley on their way home and Pak spoke 'impolitely' to Kang,

apparently mistaking his senior as a friend, police said. Kang allegedly beat
Pak in his face and trampled him when he fell down.[17]

The story does not really indicate what happened, but it is possible that
poor Mr Pak may have annoyed Mr Kang by inadvertently using verb
endings normally used for pals and kids.

The language lays itself open for such misinterpretation. Koreans do not
use language to convey literal meaning to the extent that we do. 'If I say I'll
kill you to a stranger in English, he might take pre-emptive action,' said
Shim Jae-hoon, a journalist fluent in English. 'In Korea, you're just expressing a feeling. Korean is not a good language to argue in because there are so
many shades of meaning. It is so easy to be misunderstood. English is a language for clarity and logic. It's a beautiful language to argue in. My wife and
I switch to English when we want to resolve a disagreement.'

Koreans can indeed explode in anger very easily. But, often what
appears to be spontaneous is actually very strategic. I remember once seeing some Koreans in Hong Kong airport yelling and screaming at the
unhappy representative of Korean Air, which had overbooked their flight.
They simply did not believe that there were no seats and seemed to
assume that, once their protest reached a certain volume, seats would
miraculously be produced. What happened was that the airline official, a
Korean, disappeared. Then foreigners got upset because, 'At least the airline should take responsibility and come and explain what has happened.' The next foreign complaint was, 'Why don't they apologise and
offer free tickets to anyone who surrenders their seat, like other airlines
do?' Ah-ha. Typical criticism. But the foreigners don't understand. First,
only a fool apologises. It's like saying, 'Now you may execute me.' Furthermore, the official knew that his presence would only escalate the
strategic anger and that free seats wouldn't be enough to appease them.
Best to leave them muttering among themselves.

Letting rip with strangers is one thing. But when there is a relationship,
there are certain considerations which are complex for the foreigner to
follow. For example, a customer can abuse a waiter, the latter being an
inferior because he is offering a service. I used to spend a lot of time in the
1980s in coffee shops with oppositionists and democratic dissidents. In
those days, shoe-shine boys would come round trying to get your custom
and old ladies would come round selling chewing gum. It never ceased to
amaze me how dismissive these democratic champions were of inferiors.
But sometimes the rules appear to change. For example, managers take all
kinds of abuse during strikes and negotiations from unionists and are

supposed to just sit and take it, like a wise parent absorbing the tantrum of a child. Woe betide anyone who rants back. That would be breaking the rules and, when done by a foreigner, can easily be taken as an insult to the Korean people. The thinking is that union leaders aren't inferiors but are superiors because they represent the working masses, or, in the case of foreign companies, the entire Korean nation, past and present. During a strike at a foreign bank, one Australian manager, returning from a three-Martini lunch, playfully tap-danced on some of the union posters which had been stuck on the bank floor. The workers' outrage lead to new slogans such as 'White Australia policy out of Korea.'

Koreans are only beginning to develop the democratic attitudes and institutions to resolve conflict. Hitherto it has been done by power. Hence the need to yell and make ridiculous demands. It's negotiating strategy. It may be noisy but it's logical. Sometimes things go wrong. Once a British motorist had a scrape with a Korean. Both got out to inspect the damage and it was not clear who was at fault. The Korean began yelling and demanding immediate cash payment. The strategy here was to bully the foreigner into accepting guilt and, by making outrageous demands, get him to compromise at a lower, but still unfair, amount. The Korean, still making his point, grabbed hold of the foreigner's tie. At this point, British culture entered. For many Britons, especially if they're drunk, even eye contact can signal aggression. Grabbing a tie is certainly the start of serious assault. The Briton reacted swiftly and knocked the other man to the ground. For Koreans, this was rather a shocking thing to do. I mean, they were only having a discussion. The Briton was arrested and fined for assault.

Korean men who are angry can be something to behold. They bellow from the pit of their stomach, not from their throat. I tried it once. It is very therapeutic. Student demonstrations can be extremely exhilarating when there are five hundred men roaring the same slogan in this fashion in unison. The counterpoint provided by female students is drowned out by the neanderthal male roar. You can see why men rule in Korean society.

With their expressiveness comes a natural acceptance of other people's emotions and lapses. The Koreans have a nice habit, when a drunk gets on to a bus, of getting up and giving him a seat instead of condemning him or punching him out. After all, he could be their friend's dad on the way home from work. Thus, they give you space and allow you your tears and your anger, provided you are not attacking them.

One of the most extraordinary pieces of television I have ever seen was in 1983 when the state-run Korean Broadcasting System put on a live, one-hour programme to reunite families separated thirty years earlier by the

Korean War. In the studio, middle-aged and elderly people stared at the camera holding a board identifying their name, home town and whom they were seeking. Most were looking for parents, children, brothers and sisters and each got about ten seconds on camera. It was a wee bit boring at first and the two anchors tried to break it up by questioning one or two people. After a few minutes, the phones started ringing. A woman in the audience was rushed to a phone on the set. With a few hesitant questions, she established that it was her sister, whom she had not seen since they were children. She began to cry in a way I had not seen publicly in Britain. Her voice was not quivering and cutting out and her face was not twisted up. This was a different kind of crying. Tears streamed down her face, but the conversation continued with the woman bellowing into the receiver without any self-consciousness. She was oblivious to the camera that had been shoved in her face to catch the moment.

Soon people who recognised their relatives on TV were rushing to the studios. One man found his sister. He was a taxi driver. His face awash with tears, he strode up and down the studio with his elderly sister on board, her arms and legs wrapped around him and completely beside herself with emotion. His arms were thrust into the air as if he had scored the winning goal in the final of the World Cup, and he was shouting 'Long Live KBS!' It was impossible to watch this without getting gripped by the passion. Within hours, thousands of people looking for relatives had descended on the KBS studios. They camped out, hanging signs with the names of the people they were looking for on walls. All normal programming was pushed off and this live campaign went on for forty hours in the first five days. The programme continued with satellite link-ups with Koreans in America and other countries.

The campaign ended a little under five months later. KBS said that over 100,000 people had appeared on the show and that there had been 10,180 reunions. And these were just people who had become separated in the chaos of the war within south Korea, infants who had fallen off trains or got lost in crowds, adults who made it to the South and assumed their families were still up North, children who had been put in orphanages. When you consider that an estimated one in seven of the 70 million Koreans in the two countries are from families which have been directly split by the war, you get a picture of the unbelievable human dimension to this tragedy. The Koreans are truly a broken-hearted people.

Despite their individual expressiveness, in another sense their collective pain is suppressed. The divided families are a case in point. Millions of Koreans have just put this behind them, and carried on with life. But where does all this emotional pain go? Korean national character is informed by the historical battering the country has received over centuries. In an effort to deal with it, psychiatrists, political theorists and artists refer to a specific psychological condition, which they attribute to this collective experience. Called *han*, it is a kind of rage and helplessness that is sublimated, and lingers like an inactive resentment. There is an unusual emphasis on this notion in the popular culture.

Han first emerged as a topic of literary criticism in the 1940s and '50s. Its expression was seen in songs and tales of unrequited love in old Korean literature, as well as from colonial-period writers, like the poet Kim Sowol. A more explosive version of *han* entered the popular, political realm in the 1970s, when it was identified as a national characteristic. It became a key component of modern novels, a new popular folk theatre, and of *minjung* (masses) theology, which could be loosely described as the Korean version of neo-Marxist Liberation Theology.

Most Koreans feel it is something unique and something that foreigners are ultimately unable to fathom.[18]

'What is unique to Korea is the emphasis itself,' says the historian James Freda. '*Han* in the modern era became widely used as a way to make sense of Korea's modern traumas. In other words, Koreans have felt a need to make sense of the injustice and suffering they experienced. While people commonly have to work through such traumas individually or, when they are overwhelming, as in the case of the Holocaust, often take the option of denial and repression, discourse on *han*, in my opinion, demonstrates a collective effort to face, deal with, and work through all sorts of social suffering.'[19]

Paik Sang-chang, chairman of the Korea Social Pathology Institute, says he watches out for the manifestation of *han* in individual patients, and tries to explain it in terms of modern psychiatry.

'Western history, you could say, is a history of disobedience. It tells of the struggle for individual freedom,' he says. 'But our history is one of the struggle to obey.' Korean heroes are the loyal subject and the filial son, whose exemplary virtue is their suppression of self in the course of obedience.

'Psychoanalytically speaking, this means prohibition of one's own instinctive urges,' he says. 'According to my observation of patients, *han* is very static. Traditionally, Koreans do not let it out. If a man loved a woman, but his parents ordered him to marry another, he would obey, and live with *han*. This is a typical Korean experience. *Han* has hung like a tranquil mist in the valley of our hearts.'

But, Dr Paik believes, the historical traumas of the last hundred years have disturbed this tranquil mist. First the national psyche was gripped by a collective hostility towards Japan. Then, with the division of Korea, when those you loved from the same family, school and home town became ideological enemies, there was a collective ambivalence. 'Ambivalence is a major symptom of schizophrenia,' he said. 'Your love and hate goes to the same target, like a jealous woman. In this way the division of Korea invited a kind of collective madness.'

Finally, south Korea became gripped by a 'survival complex', meaning that people became fixated on immediate survival needs.

'These three traumas acted as a chemical change, turning our static *han* into dynamic *han*,' he said. The mist blew up into a storm. 'The id impulse is no longer suppressed. Instinctive demands surface. Koreans want it all now. These desires are behind the drive for economic growth and political freedom.'

If the Koreans are explosive, and even a bit mad, they are also exquisitely sensitive. In fact, they tend to dwell too much for our liking on their delicate feelings. The *kibun* (feelings, or state of mind) is of prime importance. Not only does feeling good make you feel good, but also it's better for your health. When you feel bad you are justified in behaving badly, rejecting business proposals, barking at your wife and secretary. The *kibun* is translated as mood, but is accorded higher importance than we would accord that word. It is perhaps best described as that part of you that extends beyond the physical body, your inner atmosphere or, perhaps, your continental shelf. This invisible part of you can be damaged by loss of face, disrespect, bad news or unhappiness. Or by the appearance of someone who threatens you, or who damaged your *kibun* before.

With their awareness of the 'inner man' and the appreciation of harmony to avoid *kibun*-damaging, Koreans are very adept at sensing people's character and mood and at helping you out of a foul temper, be it by giving you space, silence or gifts. I once had a bit of a disagreement with a colleague in the office. When we'd finished disagreeing, I carried on working in seething silence. He went off, presumably feeling the two fingers I was mentally flipping at his back. Ten minutes later he came back. He'd been and bought some apples. He quietly cut them up and came over and sat down beside me and offered me a small fork to dig at them. This wordless gesture washed away all my irritation and impressed me very deeply. My priority had been with proving the correctness of my opinion, whereas his was with the relationship and office harmony.

Here lies a cultural difference that invites great misunderstanding, for it is not easy for one side to see the virtue of the other. When is one individual being correct more important than a group being happy? Obviously sometimes, but much less often for the Korean who places his emphasis on ethics in relationships, and less on the individual and his or her conscience. The Korean naturally seeks harmony in relationships over objective truth and goodness. So *kibun* is high on the agenda.

Its importance for Koreans cannot be underestimated. Koreans can make decisions, which we would consider extremely important and requiring rationality, on the basis of it. Like, for example, whether to build the factory on this spot or that one. With *kibun* being an important factor, there is a lot of talk about 'timing' and 'feeling right' by Koreans when they are making decisions. At its best, this tendency can indicate a great intuitive sense. At its worst, it is timidity over common sense. For example, your dry cleaner, now that you are not treating him like a devil-worshipper, might mumble 'yes', if you ask if your dress will be ready tomorrow. A minuscule hesitation in the 'yes' indicates a *kibun*-sensitive 'well, actually, no, but I neither want to upset you nor lose your business.' So, you conspire in your own frustration by saying 'good', and giving him the dress. While the foreigner may only see the script, Koreans live between the lines.

We should not assume that *kibunists* are irrational. In fact, Koreans can be remarkably rational and calculating on issues which we westerners tend to consider as emotional.[20] Take choosing a life partner, for example. A significant number of spouses still meet through matchmakers, professional or amateur. They may factor in all considerations, as well as attractiveness and character, and mix it up with their intuition and make a decision that we tend not to be able to make because we may not think of marriage until we've fallen in love, by which time it's too late to retrieve ourselves. In business, on the other hand, sometimes decisions are made without research or forethought.

Chapter Four

SHAMAN UNDER THE SKIN

South Korea is a multi-religious society. Between a quarter and a third of the population is Buddhist and around a quarter Christian. Shamanism and Confucianism also figure, although they are difficult to quantify as there is no exclusive worship as a means to measure adherents. There are no Jews or Hindus in Korea, but there are several thousand Muslims, mostly men who converted when working on construction projects in the Middle East in the 1970s and '80s. Several hundred thousand people ascribe to a variety of native faiths, including one which worships Tan-gun, the mythical founder of Korea, and many small syncretistic sects with Christian, Buddhist or shamanic roots.

Occasionally these clash, such as in 1989 when police had to use tear gas to separate students from the Unification Church and local Protestant churches in the town of Chonan. The Protestants were protesting the government's approval of a Unification Church application to turn a seminary in the town into a university. There have also been some startlingly bloody clashes between rival factions within the Chogye Order, the largest Buddhist order, resulting from struggles over temple finances and control. This violence can be traced back several decades. With the military coup of 1961, many hoodlums who had been active with the police fled to remote temples and became monks. Some rose up through the ranks and resorted to their old habits when reformist monks threatened to remove them. The image of shaven-headed bonzes, their grey robes flying, battling riot police with iron pipes doesn't fit, but Korean Buddhism has been undermined by its willingness to give all comers a chance to improve themselves in this life. It'll take anyone as a monk.

But these are mild affairs when measured against the political violence of recent history and, anyway, are exceptions. In their religious life, Koreans of different faiths coexist. In fact they often coexist within the same family. It is common to find a husband who could loosely be called Confucian, a Buddhist wife and Christian children. What is striking is how similar Koreans are, whatever their formal religious affiliation. 'Koreans are Koreans first. They take the system of a religion and make it their own,' says Brian Barry, a Buddhist convert and a temple artist.

When you examine this Korean-ness, you find in fact that the values of all the religions that have influenced Korea exist within the Korean mind. Each has deposited its sediment. Buddhism was the predominant faith in Korea for almost a millennium up to the end of the fourteenth century. The Zen concept of no past or future, just a constantly flowing present, can be seen behind the immediacy and impatience of Koreans of all faiths. Also, the Buddhist idea that the spiritual and physical worlds flow into one another is more pragmatically appealing to many Christians than the idea of waiting for an afterlife. Many Christians consult with Buddhist and shamanic fortune-tellers to tap into the spiritual world for advice.

Because of traditional poverty, both Buddhism and Christianity have a dominant blessing-type mentality. Instead of emphasising Buddhist compassion and Christian love, the stress has been on buying your way into paradise. The Full Gospel Church, which claims over half a million members and has the single largest congregation in the history of Christendom, has a very simple appeal. Accept Jesus and guarantee your health and wealth, the two items which always figure on top in opinion polls about what Koreans most worry about. The founder, Cho Young-gi, had a beautifully simple strategy for growth. The congregation burgeoned, with the massive influx of people from the villages into the cities in the 1970s, around home groups, mostly of women, who met once a week to study a Bible text and pray for sick members and for their husbands' promotions. When the numbers approached twenty, a cell split into two. On Sundays, hundreds of these small groups descend on Yoido Island in Seoul, where Rev. Cho has built a church which is like an indoor stadium. Throughout the day there are consecutive services with tens of thousands at a time. A section for foreigners provides simultaneous translation in several languages via headphones.

Taoist ideas also feature in the Korean mental make-up. In particular, the Taoist ethos that 'the way that can be discussed is not the way' figures in Korean attitudes. There is a deep animosity towards discursive argument.

From the late fourteenth century onwards, neo-Confucian scholar-bureaucrats eclipsed Buddhism. Through education and social regulations,

Confucian ceremony and values reached all levels of society. This influence went deeper than it ever did in Japan or China and it remains today. While many reject Confucianism for its association with an old class system and with authoritarianism, Koreans still adhere to many of its principles and rituals.

Confucian precepts, with their emphasis on vertically ordered human relationships, have informed Korean thinking and social organisation for centuries. However, as we have seen, the Koreans are not what you would expect pure Confucians to be. They are not restrained, mannered, thoughtful moral engineers, seeking through self-cultivation to change both themselves and their society. There is a contradictory passion and earthy sensuousness to Koreans. These sage-like gentlemen stamp their feet and belch and fart in public. You would think this kind of behaviour would have been outlawed by Confucians and relegated to the unwashed masses, but not so. This is because of the existence of a deeper sediment in the Korean psyche – shamanism.

From ancient times, Koreans' beliefs about the nature of existence and the practices that defined their response to it were ordered by shamans. Shamanism is not easily defined and its history is undocumented. The term loosely covers multi-deity religious practice and superstitions that began in prehistory. In ancient Korea, the rulers served as shaman-kings. In theory, shamanist belief was very holistic and tolerant. It did not propose the contradiction and conflict that we see in other faiths. There were no divides, such as good–evil, body–spirit, physical–spiritual worlds, perfect God–frail man. Life was a continuum. The individual was seen as a whole and all, men and women, were seen as being of equal value. And even within each person, different attributes were not singled out and given superior value over others. Whether more courageous or more sensitive, you contained both qualities in a way that was valid because you were you. Wind was wind, and became part of you, whether it came out the front or the back, so to speak. And why not let it out?

The shamans did not claim to know how and when existence began. And they ruled out an omnipotent deity.[21] Rather, in their view, human beings existed as notes in nature's rhythmic tune. We are here before we are born, and we remain as part of nature after we die. Thus life should always be lived to the full. To be truly human, you must act with all your energies.

Koreans have certainly hurled themselves into religion. Korea outdid its mentor, China, in its application of Confucianism. North Korea has outdone Stalin and Mao in its application of the communist personality cult of Kim Il-sung, who ruled as a kind of shaman-king figure. Korean

Christians have an international reputation for devotion. Many women go to 5 a.m. worship services before starting their housework and sending the children off to school.

On the fringe of Christianity, there has been an intense messianism. The most dramatic example of this is the *Tong-hak* movement of the second half of the nineteenth century, which developed as an alternative to Catholicism. The *Tong-haks* manifested a particular boldness that is apparent in some alternative Korean theologies, by reinventing God in a way that appealed to the ordinary, oppressed man. God existed, not in a distant heaven, but within the mind of man. Man was not a sinner, but a manifestation of God, even you, the peasant. This positive thinking appealed to many in the lower classes, who armed themselves and staged several bloody revolts.

There have been numerous obscure groups, with thoroughly heretical views. A sect in Pyongyang in the 1930s and '40s, expecting the return of Christ, hand-sewed a set of Korean and western clothes for Jesus for every three days of his life from birth to the age of thirty-three, as an act of devotion. Hundreds of people were engaged in this endeavour. Their leader was a woman, who once made her husband bow to her several thousand times throughout one night as an act of penance.[22]

By some guesses, there were at least seventy messiahs with followers in south Korea in the early 1960s.[23] The only internationally known among them is Moon Sun-myung, the founder of the Unification Church. Moon's view of God is quintessentially Korean, combining shamanist passion and Confucian family patterns in Christian form. His God is the miserable parent who suffers in lonely agony in a world of unfilial and evil children. As a teenager, Moon has said, he prayed for 'wisdom greater than Solomon, for faith greater than the Apostle Paul, and for love greater than the love Jesus had,' and developed a Christ-like mission to heal what he perceives as the broken heart of God.[24] Although presumptuous and implicitly blasphemous to Korean Christians when expressed in religious terms, this kind of Olympian ambition is characteristic of many Korean men, especially in business and politics.

Despite its high profile and international activities, the Unification Church has never had a large following. A more successful messianic figure in this regard was Park Tae-sun. A charismatic healer, Park was expelled from the Presbyterian church in the 1950s for heresy. Eight years later his Olive Tree Movement claimed almost 2 million followers in over three hundred congregations. The denomination which had expelled him had a membership of only 100,000. Although his numbers claim was obviously exaggerated, Park demonstrated what energetic leadership can achieve in Korea with government approval. Under the 1948–60 government of Syngman Rhee, who was a Methodist, Park Tae-sun was jailed several times on charges ranging from 'murder' to 'pro-Communism'. But under Park Chung-hee (no relative) in the 1960s and '70s, he flourished.[25] He built two towns for 20,000 followers (probably closer to the actual membership figure) and set up heavy industry. Believers were very disciplined in sexual matters and avoided tobacco, alcohol, pork (because pigs are greedy) and peaches (because, Park revealed, it was this fruit, not the apple, that caused the fall of man). Devoted followers used to drink the water that Park washed his feet in. Their services featured vigorous hand-clapping, often for hours.[26]

A contemporary messianic couple called the Two Incarnations teaches that Korea has a providential mission to heal mankind's spirit and revive its original vitality or *ki*. Korea was chosen for this mission because the country is located 'in the best place on earth' from the point of view of global geomancy.[27] They teach that the shape of Korea is also extremely significant. It is like a rabbit with large ears – 'to listen to the voice of the creator' – and also like a penis hanging out of Asia. It's female equivalent is rabbit-shaped Paraguay, which lies snuggled between its Latin neighbours 'like the pubic region of a woman'. The couple have visited Paraguay and held healing sessions there. They teach that the Korean people have kept their blood pure by not marrying foreigners. Traditional forms of working, such as carrying water jars on their head, and recreation, such as jumping on seesaws, have been heaven's 'secret methods' to keep the people's *ki* strong. With such insights, ambitious healers tap the Koreans' traditional sense of their own uniqueness.

In shamanist thinking, causing emotional pain is a great moral crime because it blocks other people from being fully human. In shamanism, there is no objective God setting absolute rules. Thus moral judgement becomes a matter of relative emotional hurt. Stealing money is less of a wrong than shaming someone. Unless of course by stealing from them you really damage them in some way. Then your defence would be, 'but I didn't mean to hurt them'.

Confucianism brought new values but these were still relative, because the religion laid down rules for human relations and did not propose an objective source of absolute standards. It was not until Christianity planted its stake in the Korean soil and modern concepts of law and rights were introduced that this relative world began to be challenged by the idea of an objective standard of values that existed outside of relationships. However, that stake has not yet been driven very deep.

The shamans believed that negative emotion needed to be assuaged because it could cause damage. Vengeful women were often blamed for mishaps. The unhappy dead could influence nature and bring calamities down on the living. Single women who died unfulfilled were also seen as especially problematic. After a Korean airliner was shot down in 1983 by a Soviet jet, the spirits of two stewardesses were married to two young male victims in ceremonies arranged by the bereaved parents to ease their imagined frustrations.

The most vicious form of vengeance by spirits would be to attack a victim's lineage, especially his children. But the worst thing the living can do to someone they hate is commit suicide because of them. Suicide as a form of protest has a terrible emotive power in Korean society. Instead of evoking disgust, it may stir people to take vengeance. Thus in 1970, a 22-year-old textile worker called Chun Tae-il struck against employers and against the regime of Park Chung-hee. Chun killed himself after his protests against abuses in Seoul's Peace Market led to beatings and humiliation by employers and police. His name became a rallying call for union activists. In the 1980s and '90s, several workers and students immolated themselves or jumped off buildings, or both simultaneously, as acts of protest. When protesters occupy a building, police often place mattresses around it and arm themselves with fire extinguishers before storming it, in anticipation of suicide attempts.

There has been a traditional idea that the dead feel as we do. They get cold and hungry. Food is put out for them and they are believed to consume its essence. The shamans said that the spirit decayed slowly with the body in a natural process. This idea lies behind Korean aversion to organ donation and cremation. Also it was the reason that a body had to be buried in a propitious place. Even in the early twentieth century, you would come across bodies wrapped in mats, festering in the sun while the family searched for a site. The consequences of burying an unsettled spirit were worse than the risk of disease.[28] The notion of what actually happens at death may vary from faith to faith, but a common Korean concern is that the children of the deceased show their filial love and that the spirit not be lonely. A friend described the funeral rites of her uncle, who died in a Korean hospital after a long struggle with cancer.

The body was immediately (within minutes) dressed in beautiful silk hanbok, the head was wrapped in rice paper, hands and ankles were tied with coiled rice paper, to keep the body in shape. After two days, the clothes were changed into soft hemp hanbok (apparently hemp deteriorates better).

His children, my cousins, sat in the wake room for three days to receive guests who came to pay respects. There are a set of rituals here also but one of the most important is that the incense is kept burning the whole time. The oldest son is not supposed to wash or change clothes until after the funeral.

Then on the third day, came the burial. The burial itself was a long series of ceremonies supposed to help the journey into the other world. He (the spirit along with a picture of him) is at a Buddhist temple for forty-nine days. According to the Buddhist belief, that's how long the spirit lingers in this world before starting the journey to the next. Once a week, the family goes to the temple for another set of Buddhist ceremonies. Then on the forty-ninth day, everything will get burned at the temple grounds accompanied by dance, music, and other Buddhist rituals.[29]

Despite the absence of churches and scriptures, shamanism is still quite widely practised. Modern shamans perform rituals of chant and dance to invoke various gods to exorcise evil spirits and to seek their aid. Some summon up ancient Korean and Chinese warriors to draw on their strength and protection. Back in the 1980s, there was a shaman called Hyun Myung-boon, who venerated the late American general, Douglas MacArthur, in this fashion. Mrs Hyun lived in Inchon, which was the site of MacArthur's brilliant counterinvasion against north Korea in 1950 during the Korean War. Once she featured in a TV documentary, and was interviewed before her altar. An observant policeman watching the programme spotted a carton of Marlboro cigarettes on the altar. Possessing foreign cigarettes had been a crime since 1952 when the government sought to clamp down on the black markets outside US military bases. Mrs Hyun and the TV producer were arrested. They were released after convincing police that the cigarettes were not for her, bu. for General MacArthur.[30]

There are thousands of fortune-tellers of various faiths or mixtures of faith. Fortune-telling can be big business, especially for those with the good fortune to get some of their predictions right. Would-be politicians often consult them to see whether the time is right for entering politics and even which party they should join.[31] Publicly, people pretend to be above such superstition, so during election campaigns, politicians often send their wives or secretaries along to the soothsayers to check on their progress. In the 1980s, one fortune-teller rose to prominence for having correctly predicted that an obscure lawyer would one day become prime minister. As an indication of the potential power such people can wield, the internal security agency began to monitor the fortune-teller. As part of his surveillance duties, the agent assigned to the job went along to have his own fortune read.[32]

One of the most prominent fortune-tellers is Lee Kyu-suk, whose services are more sought after by Korean politicians than those of professional pollsters. I went to see him a week before the 1992 American presidential election.

'Clinton will win. Bush's failure is in the stars,' he promised. His intuition presented itself to him in the form of mythic imagery. America, he said, was emerging from a long 'wild beast' era into a hundred-year 'era of the dragon'. The new-age dragon figure was Bill Clinton. George Bush, fine fellow though he was, was a tiger.

'Naturally the tiger fails when the dragon appears,' Lee said. I was still assuming that, because of the Gulf War success and questions about Clinton's sexual behaviour, Bush would win.

'How do you tell a dragon from a tiger?'

'It's in the face, and the shape of the head and body,' he told me. 'The dragon lives above the clouds. It's very different from animals on the earth, which means that Clinton has very special leadership qualities. His main concerns will be for the environment and for the promotion of freedom and democracy around the world. His idealism will be very good for the young people of America.' He said that previous presidential dragons, Abraham Lincoln and John Kennedy, were murdered in office because they were 'dragons in the era of wild beasts,' a problem Clinton would not face because of the new era.

What about the character issue and allegations of adultery? Not important.

'He is the best person, a very special person, and such people always have scandals. But scandals are just scandals,' he said philosophically.

And the next election? 'Clinton will win twice,' he said with confidence, and foresight.

He was also predicting that Kim Young-sam of the ruling party would win the Korean presidential race in 1992. My reason for visiting Lee was that he was reputed to be close to Kim Young-sam's son, Hyun-chol, around whom rumours of power abuse were already circling. I sensed his prediction, although it proved correct, was made more out of self-interest than any deep intuition. Given his connections, which he confirmed, he could hardly predict their ruin. As he accompanied me to the elevator outside his office after our interview, he shook hands politely and, just before the elevator doors closed, clenched his fist and winked conspiratorially and said, 'Please write well and help Kim Young-sam win. It will really help me.'

In addition to modern medicine and Chinese herbal remedies, faith healers of varying spirituality abound. I visited one once for a foot problem. I had a slightly swollen big toe, which was causing an ingrowing toenail. I'd already had it yanked out three times in clinics. These mini-operations, and two painful experiences at the hands of doctors earlier in Britain, had made me very open-minded about alternative medicine.

'Please sit down,' she said. Mrs Kim was a jolly Christian woman with large hands. Her story was interesting. Once grossly overweight, she had tried all kinds of diets. But nothing worked until one day she went to the mountains to pray and received a revelation that she should slap herself, continuously and hard. This had worked. She was proposing to do it to me.

'It will bring the bad blood to the surface,' she said.

She explained that the body is often blocked from healing itself by the collection of bad blood in certain places. The slapping drives this bad blood to the surface in a bruise and it disappears in a few days. I liked this theory because it didn't involve intrusive instruments. But the slapping was something else. She began attacking me with shamanistic gusto, raining stinging, rhythmic blows with the palm of her hand down on the back of my knee, where she reckoned the bad blood was blocking the good, healing blood from reaching my toe. It was excruciatingly painful. *In extremis*, I gripped the mattress and whimpered.

'Ah, we have black blood,' she announced, still slapping.

We did indeed. It rushed so eagerly to escape that it broke the surface. She stopped after a few minutes and wiped my leg.

Soon I was back at the hospital with another ingrowing toenail. A new doctor proposed a different remedy. He suggested I roll up a strand of cotton wool and place it under the nail and change it daily, so that as the nail grew, it would be trained upwards and wouldn't go digging into the toe. This simple solution worked. Later, a blood test revealed I had gout, and that the swelling of the toe was caused by excess uric acid in the blood. So, it was in the blood after all.

In east Asian interpersonal relations, you begin by knowing your position, and Koreans find nothing is more reassuring than having 'seniors', and nothing more balancing than having 'juniors' to whom you are obliged.

Life's training, quite naturally, begins in the family. The glue that holds the Korean family together is a fixation on blood lineage. This attitude begins with a view that could be expressed as 'you are your DNA'. In other words, you are part of a continuing stream. Your parents flow into you and you flow into your children. There is a mystical strength to this flow wherein lies the source of our meaning in life. A man's single most important duty in life is to father children, a woman's is to bear children.

However, these attitudes are more tribal sociology than biology. Until very recently, it was illegal for two Koreans from the same family clan, such as the 'Andong Kims', to marry, even though any common ancestor may have been ten or twenty generations distant.[33] The stricture applied only along patrilineal lines. There was very noisy opposition from a substantial, conservative segment of society to abolishing that ban. Confucianists in white robes demonstrated outside the National Assembly when the bill was being considered.

As a result of their mystical DNA thinking, Koreans have a different idea of where their ego, and their rights, start and stop than we do. Korean family members merge into one another, interfering and clinging and depending to an extent that would drive us to the therapy group. Close physical contact is the norm. Infants spend half the day strapped to their mother's or grandmother's back. Prams and playpens are uncommon because they separate parent and child. Children have the same bedtime as their parents and sleep in the same bed until they're about five.[34]

Traditionally, the father is not so involved in family life. In many ways, he is a peripheral figure, making his appearance only when the child, especially a son, is a bit older and needs direction. Thus Koreans have deep attachment to their mothers and can be reduced to tears recalling their devotion. A father is often more fondly remembered for the guidance he gave and the sacrifice he showed towards a noble cause, like Korean independence or democracy, than to what he invested in the family.

Recently, though, these patterns have begun to change. The extended family no longer lives together. Wives no longer quit work on marriage, and have only one baby, maybe two, not five or ten like their mothers did. And it is common now to see a young father with his baby strapped to his chest in a harness.

Korean children are endlessly indulged. Korean boys, especially, are not taught to defer pleasure. You notice that, as adults, they still want everything right now. They are impulsive and focused on the short term, and they throw tantrums when they don't get their way. A western observer will note that Korean parents seem to be much more tolerant of their children. They don't lecture their children all the time like we do. They don't even explain things. As a result children learn by imitation and by knowing what makes Mum and Dad get mad. Instead of being taught abstract principles – like, no you can't have that, because it's wrong to eat between meals – they learn that some things are wrong in certain situations. You can't have it, because Dad's in a bad mood right now. The presence of older and younger brothers and sisters, and grand-parents, all in the same house, used to provide a natural form of disci-pline. But this is often lacking in modern one- or two-child families, with the result that many adults complain the nation is raising a generation of spoiled brats. Primary school teachers now report that their biggest sin-gle headache is that pupils lack the discipline and manners of old.

Another problem that manifests in the modern era of the nuclear fam-ily is lack of communication. It is not done for Korean children to bring their problems to their parents. When families were large and extended, it was bad form for parents to demonstrate too much affection. Father may have been an austere figure and Mother a saint, but physical affection and joy was experienced with siblings. Thus Koreans are not accustomed to seeing their parents as human beings with the same needs for love and fulfilment as they. As illustration, several years ago there was a case in the newspapers of a forty-three-year-old man who committed suicide because his mother remarried. She was seventy-three and her new husband a seventy-seven-year-old widower.[35]

The emphasis in the parent-child relationship is on duties. Until recently, parents were required to work like slaves to provide for their children, to correct them when they did wrong, and set a good example. In return, they got total loyalty from their children. Children, and partic-ularly the eldest son, took care of them in their old age. Many Koreans are most deeply motivated to succeed in life or do what they do out of a sense of repaying the suffering and sacrifice of their parents. When parents are seen as victims, of the Japanese, of the military dictators, of poverty, this repaying becomes the motivating source of great filial energy. Since their country began to industrialise and democratise, Koreans have had oppor-tunities to achieve greatness that were denied their impoverished parents. Every biography of an achiever describes the virtues and sacrifice of the parents. When Kim Young-sam became president in 1993 and moved into the presidential Blue House in Seoul, the first person he brought along to see it was his widowed father.

It is not easy for Koreans to extend their trust beyond the confines of the family and close friends. The abyss between those closely connected people and the rest of humanity is so wide that the scholar Mark Setton characterises it as a 30,000 foot-deep Mariana Trench.[36] Individuals, he says, may stick out like islands in life's ocean, but they are connected under the water to their family. In fact, this connectedness is more important in east Asian thinking than the fact of individual outcrops.

The pattern of these ties is expanded to the extended family, close friends, alumni and home town. I found a lot of these attitudes rubbing off on me after a few years surrounded by Koreans. You start looking for common ground and expecting favours when you find it. I strategically introduced myself at a reception once to Yun Po-sun, who had been the president at the time of Park Chung-hee's coup, knowing he had graduated from the University of Edinburgh about fifty years earlier than I did. He responded as if he felt an immediate bond. He invited me to his home a couple of times simply on the basis of this common connection.

'The family is the key to understanding Korean society as a whole, including politics, which in Confucianism involves the extension of family ethics,' says Setton.

Going beyond the Trench to the broader society, where there may be no obvious connections, is scary. People out there are 'non-persons' and there is no sense of obligation to them. There is no guilt about behaving unfairly or rudely towards someone who is outside. Once the managing editor of a magazine showed me a pile of about fifty job applications he had received. He proceeded to pull out all those applicants who came from the south-west Cholla provinces. 'We don't want them here,' he said with a conspiratorial grin.

'Why not?'

'They wouldn't fit in.'

Koreans can be extremely rude towards non-persons. Thus there is a remarkable lack of civic-mindedness. There is, if the truth be told, a distinct lack of patriotism in Koreans. There may be nationalism, a fierce adherence to an identity, but there is not love of country. Korea has often struck me as a country made up of small tribes.

The Koreans can also be extremely cruel to non-persons. In the Vietnam War, the Korean troops fighting with the Americans gained such a reputation for merciless brutality that entire villages would empty when word got round that Koreans were in the region.[37]

Extended families know how to party. In families where there are many siblings and cousins, gatherings are often great sprawling events that may begin with ceremony – a wedding, or a visit to an ancestral tomb – and progress into gargantuan meals with, for the men especially, gallons of alcohol. If relatives have travelled a long way, the men may all crash on the floor of one room and the women in another. But this heaving – and often there is heaving – jollity among blood relatives does not mean that there are not conflicts and resentments. Relationships between mothers and daughters-in-law are traditionally fraught with tension. Also many first sons fail under the pressure of expectation. Other siblings may resent the love and favours bestowed on the eldest. It is common for family members to cheat each other, especially when there's lots of money around. If a relative or a close friend is borrowing from a bank and has no collateral, he may ask you to help out. It may be difficult to refuse without damaging the relationship and, anyway, the borrower may present it in a way that makes it appear like just another example of meaningless bureaucracy, a signature on a bit of paper. When he defaults, the bank takes whatever you put down as collateral. I know of one couple who lost their house in this way. They and four others had guaranteed a £75,000 loan for a man who was a small, and not very successful, businessman.

Given their concern for blood lineage, Koreans are not big on adoption. Even modern Koreans exhibit an unconscionable disregard for discarded babies and it has often been foreigners, Christian missionaries and American soldiers who have stepped in to assist them. Thousands of Korean orphans have been adopted in North America and Europe.[38] In 1989, the government came up with a plan to completely phase out foreign adoptions over seven years out of shame at the accusation that Korea was 'selling its babies'. The plan was dropped in 1994 due to the low rate of adoptions by locals. In the 1990s, around 3,500 children are deserted each year, 80 per cent of them by unmarried mothers. Two-thirds of these infants are adopted overseas.

These figures for local adoptions are misleading for they do not include the childless couples who adopt from family members. Also, there is no way to measure the numbers of adoptions where documents are falsified from birth. When a couple adopt a non-blood child, it is always done with great secrecy. Often only the husband, wife and the doctor know. The couple may move house. The woman will fake pregnancy, complaining to her friends and in-laws about morning sickness. In some cases, clinics act as matchmakers. When the time comes, the woman will check into a clinic where an unmarried woman is having a baby and has agreed to give it up. The two mothers may not actually meet. The clinic will write out the birth certificate in the adopting parents' names and hand the baby to them.

'In a way, loyalty to ancestors prevents people from bringing someone else's child into the family,' says Park Young-sook, who has pioneered foster-parenting in Korea. 'We're so tied up with the blood line, the family tree and me-first. There's a saying that you can't "raise something with black hair", which means that you can help cats and dogs, but not people because they'll always repay your kindness with evil.

'Lots of adopted families have problems with their adopted children because the parents expect too much. They adopt for very selfish reasons. People adopt because there is no welfare system. If you don't have children, when you're old, you'll starve. If it doesn't work out, they complain that it was not a worthwhile investment. People do not realise that adopting a child is not a business or something you do for your own welfare.'

Children are not told that they are adopted because there is a fear that they will not support parents if they know.

'If you're not the same blood, you're the enemy,' Park says. 'That's the thinking. They don't want the child to know he is not of the same blood.'

Not surprisingly, in-vitro fertilisation is booming in Korea. There are no regulations limiting the number of fertilised eggs a woman may carry, thereby increasing the chances of success. There are around 8000 in-vitro births a year with some clinics reporting success rates of up to 40 per cent.[39] With artificial insemination, men want semen from a brother or a cousin, rather than an anonymous donor.

'For a family to keep the blood flow is more important than anything else,' says Roh Sungil, the director of the Jeil Women's Hospital in Seoul.

The real desire for parents entering in-vitro programmes is to have a boy. One of Dr Roh's patients has been trying for over ten years to have a boy. 'This was a couple which already had a daughter. They had a son but he was killed in a traffic accident. They wanted to have another boy, but found they could only do it through in-vitro. They tried and tried but still it has not succeeded. They are quite wealthy and the husband gave up his job and no longer works. For years, this has been their only goal. It's a special situation but it shows a typical concern.'

The reason for the need for sons is that blood still flows through the male. Traditionally, a daughter becomes a member of her husband's family on marriage and is therefore not in a position to take care of you when you're old and maintain the rituals for you after you die. The strength of the preference for sons has dissipated somewhat in modern Korea, where government population campaigns and modern urban lifestyle have reduced family size to one or two children. But still you can see the shadow of ancestral accusation pass over a man's face when he reveals that he has only daughters.

The traditional preference most clearly reveals itself in the form of pressure from parents. Ironically, women are themselves as much a source of prejudice against their own gender as men. In some cases, if a daughter-in-law fails to produce a boy, a mother may encourage her son to dump her or take a concubine. Modern science has provided these bigots with a way to gender-cleanse the unborn in the form of selective abortion. This problem first showed up a few years ago when teachers noticed a shortage of girls in kindergartens. The trend was traced back to the arrival of the Ultrasonogram and other tests that can identify the gender of an unborn child. Females were being aborted.

It is now illegal for doctors to reveal the sex of a foetus. But tens of thousands of these selective abortions still happen every year. This, despite the fact that abortion itself is illegal in most cases. In 1997 there were around 107 boys born to every 100 girls, an improvement over the figure for a few years earlier when it was reaching 120:100. But in some areas, patients are clearly getting to the doctors. In Taegu, for example, a city noted for its conservatism, media reports said the figure was 130 boys per 100 girls in 1997.

'In the past, people didn't think anything of having abortions,' says Dr Roh. 'Some women had as many as ten or more. In those days, people were only concerned about eating and how to get rich. But now, when younger women see the foetus on the Ultrasonogram, they hesitate. They may still want an abortion, but they raise the question more shyly and feel they must apologise to the doctor for asking.'

Girls who survive find a different world from the one their parents and grandparents knew. The preference for boys does not mean that girls are neglected as they used to be. They all have schooling, and parents will pull out all the stops to ensure they marry well. But they face discrimination when they go out to work. Many women experience humiliating hiring procedures where they are selected for their looks. In executive suites, if you have a keen eye for secretaries, you can often see the preference of whichever director it was who did the interviews. This is ironic because it is my personal observation that women office workers are often more capable than men because they are less inhibited by a concern with status. As their abilities are ignored, Korean women easily become obsessed with their looks. Plastic surgery to westernise their eyes is a common procedure. Another is colouring their hair, which is extremely common. With such modern fashions and improved diet, young Koreans look completely different from their parents. They also think differently.

Chapter Five

THE GENERATION GAP

In this century, Korea has been in such constant upheaval that each young generation has found itself faced with a completely different world from that of its parents. Christianity, Communism, colonialism, national division, war, industrialisation and communications have wreaked havoc on the old structures. So far, the expressive character of Koreans, their strong relationships with the emphasis on lineage and parents have remained intact. But even these appear to be under threat. Koreans are facing the same kinds of issues of post-industrial society as we do. With increased mobility and communications, we are all turning into earthlings and it is difficult to say what will remain distinct about Korean attitudes and values in the global village, any more than one can seriously draw distinctions between provinces within the country today.

Lynne Kim, an American, has witnessed great changes in Korea. She says that when she settled in the country in 1972, she found the men generally unattractive. 'In those days, they were a lot shorter. I must have been one of the tallest people in the country then. Men were impolite, egotistical, pompous stuffed-shirts.' She nevertheless married a Korean man, and became a celebrity when she wrote a no-holds-barred book about their relationship and played herself in the TV drama version. On one occasion, they were invited to a TV chat show about marriage and ended up having a row in front of millions of viewers.

'My husband is the old-fashioned type,' she says. 'The older traditional generation is completely Confucian and sincerely believes that the male–female relationship is vertical. The woman is below and must obey the man whether he's right or wrong. She shouldn't express her opinion and it's not appropriate that he discuss things with her. I've resisted at times, but it's a waste of time. As a westerner I used to want to talk it out, but this is not in my husband's capacity. I'm his wife and I'm supposed to follow happily. Actually I do believe in a difference of roles, that a man provides for the family and a woman takes care of what he provides. What you find yourself doing when discussion is not possible is saying "Yes" and then doing what you want. This is what Korean women do. If he were a western man, his attitude would be wrong. But he is a Korean and he feels deeply he is in the right. So it's a process of accepting this. I accept that he won't change.

'But generally, things are changing so much in Korea. I have given lectures on east-west cultural differences to groups of businessmen and I like to ask them whether they think the woman should follow the man. The over-forties all raise their hands with confidence. With groups in their thirties, three or four don't raise their hands. They've usually studied overseas. Three or four more look around before they raise their hands. But with the twenty-year-olds, only half raise their hands and they do so hesitantly.

'Unmarried young men, especially, have changed radically. I tell them I'll come back and see what they're like in ten years' time. I don't think they will become conservative. Power and position of course change people, but we're talking about profound changes in the system and thinking in recent decades. But I think you have to look at it reasonably. Those men at the top who bark orders are not being obnoxious boors. In their society, they are fulfilling their positions. That's how authority was expressed. Young people now don't have the same attitudes.'

Psychiatrist Lee Na-mee says that in modern households women's power is much stronger than it used to be. 'Men yell and beat more, and appear to be in charge, but they're not. Women control the budget and have the main say in raising the children.' However, this is subtle control, rather like saying that the banker, not the politician, is really running the country. It is not enough for women's activists, who campaign to change deeply rooted attitudes and for equal rights under the law. 'There's no such thing as too much feminism in Korea,' says Yu Gina, a film critic and feminist.

Lee Yoon-sang, a thirty-one-year-old male office worker, has one child, and wonders if he and his wife, who also works, can afford to support another. 'My friends all ask this kind of question. Can we afford another child? This is a big change because traditionally even poor people used to have big families. Unmarried men are even wondering if they can afford to get married. Until now, the groom has had to provide the housing and the bride supplies what goes in it. But people can't afford this any more. So you'll see more change.'

His world is a long way from the one he remembers a child. His mother was the daughter of an upper-class landlord family who escaped from north Korea, bringing their gold with them. She went to prestigious Ehwa Women's University, but never worked after marriage. His father was the son of a poor peasant who studied hard and entered an elite school and went to Seoul National University. His father entered government service and became an assistant minister of culture and information. They had two sons.

'Our family was smaller than most,' Lee says. 'My parents were strict with my pocket money and curfew, but they let me study what I wanted at university. This was unusual and considered quite western. Most of my friends' parents interfered much more in their lives. One of my friends got a job offer from several hi-tech companies but his father refused to let him accept them and made him apply for Hyundai instead. Now, five years later, his father's telling him to quit because he's making half what he could be earning. For that generation, the big name provided security and reputation. For my generation, it doesn't.'

There are also changes in how husband and wife relate to each other.

'My father used to run the house. He'd give my mother some money. I remember when I was growing up my mother would say most mornings as he was going to work, "Oh, I need thirty thousand Won for this or that." He'd get irritated and say, "Why ask me just as I'm off to work?" Now there are so many things to spend money on that the husband can't keep up with it all. I give all my money to my wife and then ask for pocket money. I'll say, "I'm meeting my friends tonight. I need fifty thousand Won." My generation is like that. We recognise that giving money to our wife is the best way to save.'

Their combined monthly income is 4.5 million Won, about half of which is saved.[40] Their baby stays during the week with his mother-in-law and comes home at weekends, a common arrangement for young couples.

As work patterns change, so do relations at home. In the 1960s, '70s and early '80s, men who lived in cities would arrive home after working late or socialising with colleagues, itself considered part of their work obligations, and flop into bed. If they weren't back by midnight, they would have to stay out until after the 4 a.m. curfew. Then they'd be up at 6 a.m. Sexual activity was not a major pastime, at least not at home. It was common to see people dozing on buses and at their desks. Now office workers are usually home by 7 or 8 p.m.

'You've got a few more hours before bed. What are you going to do? Rent a video?' Lee asks. Divorce rates are rising. About one-third of marriages in the mid-1990s are ending in divorce. The major factor is economic change, which allows women to find jobs and end their dependence on unfaithful or violent husbands.

Sexual mores are rapidly changing. For the older generation, women often went without and men would pay for it. Today the young generation is more free. However, there is much less casual sex in Korea than there is in, say, Japan. Several western male specialists in this field have reported to me that Korean women are extremely passionate and uninhibited. This energetic involvement is based on an expectation of commitment. When this is not forthcoming, a man can find himself the object of devious plots or great fury. One American friend suffered extreme anxiety when a lady he had taken out turned up a little while later pretending she was pregnant, in a ploy to secure his commitment. Another actually fled the country after a Korean girlfriend discovered she had a Japanese counterpart. The two-timer was attacked with a knife and flew home out of fear that the woman, whose brother was a policeman, might have him arrested. It is a crime to make false promises of marriage.

At other times, women may offer sexual favours in expectation of some return. One foreign scholar I know was extremely embarrassed when a young woman in his class invited him to a coffee shop and strongly intimated that she would be happy to provide sexual services if it would help her grades. I've known others who don't find such offers embarrassing. Males in authority, such as bosses, teachers, university professors and church ministers, frequently abuse their positions in this way.

Transvestism and homosexuality remains low-profile in Korea and there is no attempt to gain recognition, with the result that few Koreans are aware of them as anything but an issue in foreign countries. One or two rather prominent people feature ambiguously on the Korean public scene. Andre Kim is a leading fashion designer who turns up to functions full of conservative men and women, wearing a white trouser suit and frock and heavy make-up. Kim Ok-sun was for many years an opposition member of parliament and one of the few women in politics. The unusual thing about Ms Kim was that you had to look twice to see she was a woman. She set her hair like a man's and wore a man's suit without any flair or make-up. It is unusual that such figures are so uncritically accepted in society. In part it is because both, in a sense, wear a uniform in keeping with their professional status. But the most likely explanation is that other people do not appreciate that they may be homosexual and stop to ask what practices this might involve.

Another sexual issue that has appeared in recent years is incest. Psychiatrists say that this has always existed, but that only recently have women been able to confront it. Of 663 cases of rape reported to the Korea Sex Violence Prevention Centre in the first ten months of 1997, almost one-fifth were committed by family members.[41] Of sixty cases involving fathers, only six led to prosecution. Of nearly five hundred complaints of sexual molestation, fathers were responsible for thirty.

One marked example of the generational change in the 1990s came when the local media discovered the free-spending offspring of the nouveau riche. These rich, college-age, young people outraged Korean society by breaking traditional norms which forbid the flaunting of wealth. Many of them also drove foreign cars, the ultimate mark of a traitor. On average, they received a minimum of a thousand pounds a week pocket money from their father. They were dubbed the 'Orange Tribe'.

Over several nights I went looking for them. I began in a very smart bar called Zippangu, in the fashionable Apkujong part of Seoul. The owner was, surprisingly, a foreigner, a Korean-Japanese called Takashima Ryuichi, who explained that the attack on his wealthy customers was part of a broader government crackdown on corruption. The new president, Kim Young-sam, had launched a campaign, and the Seoul City bureaucrats were showing their zeal in order to avoid becoming targets themselves.

'The city government says that foreign-language signs outside coffee shops and bars are a corrupting influence,' he said. 'The names in English must go or at least be accompanied by a sign in Korean. The government wants to make this a cultural area,' he said. 'They reckon there's too much foreign influence.'

It was a bit late for that. The main Apkujong Street is known informally as Rodeo Drive. There's McDonald's and Pizza Hut, and fashion houses like Boss, Gucci, Giorgio Armani and Valentino. You can't blame the local bars and restaurants for wanting to sound exotic, too.

Takashima explained that the term 'Orange Tribe' was itself a foreign import. It came from Japan, where male university students used to throw an orange at a girl they liked. 'If she caught it, it meant she was willing to date,' he explained.

Plainclothes policemen with portable phones lurked outside discotheques, taking down the numbers of expensive-looking cars, and handing information to the tax authorities for investigation. I found two problems. One was that no one would admit to being a tribesman, and the other was that no one was willing to defend their right to spend their money as they wished.

'I don't like seeing them spend so much money,' said Kim Soon-bum, who claimed to be a simple student as he sat drinking in an Apkujong bar.

'If you have money you can get everything. If you have no money you get nothing. That's Korea.'

'The campaign is good for the country but it's hurting my business,' said Sohn Kwang-jin, the manager of the Hilltop discotheque in southern Seoul, which was said to be a favourite Orange Tribe haunt. 'The real big spenders have gone to the Hongik University area to avoid the press and the police.' Was this a tip? Or a way of getting rid of me?

I caught up with them a few nights later near Hongik University, in a fashionable part of western Seoul. This time I had two companions, my secretary, Jung-hee, and Suh Joon-sik, a human rights activist. We had driven up from a provincial prison where earlier that day we had met some political prisoners who Suh had campaigned for. A thoughtful and self-effacing man, Suh had spent seventeen years in prison himself as a suspected communist. He told me that he spent a lot of his time in solitary confinement after beatings meditating about love and wondering why human beings were so cruel to each other. He was interested in my pursuit of the Orange Tribe.

I parked my old-fashioned Hyundai Stellar. Jung-hee, a fearless former student protester, leapt out in front of two young people and demanded to know whether they were Orangemen. Suh and I started giggling. We spotted two men sitting in a white sports car. Both looked the part but wouldn't say if they were Orange. 'This whole Orange business is exaggerated,' the driver said. 'We just like to meet in nice places, have coffee and maybe a drink and then we go home,' he said.

We settled into a fancy pub called Heidelberg House. 'I come here for the drinking and dancing,' said Lim Ho, a wealthy-looking twenty-four-year-old who said he was a drama student. 'Am I an Orange? No, I'm just a tangerine.'

'I've never been to a place like this before. People live such different lives,' said Suh. 'But everyone has rights.' He was the only person who I found at the time who was willing to admit that rich young people should be allowed to waste their money unmolested.

Around midnight, we noticed several sports cars cruising up and down the street outside.

'They're looking for drunk girls,' said Kim Soon-chul, the barman. 'They offer to take them home.' This practice led to a new title, the *Yata*. This came from the Korean words *Ya* (hey) and *tada* (to ride in a vehicle) and meant literally the 'Oi, Hop In' Tribe. I was sure these were real Orange Tribespersons, for 'Oi, hop in' is the Korean man's equivalent of tossing an orange. But we were too late to talk to them. They were already at work.

61

The campaign against the Orange Tribe was brief and made no difference to anything. Much could be made of the fact that there was a lot of envy involved. Everyone had a reason to dislike the rich kids, and because they didn't approve of their behaviour, no one, lawyers or politicians or journalists, jumped in to defend their rights. It was also never pointed out that we had three of the most corrupt institutions in modern Korea – the civil service, the police and the media – posing as champions of morality and pointing the finger at the children of the nouveau riche.

Some did point the finger at the parents.

'Actually it's the parents' fault,' said Kim the barman. 'They only care about making money and they ignore their kids.'

It interested me that this comment should come from one of the young men behind the bar. The barmen and waiters saw these rich new Koreans close up and were able to understand them, for Korea's twentieth-century class upheaval meant that they are probably only half a generation away from each other in status. His parents, and those of the Orangemen cruising in their sports cars, could well have been neighbours in the same village. What distinguished them may have been a move twenty or thirty years earlier to the city and some opportunity that allowed them, through luck or corruption, to buy property. The parents of the Orange Tribe were people who in the main owned buildings and became multimillionaires during the 1987–90 property boom.

Even those who didn't become millionaires found themselves suddenly relatively wealthy. Yang Soo-kil was married in 1975. His father provided a small one-room flat in Seoul. His wife, like so many Korean women, was very astute with finances and they made strategic moves at the right time. He was too young for the first big property price rise in 1968, but caught the second in 1978 and the third in 1987. By 1988, he was living in a £300,000 house which he had designed with the architect. He also caught the 1989 boom, and in 1990 sold his house, moved to a smaller flat and financed his two daughters' education in the United States. At this time, his monthly pay packet was never higher than £1,500.

'I was lucky,' he said. 'Some of my friends married around the same time and preferred to rent flats so that they had more money for drinking and going out.'

The most common form of rent involves 'key money'. Under this system, you give the owner a one-off deposit, usually around a third of the total value. When you leave, you get it back from the next person coming in. (If you don't have the whole deposit you can pay full or partial monthly rent, which is calculated at 2 per cent of the unpaid amount.) In 1985, I paid

£9000 in key money for the three-bedroom first floor of a house. The owner lived on the ground floor. By 1996, I was in a three-room flat in a fifteen-storey block, which required a £65,000 deposit. This was middle-class Korea. Expatriate diplomats and business people who rent houses may pay up to £7000 a month in rent for a good house.

The problem with the rental system for the late-starters in the booming economy is that it is more and more difficult to get into the ownership pipeline. Many Koreans, desperate to avoid the slide down the status scale, get into all kinds of financial difficulties, borrowing money they cannot repay, accepting huge bribes, losing family fortunes on the stock market, swindling relatives, embezzling from their companies. The honest, but financially challenged, find themselves being pushed to the edge of the city with the poor. Working for the right company can really help. Many companies build apartments and sell them cheap to their employees, who can then sell them for profit and get started. All of this creates a strong disincentive to work and has been a huge factor behind the increasing reluctance of Koreans to work as hard as they used to.

Many wealthy parents, especially of Orange Tribe children, were so fixated on their own progress that they effectively paid their children to keep out of their way. But even children you ignore have to be educated, regardless of how wealthy you are. If the children were not so smart, parents would either make under-the-table donations to colleges to take them or pay for them to go abroad to study.

Education has always been the important consideration in Korea. We read of a *Dae-hak* ('great school', now the word for 'university') in the year 372 and a *Kuk-hak* ('national college') in 682.[42] In the year 992, an institution called *Kug-jagam* was set up to replace the earlier schools and education changed its focus to help prepare upper-class youngsters mostly for civil service careers. In 1398, the new Confucian regime replaced it with the *Sung-kyun-kwan*, now Korea's oldest surviving university. Traditionally, an ambitious boy could rise to the top – which meant becoming a government official – by memorising the Chinese classics and passing the civil service exam. The central theme of this learning was ethics. In reality, though, the system stifled development. It took the arrival of Protestant missionaries in the 1880s to begin the process of change. Within a few years, they had established Yonhui (later renamed Yonsei) and Ehwa colleges in Seoul, and Soong-shil College in Pyongyang. A few years later Korea University was established by a private citizen and Buddhists founded Dong-guk University. Future leaders of Korea emerged from this handful of campuses.

Until recently, most lower-class Koreans remained uneducated. In fact, although the Japanese colonial government had introduced a modern system with both private and state-run primary, middle and high schools, many parents were able to afford only a few years of the old-style, village Confucian tutoring for their children. By 1945, only 20 per cent of Koreans on the whole peninsula had received any formal education.[43] Seventy-five per cent of Koreans now complete high school and 35 per cent go to college.

After independence, resources were severely limited. During the Korean War, these were further depleted when many teachers joined the north Koreans or were forcibly taken north. Some of those who remained fled to Pusan to escape the invading north Koreans, where they started up classes in refugee camps. The government set up a Wartime Union College in Pusan, and opened state-funded universities in provincial capitals freed from north Korean forces. Teachers and children huddled in overcoats, often in war-damaged buildings. They were short of textbooks, paper and pencils.

The 1950s were a time of sheer struggle to survive, and the kind of opportunities that arose were often taken by the forceful and the enterprising, not the educated. For example, the founder of the giant Hyundai conglomerate, Chung Ju-yung, was a barrow boy and car mechanic who did just a few years in primary school. Kim Sang-hyun, a long-time opposition politician, was a shoe-shine boy. These people knew what it meant to go hungry. But they went on to surround themselves with better-educated assistants, the boys who had broken the ice in their inkwells on winter mornings and shivered through their lessons, and then gone on to get their PhDs from Harvard and Yale.

'Without the educated manpower to plan the development, the wisdom to put it into effect, and the educated skill to do the work, the economic development would never have taken place,' said Horace Underwood, a professor at Yonsei University.[44]

By the late 1970s, Korea had the highest level of education vis-à-vis wages in the world. Today, literacy is almost 100 per cent, thanks to a rational spelling system that you can learn in a week. (It would be 100 per cent if south Koreans followed the north Korean lead and dropped the basic fifteen hundred Chinese characters still in wide use.)[45]

For those who grew up before the 1960s and were too poor to receive an education, high school and college were a dream that their children could fulfil for them. 'We all save hard so that our children will have better lives,' says Ko Soon-ja, a fifty-year-old woman from Sungsan village on the south coast of Cheju Island. She has spent her adult life diving for sea slugs and abalone to supplement her husband's income, but is happy that her daughter will not have to do the same for a living. 'She has graduated from university and I'm now looking for a good son-in-law for her to marry.' A good son-in-law means, of course, a university graduate.

In Korea today, education is the single most important key to status. Failure to achieve can mean a serious slide down the ladder, even for the children of the middle class. The reason for this is that school and university provide Koreans with the most important social network in their life. Old Boyism works rather like the public school and Oxbridge system in that the higher the establishment on the scale, the greater the sense of mutual support. If you are a graduate from a top university you can be confident that there are tens of thousands of 'seniors' out there who will do favours for you.

The pressure to succeed at school begins early. Choice of kindergarten is important. There are now some in Seoul that operate in English, for experts have said that language learning is best started early, a fact I learned when my four-year-old bilingual son started correcting my accented Korean. At primary school, you don't waste time. The family is prepared to make the sacrifice because schooling has become its main priority. Parents will make their schedules around children's study routines, and frequently move house in order to be near a better school. After school, most primary pupils go to institutes to study piano, maths, ballet and other subjects. This extra tuition can be very expensive. In high school, these expenses mount. Most pupils work so hard that they seem to see little of their childhood. Even fourteen-year-olds are in school by 7.30 a.m., and after a full day's classes may do private study until midnight or later. Many make do with only four or five hours' sleep. Many also study with private tutors. This tutoring has been banned at different times because it favoured the wealthy and the government wanted to stop the flow of money outside the official educational system. But it remains widespread. Tutors are usually university students, earning their own tuition fees by private teaching. But the highest paid are former high school teachers, called 'tweezer tutors' because of their ability to pick out the questions which are likely to come up in exams. These experts may get paid up to £400 for just one weekly lesson in one subject. Tutoring at institutes is legal, but fees have been controlled, since a survey in the early 1990s calculated that the parental contribution to education in the form of school fees, extracurricular activities, extra tuition and under-the-table cash to teachers equalled the education budget itself.[46]

The unsung heroine of your success in life is your mother, who plies you with coffee at night and is already up, having made your breakfast, at 5 a.m. If she's a Buddhist, she may be down the temple, making donations and releasing paper boats on to the river for good luck before exams. She will also be monitoring her dreams for portents. Chang Young-hee, a literature professor, overheard two women in a dentist's waiting room talking about their children. One woman had dreamed that she was drowning in a brook and that an old man in white appeared and held out his cane to her. Drowning in water? Cane? Professor Chang was thinking Freud:

> ... a typical dream of a sexually repressed woman: the water represented the womb, and the cane, of course, was a typical phallic symbol. My amateur psychoanalysis was just about to get serious, when the other woman, who was all ears, started her own interpretation.
>
> 'My, my. What a wonderful dream! The water you bathed in was clear, right? Gosh, I wish I had that kind of dream. Bathing in clear water means you'll have good luck, and I bet the old man in white was one of your ancestors. He was there to take care of you. I bet your son will get into university with no problem. I think my Jong-ho will fail this time again. Last night in my dream one of my molars fell out ...'[47]

The reason for all the money, prayers and effort is the university entrance examination. This is the tail that wags the educational dog. The entire system accommodates itself to its needs.

Every year in December, 750,000 high school students sit the Scholastic Achievement Examination for College Entrance. They're vying for 250,000 places at over one hundred universities. A quarter of a million who fail, or who succeed but want to get into a better college, become next year's 'repeaters'. So great is the pressure that, each year, several of those who fail commit suicide.

Competition is further intensified by the preference for a few top universities. Many who go to smaller universities carry a burden of failure or mediocrity. To be somebody, you have to get into one of a small group of prestigious universities. And even they have departments which are more prestigious than others. The lowest rung starts with provincial universities, climbs up into Seoul, to reach the law, business administration, medicine and dentistry departments of Seoul National University. Those gaining access to the top few rungs can be sure of a guaranteed place in the exclusive club that makes up top Korean society, because once in, it is very unlikely that they will fail to graduate. Korean universities, like Japanese, and indeed like Korean organisations in general, are very difficult to be thrown out of. Sogang University in Seoul, which was started by American

Jesuit missionaries, became notorious for actually failing students who never attended classes. Because organisations seldom remove people, the great difficulty in Korea is securing entrance.

On the fateful day of the exam, trucks carry the papers in sealed envelopes to thousands of test sites around the country. Office workers go to work an hour later than usual in order to prevent rush-hour traffic jams which may delay students, and police patrol cars are on alert to rush latecomers through the traffic.

The exam itself consists of 230 multiple-choice questions. Usually, there are three obviously wrong answers and one obviously right one. The design of multiple-choice questions is a job for experts who try to create good wrong answers. For example, Hamlet is the Prince of a. Prussia, b. Denmark, c. Finland, or d. Stratford. But the Korean test is written by teachers and is usually less sophisticated, although not easy. One occasional problem which reveals a weakness in the tendency to see knowledge as a matter of black and white, occurs when there might actually be two right answers. For example, is Hamlet a waverer, a prince, a rock star, or a cigar? In the English section of the exam in the past, there have occasionally been two possible right answers to a question, but the markers accept only one. For many years, high school English text books had the phrase 'as possible as I can', a mistake for 'as much as I can' or 'as much as possible'. If it ever came up in the university entrance exam, a fluent English speaker had to remember to use the wrong phrase.

Even though the government has sought to relieve pressure by allowing universities to hold their own additional entrance exams, there is reluctance to change the national exam because, ironically, it is so fair. There is no room for subjective marking and, for this reason, teachers, parents and students can accept the results as fair. (The scholars setting the questions are whisked away in the middle of the night in November to a secret government safe house somewhere in the countryside. They are locked up for a month. Nothing comes out of the building. Literally. Not even the rubbish. Their job is so top secret that not even intelligence officials are permitted access. If the restrictions seem dramatic, consider the awkward position of the teachers making up the questions. If they have children, relatives or children of friends sitting the exam, and the chances are high that they do, they are failing in their duty not to do their best to somehow leak the questions. Honesty is certainly valued by Koreans, but not as highly as loyalty.)

This fairness appears almost cruel, when you consider how in other aspects of life Koreans are used to bending the rules and using connections.

Given what's at stake, it is remarkable but true, that the driver's son from Cheju Island has as good a chance as the son of the president.

A malignant side effect of the parents' desperation for their children to succeed is the corruption that permeates the rest of the Korean education system, from the kindergarten upwards. In its broad-reaching anti-corruption campaign in 1993, the government unearthed numerous cases in which parents paid up to £100,000 to buy places in colleges for their children. Parents routinely give teachers extra money as indirect insurance that the child will not be ignored in class. Often parents form an informal association and take the teacher to nice meals and give a collective cash gift, the idea being less to ensure their own child's advantage over the others than to generally make sure that the teacher is focused on the job. The lengths to which some colleges go in their entrance procedures to appear fair gives an idea of the kind of abuse that Koreans are used to. For example, at one college, candidates sitting the practical part of music exams were screened off from the examiners, so that an examiner who may have been bribed would not know who was on the other side. Whether it is teachers doubling their salaries with cash from parents, professors buying teaching posts, or mature students paying people to write their theses, corruption appears all the more cynical when perpetrated in association with students with such a zeal for learning as the south Koreans have.

But the quality of the education they are torturing themselves to receive is questionable. In school, young Koreans are taught a number of things about life that we would find objectionable. For example, that in the world there is one way to success. This is not a culture in which diversity is seen as a value or an ideal. Koreans see virtue in unity: one mind, one people, one system, one race, one path. The education system reinforces this idea. The artistic but ill-disciplined student, or the creative thinker who wants to challenge established thinking, may have nowhere to go. Another lesson is that education is what is in high school texts and what may be in the exam. It doesn't mean life experience, critical thinking and creativity.

Language teaching is especially flawed. It tends to focus on grammar and learning of obscure vocabulary for the sake of being able to read textbooks, rather than for conversation. Thus, students of a university *Time* magazine-reading club may struggle when you ask them the way to the station. I taught an opposition politician English conversation many years ago. He was not a highly educated man but he had decided in prison that it would be good for his career if he learned English. When we talked, he had an odd habit of getting words almost right. For example, he'd stumble to reach for an unnecessary big word like 'dissimilar' and say 'er, distort, no, dissipate, no ...' before he got to it. I asked him how come he knew all these big words.

'I learned the dictionary in prison,' he said. He had rote-learned whole pages.

Classes are very much a top-down affair, and discussion of the shades of grey in life often do not start until students are on MA or PhD courses. For these reasons, degrees in Korean universities are not highly rated internationally. There has, therefore, been a long-standing tradition of students who need substantial qualifications going overseas, mostly to the United States, for advanced degrees. This they do in large numbers.[48]

Wealthy parents also send their children to English-speaking countries, including Britain, for secondary education. These children are not always so bright, and often find it difficult to adjust to a life in which their parents are not around and teachers do not provide the strict guidelines they are accustomed to. However, brighter children excel overseas, especially in mathematics and sciences, subjects in which habits of hard work and memorisation pay off.

When Park Yong-soo was assigned to London in 1982 as chief of European operations for a Korean conglomerate, he placed his elder son, whose western name was John, in Haileybury Preparatory School in Windsor. To help him in his struggle with the lessons, John's mother took English language classes with him after school. Three years later, John became the first oriental boy to ever win a King's scholarship to Eton. At the prep school Speech Day, the headmaster told assembled parents and pupils that three years earlier, John's English had been so limited that he had had to use sign language when asking the teacher if he could go to the toilet. The audience rose to their feet and applauded and John's mother burst into tears.

Two years later, his brother Paul smashed all records when he became the first foreigner ever to come top in the Eton entrance exam. Both boys went to Cambridge University.

Despite their achievements, Park insists his sons are not geniuses. 'They are just normal boys. They worked hard and the result came,' he said. 'When they were young, my wife and I decided to create an environment to encourage them to study. First, we decided that we would never both go out and leave the boys at home alone.' One unintended result of this was that when Park was chairman of the Korean residents' society in Britain, rumours spread that his wife had left him. The other decision was that in the evenings, husband and wife would sit at the large table in the study reading or writing, rather than watching television.

'It meant that the boys could not just put on the TV because Mum and Dad were reading. They naturally picked up their books.'

But, he said, it was really his wife who helped the boys most. 'My wife gets the credit. She really devoted herself.' This is an understatement. Not only did she study with them, listening to their problems and supporting them. She even sat three A-levels herself while the boys were at school and remained in Britain, when Park was reassigned to Seoul, until their education was complete.

In Korea, once accepted into a university, many students breathe a huge sigh of relief and do as little as possible. They relax and go out on dates. The English word 'meeting' has been hijacked and mutilated to describe the various types of dates that the awkward young engage in. Some 'meetings' begin as group affairs and couples pair off. 'Goating' is a popular type of date. Vulgar though it may sound, it combines the '-co' of the word 'disco' and the '-ting' of 'meeting' and refers to a night out dancing.

One puzzling, but revealing, phenomenon is that students may not bother to read books, but they usually don't skip class (unless they're participating in demonstrations). When I was a student, it was the other way round. I hardly ever went to English literature lectures, but went to the library instead to study. The reason for the Korean behaviour goes to the heart of why he or she is there in the first place – to network. The class is the group and it's linked in the ancestral alumni chain to tens of thousands of graduates who have fanned out into influential positions in society. Sometimes, an entire class will inform a professor that they will not be there at the next lecture because of a demonstration, a class picnic, a party or a 'sandwich day' (a working day caught between the weekend and a holiday).

The quality of education, then, even at the top universities is poor because there is no pressure to perform as undergraduates. They are taught in classes too large for personal attention and in which there is little discussion. Sometimes they are assigned essays to write, but feel no compunction about plagiarising them because they are neither taught how to research nor that their personal opinions might have intrinsic value. Another problem is cheating at exams. Grading papers is also often a dilemma. Colleges are reluctant to fail students because to do so may ruin a young person's life, indicate the school erred in accepting them in the first place, and also cost between two and three thousand pounds in lost fees.

Halfway through their studies, men usually go off to do military service, which is still compulsory. The basic period is twenty-seven months, with reductions and exemptions for only sons, breadwinners, boys without fathers and the disabled. This last category offers possibilities for the reluctant soldier: aside from the obvious handicaps, having bad eyesight and being overweight (90 kg) are also causes for exemption. Those exempted are not missing out on anything too important. Shared military experience for non-professional soldiers does not create the same type of bonds as family, home town and school. After basic training, students are assigned to bases, including front-line units along the DMZ. In these units, youngsters are thrown in with people from all kinds of social and educational backgrounds. The experience is sobering and students return to campus matured and more committed to work hard for their future. They also find the girls they knew in the first year have moved on, and the girls in their classes are two years younger than they. It's time to think of love and marriage and, free of military duties, they are now able to commit themselves to more stable relationships.

PART TWO

History

Chapter Six

ANCIENT TRIBES

Through a great sweep of history, much longer and better chronicled than our own European story, the Koreans have remained a distinct people. They have a tradition, language and identity of their own, preserved thanks to geographic isolation, and through warfare, strategic subservience and sullen resistance. To help us understand modern Koreans, this national biography is best read in three broad periods: the long era from prehistory until the arrival of the Confucian state in 1392; the 500-year experience under China's wing; and the twentieth-century colonial rule under Japan, during which they lost their sense of national self-worth. This brings us up to the division of their country and the question that underscores everything about modern Koreans: how will they become one country again and recover their national identity?

That identity goes back a long way. Scholars believe that today's Koreans are descended from the Neolithic families which came into the peninsula in what was probably three successive migrations between 5500 BC and 2000 BC. There is evidence that Palaeolithic man lived 30,000 to 40,000 years ago on the peninsula. Palaeolithic ancestors are guessed to have gone back up to half a million years, but there is no evidence of their ethnic connection to present-day Koreans (although the possibility of a blood link to Seoul city bus drivers merits study). The first Neolithic Koreans grouped in clans which identified themselves by totems taken from nature, worshipped gods of the wind, rain and cloud and lived in pits and caves. It is believed that they were hunters and wore animal skins and later became farmers and dressed in clothes spun from animal furs or hemp.

Around the eighth or ninth centuries BC, Bronze Age clans made their appearance.[49] They appeared to have lived side by side with the older inhabitants, but to have been ethnically different. The evidence cited is the difference between their bland pottery and the better-designed work of the Neolithics. The less artistic newcomers, however, had better weapons, made of bronze, and prevailed. They had a habit of declaring themselves sons of heaven and of building dolmens, probably with Neolithic labour, some of which are still around. The newcomers may have been tribes of the Altaic language group of central Asia. This history is still contended by scholars who hope that further excavations in Siberia may add a few pieces to the puzzle. But two points are clear: first, there's been no ethnic mixing since on any significant scale, which makes Koreans among the most homogeneous people on earth; and, secondly, the original Koreans were ethnically and linguistically different from the Chinese tribes. Our picture of the ancient Koreans may be skewed because the historians who documented it were Chinese and may have written out of misunderstanding and prejudice towards their rough peninsular neighbours.

There is a theory that the Altaic tribes scattered eastward to Mongolia, Manchuria and Korea, and westward where they ended up in places like Hungary and Finland. But it is based on some flimsy similarities in language. The archaeological evidence is better, but there is, of course, only so much you can deduce from old jugs. And they don't offer much of a story to tell your children. As you would expect, there are other explanations for Korean origins which better suit the human need for meaning and which are better preserved by the anecdotal mind. My favourite comes from old texts recording a history which allegedly began 9000 years ago with a couple called Na-ban and A-man, from whom came the original five races of mankind. These two met at an Eden-like place where four rivers rose, which is interpreted as being either Lake Baikal in Russia or Lake Chonji, on the present-day border of north Korea and China. We're talking here about Adam and Eve, who were, according to this theory, Koreans.[50]

There is also a view among some Christians that the Han Chinese and the Koreans are one of the lost tribes of Israel. But these two theories are pretty obscure and most Koreans are unfamiliar with them.

The standard account of Korean origins is contained in the myth of the first great ruler, Tan-gun, which we should outline because both governments on the Korean peninsula make significant use of it. Furthermore, a lot of people believe it.

According to old records, Hwanung, the son of the celestial being, Hwanin, came down from heaven to Korea and lived as a king among human beings. He came with three thousand followers. At that time a bear and a tiger living in the same cave asked Hwanung to transform them into human beings. The king gave them a bundle of sacred mugworts and twenty cloves of garlic and said, 'If you eat these and shun the sunlight for one hundred days, you will assume human form.' The bear succeeded and, after twenty-one days, turned into a human woman. The bear-woman prayed for a child. Hwanung metamorphosed himself into a human, lay with her, and they had a son called Tan-gun Wang-gom. In the fiftieth year of the reign of Emperor Yao,[51] Tan-gun made the walled city of Pyongyang the capital, called his country Choson, and ruled for fifteen hundred years.[52]

There is a lot of information peeping through this tale. In particular, the year is precisely identified as 2333 BC. That was just after the Great Pyramid was built in Egypt. We can presume that 'heaven' was up north, and that the bear and the tiger were the totems of resident Neolithic tribes being usurped in Korea. It sounds to me like Tan-gun was the son of a Bronze Age chieftain and a Neolithic woman of the bear tribe. Korea's political culture is dated back to the walled-town states of this period. Their leaders were called *tan-gun wang-gom*, which suggests that our Tan-gun could have been several people, especially if the 1,500 years he is alleged to have lived were solar ones. He (or they) would have been a shaman-king.

Tan-gun is said to have worshipped on the top of Mount Mani, a peak near the coast west of Seoul. Once, I climbed this mountain on a lone search, hoping to learn something about the father of the Korean people. It was a wet and miserable day in early spring. I parked the car at the foot of the mountain and walked up through the well-trodden tourist trail. As I made it up the steep path, I got into thick cloud, appropriately, I thought, for this climb to prehistory. A wind blew in scary and unnaturally loud flurries that I fancied were evil spirits trying to frighten me off my quest. I wondered why the wind wasn't blowing the mist away. It hung there trying to spook me. By the time I got to the top I was in a really shamanistic frame of mind. Then, there it was – a large stone altar of sorts looming overhead out of the mist. When I clambered up on it, I was in for a real shock. I don't know what I had expected but it was certainly not something this new. Even accounting for some recent restoration, this construction was not 4,300 years old. In fact, most of it looked distinctly modern. Something was fishy.

Reading up the history, I discovered that the source of the Tan-gun story was a patriotic Buddhist monk named Iryon who was writing in the 1280s, at a time when Mongol hordes swept into Korea. He was quoting sources from several hundred years earlier which no longer survive.[53] But even those chroniclers were writing about events that had allegedly happened a good 2,700 years earlier, unless of course the dates then were calculated differently. Shrines to Tan-gun are believed to have been built around the fifteenth and sixteenth centuries.[54] However, the idea of him as a common ancestor with heavenly connections is embarrassingly modern, twentieth century in fact. Nationalist historians in the 1930s reworked the myth into its present shape as a counter to Japanese efforts to work Koreans into their own fictional sun-god genealogy as adopted citizens.[55] Previous rulers had sought connection to different figures. In 1948, the government declared that the people's history had begun in 2333 BC and made Tan-gun's birthday a national holiday.[56] The cement on the altar was hardly dry. Naive historian that I was, I somehow expected to see a sign of Tan-gun on that mountain top that had been missed for the last four millennia. What I came away with was an education in the rewriting of history.

Some Christians have proposed Hwanin, Hwanung and Tan-gun as a kind of holy trinity with the bear as a Mother Mary figure. Nice one. A cheekier attempt to hijack the myth to modern purpose has been made by the north Korean leadership to their captive audience of 23 million. In the 1990s they have excavated the alleged tomb of Tan-gun and are displaying his eight-foot-long bones there and those of his wife.[57] The none-too-subtle message is that the Kim Il-sung dynasty is a continuation of a long line stretching back into the collective memory and therefore the legitimate authority on the peninsula. If the north Koreans take over the world, I bet in a couple of hundred years they will discover texts proving that Tan-gun invented basketball.

Before we leave Tan-gun, we should note that, according to ancient Chinese historians, he gave his state the name of Choson, which is usually translated to mean Land of Morning Calm. Old Choson, as it is called, wasn't really a nation-state in our sense of the term, but was a territory which covered what are roughly the Pyongan provinces of modern north Korea. This name lasted, if our chronology is accurate, from 2333 BC to 108 BC. A new regime in AD 1392 revived the name, which lasted into the twentieth century. When the Japanese ran Korea they called it, in English spelling, Chosen. North Korea retains this word, rendered Choson (or Chosun) in English, while south Korea calls itself Hankuk (short for *Dae-han Min-guk*, literally, Country of the Great Han People).[58] The word we use – Korea – comes from Koryo, the name used from 918 to 1392.[59]

By the fourth century BC, the Korean tribes had narrowed down their political organisation to three kingdoms – Koguryo, Paekche and Shilla. The biggest, Koguryo, covered modern north Korea and cut an equal-size swathe into what today is the Manchurian part of China. This historical echo and the fact that there are almost 2 million Korean-speaking Chinese in an autonomous area north of north Korea today, lays a foundation for irredentism. Although dormant, this desire to recover lost territory is not dead, and was one factor on the minds of the Chinese in 1950 when they entered the Korean War on the north Korean side.[60] An adviser to the (south) Korean joint chiefs of staff once told me how shocked he was to have some young officers come up to him after a lecture asking whether he agreed that a unified Korea should reclaim this lost territory. China has been sufficiently upset by south Korean visitors stirring up nationalistic sentiment to have complained about it to Seoul.

Koguryo was aggressively expansionist, and in the late sixth century went to war against the recently unified Chinese Sui dynasty. They probably had good reason, for neighbours had always suffered when China had been unified. Koguryo struck first and later held off a Chinese retaliation of 1,130,000 troops, if we are to believe the figures. The Koguryoans prevailed, thanks to the cunning genius of their commander, Ulchi Mundok. He employed head-on attack when he couldn't lose, but otherwise preferred guerrilla tactics, strategic retreat and deception. At one point, he feigned surrender and entered the enemy camp to get a better assessment of their weakness. The Chinese accepted his peace offer and let him go. It was a costly error. The crafty general thought that the Chinese troops looked hungry, so he ordered his men, once the war started, to pretend to lose each battle, to lure them deep into the peninsula and stretch their supplies thin. 'Thus the Chinese won seven battles in a day,' says an old account.[61] A force of 305,000 Sui went confidently for the capital, Pyongyang, but were stopped and, short of supplies, turned and retreated. The Koguryoans pursued them mercilessly. According to records, only 2,700 survived. Enfeebled by this disaster, the Sui dynasty collapsed.

In the south-west of the peninsula, Paekche developed around a single tribe and instituted an authoritarian order earlier than the neighbouring states. It was allied against Shilla with Japan. In the fifth century, Paekche scholars were sent to Japan to teach Chinese classics, the start of a history of cultural transmission which twentieth-century Japanese have tried to obscure.

But it was Shilla in the south-east that would eventually prevail. All three kingdoms strengthened themselves through Confucian administrative structures as they evolved from the looser tribal arrangements into centralised monarchies. Each adopted Buddhism. Official histories were compiled and legal systems developed. Despite royal support, Shilla was the last to adopt Buddhism, due to opposition from the nobility. In the year 527, a young Shilla official called Pak Yom-chok helped the king around this by deliberately getting himself executed. Why didn't the king issue an order to build a monastery and when the nobles protested, blame Mr Pak and execute him? he suggested. Good idea. Pak prayed that his sacrifice would produce a miracle and, sure enough, when he was beheaded, his head flew to a mountain top, white milk spurted several hundred feet, the sun darkened, the earth trembled and the heavens rained flowers. The petrified officials agreed to accept Buddhism.[62] It's possible that this story got exaggerated in the telling.

This king, Pophung, instituted the aristocratic 'bone-rank' system, which still rattles in the Korean mind. Your bone rank, or hereditary bloodline, determined your job, promotion and what kind of house you could have, clothes you could wear, utensils you could use, and cart you could ride in. On the top of the pile were the holy-bone and true-bone classes, which were gradations of royalty. Bone ranks six, five and four were the nobility, and three, two and one the ordinary folk. Originally the kings were all from the Kim clan and their queens from the Pak clan. Their children were the holy-bones. Later, the royal distinctions blurred and holy-bones and true-bones got mixed.

Another feature of Shilla was its youth groups. Called *Hwarang* (flower of youth corps), they appeared to have been launched as an effort by the state to select talented youngsters for service. Some would argue that these were the foreunners of the Japanese samurai. The old histories record that the programme began with women. Several were chosen under the leadership of two beautiful girls called Chunjong and Nammo. It's not clear what their role was to be and we never found out because these two fought and ruined it for the others. Chunjong got her rival drunk and tossed her into the river and was executed for murder. After that, good-looking boys were chosen. These handsome lads were trained in warfare, poetry, music, patriotism and communal life. The core principles of *Hwarang* training were loyalty to the king, filial piety, comradeship, bravery in battle, and discrimination in the taking of life. These youth groups often supplemented military garrisons and were led by a true-bone.

One of the most famous of all the Hwarang was Kim Yu-shin, who led the key battles which resulted in the unification of the three kingdoms under Shilla.[63] Kim was a model example of the idea of fortune coming to a man who listens to God and to his mother, and subjugates himself for a higher cause. As a lad out revelling with friends, he fell for a beautiful dancing girl called Chong-wan and spent a night with her. His mother was so angry when he got home that he swore he would never be so tempted again. Once when his horse turned towards Chong-wan's house, Kim dismounted and lopped its head off.[64] As a commander, Kim knew how to inspire his men. In battle once, when his forces were being defeated by Koguryoans, Kim cried, 'We hear the saying, "Shake a coat by its collar and all the fur will fall smooth; lift the head-rope and the whole net will open." Can't I be the collar or head-rope now?' Then he rode alone into the enemy ranks and beheaded their commanding general. When he came back holding the head, his soldiers found their courage and went in and mopped up. Over five thousand Koguryo men had their heads chopped off on that savage day in 629.

Thirty years later, Kim was the commander of all Shilla forces. In alliance with the Chinese Tang dynasty, he attacked the Paekche and Koguryo states. These were bloody times. Three thousand Paekche women, all the maids and dancing girls of the palace, hurled themselves over a cliff, rather than submit to the rampaging soldiers. Shilla won its wars and then went on to defeat its erstwhile allies, the Chinese. The records say that over seven thousand Chinese were decapitated after a series of battles.[65] Thus Shilla, under King Muyol, eventually established its authority over the peninsula south of Pyongyang. Had the diplomacy and military skill failed Shilla in this hour of history, we might know the peninsula today only as part of China.

At this time, then, in the 600s, Korea was more advanced than any European country with the possible exception of the Ottoman Empire. It was already centralised, had founded educational establishments, had a highly developed culture and more advanced technology. It is important to bear this fact in mind when we consider its subsequent experience.

Most of Koguryo went to China. But in the eighth century, various tribes lead by Koguryoans set up an independent state, called Parhae, in the former Koguryo area of Manchuria and northern Korea.

In peacetime, Tang China had tremendous cultural influence over Shilla, particularly as Buddhism and Confucianism both came from China. Korean monks went to study Buddhism in China and enormous, exotic temples were built.[66] Differing Buddhist sects which placed varying emphasis on scriptural study, prayer, or Zen meditation flourished. A famous monk, Wonhyo, appealed for harmony between the sects and, as penance for breaking his celibacy vows and fathering a son with a princess, spread a simple form of the faith – Pure Land Buddhism – based on a single chant. He converted over 80 per cent of the ordinary people. At the same time, the state tried to introduce the Confucian-based bureaucratic system and educational institutes were established. In Shilla, this Chinese system came up against the aristocratic bone system and so education was limited to the aristocracy.

It is estimated that a million people lived in the Shilla capital of Kyongju in its heyday, five or six times more than now. It was a centre of great learning and creativity. One scholar, Choe Chi-won, who was in charge of drafting royal proclamations, wrote twenty volumes on his experiences in China. This collection is the oldest surviving Shilla document. Another man, Sol Chong, who was the unintended son of the monk Wonhyo, adapted a Chinese phonetic system to the Korean language. Shilla stone pagodas and bronze temple bells remain. Other outstanding items of Shilla creativity still in evidence are the royal tombs, the Chomsongdae astronomical observatory, the Pulguksa Temple and the Sokkuram grotto near Kyongju. This last is an artificial cave featuring a ten-foot granite Buddha and other carvings which remain unweathered by the centuries.

Shilla was not fun for everyone, though. A Chinese record said that the highest officials had 3000 slaves.[67] Given these numbers we can presume that a huge part of the population was in fact in slavery. Continued warfare reduced many ordinary people to poverty. Authorities took a census every three years that appears to have been remarkably detailed, recording even the numbers of livestock and trees per household. In addition to commoners, settlements of slave labourers were dotted around the state.

In the end, bone-rankism was the undoing of Shilla. The true-bone aristocrats conspired against the throne and eventually started setting their militias on each other. Head-bone intellectuals favoured the spirit of meritocracy of Confucianism over Buddhism. Rebel leaders founded separate states in areas they controlled. One of them, Wang Kon, eventually took over Shilla. His state was called Koryo, and its capital was Kaesong, in modern-day north Korea.

A warming feature of Koryo was that it generously embraced the ruling class of the Parhae state to the north after its collapse, and was diplomatically compassionate towards its Shilla foes. The Koryo leader, Wang Kon, married a Shilla princess. He also freed many slaves and gave farmers a three-year tax break. He expanded the dynasty's territory, annexing Cheju Island to the south and pushing his borders northwards to the Yalu River. Thus, in 936, the Koreans were living in a single state that was established, near enough, along the border which remained in place until 1945.[68]

Bone-rankist Shillans, generously invited into the new Koryo bureaucracy, ensured that the new state retained much of the Shilla character, although there was much more mobility in the new order. The Koyro founder unwittingly began what one historian called the 'tradition of elite continuity' which continued into the modern era.[69] Thus Koryo was less a rejection of Shilla than an alteration. Shilla noble clans would continue to dictate Koryo politics until the fourteenth century. Shilla's rigid social order, by which your bone rank determined social status and job, and its strong Buddhism characterised the new state. Koryo is best remembered in this age for its superb celadon pottery, which even the Chinese have rated as the world's finest ceramic art of old.

The Koryo kings got off to a bad start. Wang Kon's son, Hyejong, was the second leader. The main thing we know about him was his conception, which is recorded in the official dynastic history books with a striking attention to detail. His mother was named Lady O. The history book says that she dreamed of a dragon entering her womb. Wang Kon met her when he was commander of naval forces. We read that he first saw her doing her laundry. 'Because of her humble status, he did not want her to become pregnant, and so he ejaculated on the bed sheet. The queen absorbed it and became pregnant, giving birth in time to a son, who later became King Hyejong.'[70]

Hyejong didn't rule for long. He is believed to have been assassinated. His half-brother took power and was himself assassinated.

Some monarchs were quite nice. One tenth-century king made a special point of recognising and honouring filial behaviour in his subjects.[71] He cited a woman called Nambu, whose father died from a snakebite and who put the coffin in the bedroom for five months and continued to serve the corpse as a dutiful daughter. A man saw some wood that reminded him of his recently deceased mother, so he took it home and venerated it. These two were given royal exemptions from corvée labour and had special gates built at state expense at the entrance to their villages.

Koryo was endlessly harassed by marauding tribes from the north and Japanese pirates to the south. The state also suffered unrest and rebellion, due to a weak and corrupt court and abuse of power by the nobility. There was one failed coup attempt by the grandfather of a king. Not content with his role as grandfather, he married two of his own daughters off to his grandson the king to ensure that the successor would also be a grandson. Then he got even more ambitious, made a failed bid for the crown and was driven into exile. Around the same time, a monk tried and failed to establish a new dynasty in Pyongyang. In 1170, an incident in which an officer was slapped in front of the king by a civilian prompted a military coup. Rebel officers massacred many civilians and placed a new king on the throne. A military junta effectively ruled. This regime faced a rebellion by an army of armed Buddhist monks who assaulted the capital, and insurrections by peasants and slaves, seeking liberation, in which thousands were slaughtered. But for the following century, military officers effectively controlled policy.

In the thirteenth century, the Mongols invaded. The court moved the capital to Kanghwa Island and peasants retreated to mountain forts. The Mongols laid waste to the land, slaughtered Koryo's peasant troops, and destroyed cultural relics. At the height of the Mongol invasions, the court arranged the carving of over 81,000 woodblocks – needed to print the total Buddhist scripture – as a devotional project to win divine protection. Created between 1237 and 1252, these blocks, known as the *Koryo Tripitaka*, are now preserved at Haein Temple in Korea.[72] They replaced a set of woodblocks, carved over seventy years in the early eleventh century, which had been destroyed by the Mongols in 1231. The Meditation school of Buddhism, with its appeal across class lines, became predominant. There were seventy temples in the capital alone and hundreds of others built all over the country, testimony to the belief that personal, and indeed national, security was enhanced not just by meditation, but by pious observance and active involvement in ritual. In Koryo times, there were huge prayer ceremonies and street processions for peace involving tens of thousands of monks.

Eventually the military dictator was assassinated and authority returned to the king, who sued for peace. The subordinated Koryo kings now found themselves having to marry princesses of the Mongol Yuan dynasty and assist in the failed invasion attempts against the major Mongol prize – Japan. By the mid-fourteenth century, however, Yuan was in decline, under pressure from the emerging Ming dynasty of China, and the Koryo king reasserted control and purged pro-Mongol officials.

In the second half of the fourteenth century, Koryo came under attack from Chinese bandits called the Red Turbans. A hundred and fifty thousand of these raiders once briefly seized the capital, Kaesong, where, if we are to believe the disgusting accounts from old court records, they terrified the locals. They made their shelter out of large circles of wet animal skins, from which long icicles hung as windbreaks.[73] Inside these primitive camps, they drank and danced by day and at night played with naked girls and cooked the breasts of pregnant women to eat as side dishes. They were repelled by a general called Yi Song-gye. Less than 10 per cent of the bandit force survived his murderous attacks and made it back across the Yalu river into China.

Even more problematic were attacks by Japanese pirates. These had begun over a century before as coastal raids, but intensified to the point where villages were wrecked, terrorised peasants left their farms and sought refuge inland, and coastal shipping ceased operating. General Yi was called in and, in a decisive engagement, shot an arrow through the mouth of the pirate's leader.

In 1388, the king sent General Yi off on a new mission to attack China. He disagreed with this policy and turned his troops around and marched almost unopposed to the capital. The tearful king was placed on a horse and sent off with his queen and a concubine into internal exile and a new king was placed on the throne. Over the next three years, General Yi assumed political and economic control, chiefly through the introduction of a sweeping land reform. All current ownership was declared invalid, land near the capital was given to officials according to their rank and the rest remained state property. This measure destroyed the powerful nobles and undermined the Buddhist establishment, but strengthened the livelihood of the peasantry, who had new tenancy guarantees. By 1392, the general had declared himself king and pulled the curtain down, after 456 years, on the Koryo dynasty.

Chapter Seven

CHINA'S LITTLE BROTHER

I t is fitting that General Yi's coup began with a refusal to attack China. For his state, which revived the old name Choson, adopted Chinese Neo-Confucianism so fully as the foundation for both its religious ethic and state organisation that the Koreans are reckoned to have produced the most orthodox of such dynasties in east Asian history. It has been suggested that the zeal to out-Chinese the Chinese came from a survival urge by the Koreans, who sought to raise themselves in relation to the Middle Kingdom, as China called itself, from an inferior and threatening barbarian state to a younger brother.[74] Later, Choson was to survive as a vassal to China. It lasted over 500 years, right up until 1910, and its history provides profound clues to an understanding of modern Korea.

General Yi's reformist Confucian thinkers restructured the bureaucracy and society. They recalled the old notion of the Mandate of Heaven to justify the establishment of the new dynasty and the new name for the state. The notion still echoes in the modern Korean mind, despite modern knowledge, in the same way as many western Christians sense a divine hand behind changes in the weather. According to this idea, political legitimacy derives from divine backing and calamities such as military defeats, natural disasters and poor harvests are indications that heaven is angry and that the mandate has shifted.

In keeping with tradition, the general was given a new name when he became the monarch and he is now known to Korean history as King Taejo. As a victorious warrior and dynastic founder, Taejo inspired considerable sycophancy. He was a reputed archer and once is alleged to have shot eight deer running abreast with one single arrow.[75] There was of course nothing new about this kind of poetic licence. (Nor nothing old. Similar excesses by

86

writers in modern north Korea about their leaders indicate that it is human to wax lyrical, genuinely or falsely, about people who wield great power, especially if it is over your livelihood.)

An important gesture by the new order was to move the capital. A place called Hanyang was selected and renamed Seoul, and it has been the political, economic and cultural centre of Korea ever since.[76]

The intellectuals behind the new regime embraced a philosophical version of Neo-Confucianism, a doctrine which emphasised the relationship between ruler and subject.[77] They were also very intolerant and sought to destroy the Buddhist establishment. Even though some kings maintained a private faith in Buddhism, the religion was restricted throughout the period of the Choson dynasty. State and family ceremonies were replaced with Confucian rituals, but Buddhist and shamanist rites were still widely practised by women. The Neo-Confucianists sought to recreate the utopian rule of ancient Chinese dynasties. Thus politics became the supreme pursuit and other disciplines became subordinated to it. This predominance of power interests is still a notable feature of the mindset of modern Koreans.

The society they built was a rigid, caste-like structure. There were five classes. In contrast to the earlier periods, when Korea was dominated by the nobility, the country was now run by a scholarly upper class of civilian and military officials known as *yangban*. They represented about the top 10 per cent of the population. They saw their prime purpose as the devotion to learning and self-cultivation, and the only employment they aspired to was government service. Geography was also important and there were almost no *yangban* in the northern and eastern parts of the country. They were actually banned from farming, commerce and other jobs. Technical people such as doctors and translators, and lower functionaries such as clerks, were from the *chung-in* or 'middle people' class. The *yangban* elite married within their class and lived either in separate parts of the capital or in separate villages. Despite the apartheid-like rigidity of classifications, in practice there was some fluidity between these top groups, as the 'middle people' class became permitted to sit the civil service exams, some peasants became rich and the numbers of impoverished *yangban* without government office increased.

Over half the population were of the *sang-in* or commoner class. They were also known as *yangmin* (good people). These were the farmers, fishermen, merchants and craftsmen. There were degrees of goodness, with craftsmen the most highly regarded. Merchants and businessmen were widely considered as scum and struggled to scrape by. As a measure of their lowly status, they were forbidden by law to use the language of the *yangban*.

Peasants were restricted by law from leaving their land and had to carry identity papers at all times. In addition, peasant households were organised into groups of five, which were responsible for keeping an eye on each other.[78] A similar pattern still exists in north Korea as an important means of political control. One reason for this was to ensure that the government had well-distributed access to forced labour, which all non-*yangban* men were required to perform, as well as military service.

The next class was less euphemistically called the *chonmin*, meaning 'lowborn' or 'inferior people'. These were people in certain hereditary professions which the Choson state found dubious, such as grave-digging, tanning and butchery. It also included bark-peelers and basket-makers (perhaps because these were jobs often done by moonlighting butchers). This lowest of hereditary castes lived in separate villages, or existed as wanderers. The men were forbidden to wind their long hair up into a bun, or 'topknot', as the higher classes did. They had to walk in an odd jumping fashion and bow when they went past villages of commoners and *yangban*.[79] If a person of higher status approached, they had to bow, step aside and grip themselves in a cringing, inferior posture until he'd gone by. Failure to bow could be punishable by hanging. Giving their children too high-sounding names, such as *ui*, which means 'righteousness', was also a presumption punishable by hanging. They could not smoke in front of other people; they had to use honorific speech towards even the children of commoners; they couldn't tile the roof of their house, which had to remain thatched; they couldn't wear silk clothes or straw shoes.

Also in this class were shamans, exorcists, entertainers and the female *kisaeng*, the Korean equivalent of the geisha girls, who often ended up becoming *yangban* concubines.[80] These women were highly trained in poetry and the arts in order to provide stimulating company for *yangban* men.

Technically, they had the same status as slaves. And the caste included actual slaves, both government and private-owned. It is estimated that as much as one-third of Koreans during the Choson dynasty were, in fact, slaves. This is a feature of not-so-distant history which Korean scholars have yet to bring themselves to face. In 1650, prostitutes were all made government slaves. But the number of other slaves at this time had declined from a high of 400,000 in the early years of the dynasty to around half that number by the mid-seventeenth century. In 1800, government slavery was technically abolished, but *yangban* families maintained their own slaves until the turn of the twentieth century.

The *yangban* had their clan books. Some clans trace their lineage back as far as the Shilla and Koryo dynasties. Compilation of these genealogies became an urgent consideration after invading Japanese in the late six-teenth century destroyed records and left many *yangban* unable to prove their status and their eligibility to sit the civil service exams. Aristocrats searched old census records and documents, official histories, civil service rosters and tombstone rubbings with a thoroughness matched only by the Mormons in this century. It had become vital to prove your pedigree and to ascertain your broader clan connections in society. The clan books trace the family through the father's line as far back as they can. The man it stops at is identified as the lineage founder. Daughters are either excluded or registered by their husband's name. These books are still updated and handed down from father to eldest son.[81] Forgery and bribery were a significant factor behind the rather unusual rise in the *yangban* from 10 per cent to 70 per cent of the population in the 150 years up to the middle of the nineteenth century.

Slaves did not have surnames and often women of the lower classes were not even given a forename. All women were raised to understand they were inferior to men and should be submissive at all times. In their life, this meant being obedient to their father, then later to their husband and in-laws, and, when they were widowed, to their sons.

The system of justice in the Choson period was unfair, chaotic and often vicious. Prisoners were subjected to flogging, dislocation of limbs, sawing of the flesh with coarse ropes, gouging by a wooden axe, and branding. The officials responsible for carrying out punishment often received no pay and so lived on bribes from victims' families.

Disputes between communities were often settled with organised stone-throwing battles. They might involve hundreds of men and last all day. 'Missiles were flying through the air, any one of which would have done for a man,' wrote an American eyewitness to a nineteenth-century stone fight through the streets of Seoul. 'All were alive to the danger, and the rush and scramble to escape was like a stampede of wild beasts.' At one point the game was stopped with a roar 'as though a goal were scored' and a dead body was carried off. Final score by the evening was 1:1.[82]

How did such egregious inequality and violence exist unchallenged in a state whose central vision was of the virtuous ruler presiding over the per-fect system? One idea which may have justified the rigid caste-like struc-ture, and kept hundreds of thousands in hereditary slavery, was that people are inevitably born to their station, as a mouse is born to be a mouse, and that the best one can hope for is an improved reincarnation. In Confucian Korea, it is possible that many of the *yangban* believed that the lower castes had an inferior *ki*, or essence, which precluded them from becoming good and moral people.

Korea was a very ascetic country at this time. Conspicuous consumption was abhorred and no one of any social background would engage in it.[83] Thus social stability, not development, was seen as the measure of successful rule. The Neo-Confucians thought that the perfect society began not with the system, but with the personal morality of the monarch. Thus an immoral ruler created instability. Looked at the other way round, instability was indication of a flawed leadership, even when no obvious flaws were visible. A wise king's strategy was to select learned bureaucrats both for his own education and for the implementation of virtuous policy. The most important means for ensuring that the best talent rose into these positions was the establishment of selection by examination, as opposed to birthright. The most important was the civil service examination, which tested knowledge of Confucian classics, history and literature. As Confucian education was all about ethics, the state was in theory ensuring that it recruited its most ethical young men as the future decision-makers. These notions behind the arrangement of fifteenth-century bureaucracy still have strong resonance in modern Korea, including the penchant for education.

Naturally, in Choson, the establishment of schools was a priority. Young boys were educated in the five relationships of Confucius: a son's filial piety to his father, a subject's loyalty to his ruler, a woman's obedience to her husband, deference of youngsters to their elders, and honesty between friends. These first two were especially important and failure in this regard meant dishonour worse than death.

The fairy tales of the day reinforced this instruction. One tells of a young man who went fishing for carp. It was winter and pretty freezing, but he went because his parents had suggested he should. He was a dutiful son. Fanatically so, it would seem, for, when he arrived at the river and saw it was solid with ice, instead of shrugging his shoulders and going home, the young man became distraught that he could not fulfil his parents' desire. He fell on his face and began wailing. Then, unexpectedly, fish jumped out of the ice and landed right there in front of him. It was a miracle! His devotion to his parents had moved heaven.[84]

Scholar-officials were tasked with ensuring that the ship of state charted a politically correct course. One innovation of the Choson state was the introduction of offices which were required to monitor and prevent arbitrary decisions and abuse of power by the king or other officials. However, a cursory glance at the throne offers enough argument for republicanism. Despite the utopian emphasis on filial piety and blood, only six out of the twenty-seven Yi kings were first sons.

The first few years of the Choson dynasty provide a good study of how the pressures of power can shatter a family that may well have already been dysfunctional. Taejo's fifth son by his first wife, Prince Bangwon, was ambitious to succeed him. It was he who had originally suggested that his father mount the coup. When Bangwon killed his two half-brothers, King Taejo was so distraught that he immediately abdicated in favour of his second son. But this new king was eventually persuaded by his wife to give up power rather than fall victim to Bangwon's ambition. Bangwon then became king and was named Taejong. An old Buddhist monk, who had predicted that General Yi would become king, persuaded Taejo to meet his son for a reconciliation.[85] At the meeting, the old king tried to kill his son with a surprise shot, but his bowmanship finally failed him and the arrow missed.

Bangwon was succeeded by his third son, who was named King Sejong. He is the favourite of the Choson dynasty kings. There was both relative peace and plentiful harvests during his 1418–50 rule. He was a scholar and set up a research institute called the Hall of Worthies, whose great minds developed scientific devices such as rain gauges, sundials and striking water clocks. Sejong also introduced more scientific farming methods from China, including wet farming associated with the paddy field, and rice transplantation methods which allowed farmers to reap two crops a year. But his greatest contribution to history was the creation in 1443 of the Korean alphabet. This system, known as *Hangul*, is striking, coming as it does from the Chinese cultural sphere where the complex characters serve as a conspiracy by snobs who have mastered them to keep the masses illiterate.[86] As in Spanish, but in total contrast to English, one symbol refers to one sound and there are only minimal anomalies. You can learn it in a week. Sejong did not just get the credit for the work of his academics, although this is a common feature of even modern Korean scholarship. He reportedly developed many of the symbols himself by studying the shape of his wife's mouth and tongue as she formed different sounds.

As with any royal lineage, the Yi family had their share of other goodly souls and scoundrels. Sejong's first son was a gentle but sickly man and ruled for only one year before he died. He got a group of his close advisers so drunk once that they passed out. When they woke up, they found they had been carried by eunuchs to the king's chamber and covered with royal quilts. Their profound shame at this lapse and the king's kind response created a loyal bond around which the monarch hoped to create protection for the teenage crown prince. The boy became king, but was executed after a violent coup by one of his uncles. This new king, Sejo, executed numerous courtiers and Hall of Worthies scholars, and personally presided over the gruesome tortures of some other offenders.

But the most fiendish of the monarchs was Yonsan the Obscene (1476–1506). Separated from his mother at age three, he grew up as a 'dark prince who loved dark deeds'.[87] As a young boy he developed a close relationship with a young noblewoman. She was poisoned, and he later discovered that she had been his real mother, the deposed queen, who had been banished after scratching the king's face in a jealous rage when she caught him having sex with a concubine. Given such a trauma-filled childhood, it is not surprising that Yonsan became a sex maniac. He once allegedly ordered a court woman to strip and pretend to be a mare and go on all fours. When she began to nibble at some pretend horse food, he approached her from behind. As king, he trawled the provinces for beautiful women and did not discriminate between the married and unmarried. It is said that if a married woman in his harem continued to look dejected, he would have the head of her husband brought to her to really give her something to complain about. Other married women were more willing and in fact exchanged their favours to secure promotions for their husbands. At least one victim who proposed to go back for more was murdered by her husband.

How do we know all this? The palace was crawling with historians who took notes of all official transactions and even royal conversation. Eunuchs and concubines were also sources for the juicier stories. We may assume that there are considerable distortions in the stories of kings considered at the time of the writing to have been bad, and cover-ups in the case of the good kings. The fact that we have the dirt on Yonsan is because he was deposed, and the stories were written up by the new court while they were still fresh. Yonsan's lust eventually was his undoing. His last offence was the rape of his own widowed aunt. After this assault the desecrated woman took a dagger and 'slashed her unmentionable parts and fell dead with the blade thrust in her body'.[88] Unfortunately for Yonsan, the aunt's brother was the commanding general of the royal Tiger Brigade unit. He led a lightning coup of government officials, soldiers and ordinary citizens, who rushed the palace, drove the king out, executed several loyalists, and emptied the jails. Yonsan was sent off under guard into internal exile.

Another nasty character was King Kwanghae. He is believed to have slipped poison to his father to avoid losing his position as crown prince. He then murdered two of his brothers. This king preferred partying with his concubines to running the country. But the ghosts bothered him and he had his father's tomb dug up and the bones buried on another hillside. He upset the Confucian orthodoxy by inviting shamans to the palace to scare away evil spirits. Eventually, an army of six thousand rebels staged a coup and placed a royal nephew on the throne. Kwanghae fled and took refuge in the house of a citizen, who turned him in. The new king spared Kwanghae's life and exiled him to an island with some concubines and slaves.

One crown prince was so tormented by his father's abuse, that he became a psychopath. He beat his favourite mistress to death, cut the heads off eunuchs, and slaughtered doctors and fortune-tellers who upset him. Egged on by courtiers, his father the king became convinced he was plotting a coup and had him sealed in a wooden rice chest, where he died a slow, stifling death after eight days.[89]

After two hundred years of relative peace with its neighbours, Korea was once again threatened by invasion, this time from Japan. The warlord Toyotomi Hideyoshi had gained control of warring clans and turned his attention towards Ming China. When Korea refused to co-operate, Hideyoshi launched his first attack, landing 160,000 soldiers at Pusan in 1592. As his defences collapsed, the king, Sunjo, and his ministers abandoned the capital and headed north. On the way, angry citizens blocked their path and swore at them. Citizens refused to join the fight. Slaves in Seoul took advantage of the bureaucrats' flight to torch the office where all the registers of slaves were housed and, for good measure, the Ministry of Punishments. Japanese troops took the capital without firing a shot.

At this point, a regional naval commander, Admiral Yi Sun-shin, stepped to the fore. Now revered as one of the greatest heroes in Korean history, Yi was a commoner who failed his first attempt to pass the military officer exam when he fell off his horse during one test.[90] He launched his specially designed 'turtle ships' against the Japanese. They are believed to have had a spiked, iron-plated cover over the deck to prevent boarding. Cannons fired from holes in the side and clouds of sulphurous smoke poured out of the dragon-shaped bow of the vessel to both terrify the enemy and provide protective cover.[91] Admiral Yi defeated the Japanese at sea and cut their supply routes. At the same time, local 'righteous armies' of gentry, peasants and slaves sprang up to defend their villages, often under the leadership of Confucian intellectuals. Elsewhere, groups of Buddhist monks took up arms. These independent guerrilla units were supplemented by a force of 50,000 Ming Chinese. The Japanese were pushed back. Admiral Yi was sidelined by court intrigue, but recalled when the Japanese attacked again five years later. When Hideyoshi died in 1598, the Japanese withdrew completely and, in an attack on the retreating enemy, Admiral Yi was killed by a stray bullet which hit him in the armpit.

The Japanese had caused terrible devastation, especially in the southeast. The population dropped, two-thirds of arable land was devastated, and historical records, national treasures and cultural relics were looted and destroyed. The most ghastly detail concerns facial trophies. Japanese troops were ordered to lop off the ears of captured soldiers and civilians. Later, they were required to cut off noses and ship them back to Japan as proof of death. Noses were sent in batches, pickled in salt, and buried. Around 100,000 in all. A Korean scholar discovered a tomb containing 20,000 noses in a place called Bijen in Japan in 1984. In 1992, they were returned to Korea. Controversy flared when it was proposed they be buried at a temple which was a memorial to Admiral Yi. It was feared that the angry, humiliated spirits of the mutilated soldiers would cause trouble. One year later they were finally laid to rest in the town of Puan, where 3000 other soldiers had died in a battle in 1597.[92]

Resentment from this period lasted for a long time, unrelieved by any historic borrowing, court connections or exchanges that benefited the Koreans. Indeed, the notable outcome of this warfare was a civilising flow from Korea to Japan. The Japanese adopted Neo-Confucian ideas of political organisation, especially those of the school that emphasised self-cultivation and learning from experience. In addition, hundreds of Korean craftsmen taken as prisoners developed ceramic and textile traditions in Japan.

One generation later, in 1627 and 1636, factional strife led directly to invasions from the Jurchen tribes of Manchuria, who were to conquer Ming China. Korea walked a tightrope during the Ming-Jurchen struggles. Unable to refuse Ming requests for help, the king secretly ordered the commander of his troops to surrender as soon as it looked as if he would lose. This he did, thereby successfully avoiding a Jurchen attack on Korea. The king was then ousted in a factional struggle and his successor, King Injo, immediately threw his weight behind the Ming throne. A pro-Injo noble, called Yi Kwal, got miffed because he wasn't sufficiently rewarded, and rebelled. His forces were suppressed, but some escaped to Manchuria where they persuaded the Jurchens to invade. Peace was signed after the Koreans agreed to recognise the Jurchens as an elder brother and to remain neutral between the rival Chinese. The Jurchens declared a new Ching dynasty and invaded again in 1636 after Korea refused to recognise its sovereignty over Ming. There was a humiliating capitulation ceremony on the banks of the Han River. Although the destruction was not as severe as that by the Japanese, Korean hostility towards the Ching dynasty lasted a long time. In both this and the Hideyoshi experiences, Koreans felt they had been assaulted and humiliated by pagans with an inferior culture.

Choson Korea was now a tributary state. There was a cultural flow from Beijing which became the Koreans' window to the outside world. Korean officials returned with new books and ideas, such as Catholicism, knowledge of the West, modern cartography, science and astrononomy which would have otherwise remained unknown for some time.

During the early centuries of the dynasty, the failure to create virtuous politics led Neo-Confucian scholars to split into arguing factions. Some lost their enthusiasm for political office. A broad rift developed between those who held that personal experience and self-cultivation were the essence of learning and others who rated intellectual learning over spiritual insight. Scholar-bureaucrats argued over whether to always stick by the book, or to allow expediency, and they fought over court rites and succession issues. Major disputes continued over such vital issues of national security as whether the Queen Mother should mourn her deceased daughter-in-law for nine or twelve months. In this case, the nine-monthers, who controlled the government, were pushed out of power by the king, because the twelve-month reckoning was based on an analysis that gave the king higher status in his own personal family. This kind of nonsense was tamed in the eighteenth century when attempts were made to spread government posts among the four main factions.

By this time, many scholars began to take a more scientific approach to learning, refusing simply to follow tradition. They did not hesitate to attack the views of the older generations of thinkers. They proposed reform in agriculture, administration and the military and some went so far as to offer a new vision of the ideal state: an agricultural economy of free, self-employed peasants who owned and worked their own land. They proposed the abolition of the class distinctions, equal opportunity in education and selection based on merit. Others of a similar mind favoured the development of Korea as an economy based on commerce and manufacturing. These intellectuals were the first to show interest in Catholicism, introduced by Korean visitors to China. A papal ruling strictly opposing the Confucian rites of ancestor worship led to the banning of the faith in Korea. A Korean convert was executed for failing to prepare an appropriate ancestral tablet for his mother. Nevertheless, at the end of the eighteenth century there were around four thousand converts. Then in 1801 a vicious suppression resulted in several executions and thereafter it was the lower classes mostly in and around Seoul which responded to Christianity. In 1839, three French priests and several Koreans were beheaded. Thirteen years later, the first Korean priest, Father Andrew Kim Tae-gon, was executed. Father Andrew, ten French priests and ninety-two other Korean martyrs were made saints by Pope John Paul II in 1984, during a visit marking the 200th anniversary of Korean Catholicism.

Around this time, as the *yangban* grip on society weakened, the peasants sought ways to take more control of their lives. A significant concept which developed at the time were mutual help bodies called *gye*.[93] These were voluntary associations created between people with connections such as lineage, home village, same age and so on. Some were social, while others were economic self-help groups which shared resources. Such groups still function today, especially among housewives and Korean residents overseas. Typically, the members of a modern *gye* will donate a certain sum each month, with the entire sum going to one member each time.

The life of the peasant was tough. Thousands died when the harvests were bad and many became so impoverished that they left their homes and became vagrants. In the early nineteenth century some formed roving bands of brigands. At the same time there were several popular uprisings.

The most significant threat to the government came from *Tong-hak*, a religious movement which rose up mostly among peasants. Conceived as a bulwark against foreign influence, *Tong-hak*, or 'Eastern Learning', was a doctrine that ironically set in motion a chain reaction which brought the worst kind of nineteenth century imperialist power crashing into Korea. It was established by a man called Choe Che-u, the son of a poor *yangban* teacher and his concubine. He felt a divine call to rescue Koreans from corrupted Confucianism before they succumbed to the appeal of the West and its Catholic religion (called *So-hak* or 'Western Learning'). His syncretistic belief drew on all faiths. Choe taught that man and God were the same, that the spirit of God dwelt within the mind of man. Thus everyone is a 'Lord of Heaven' and should regard others as such. The first appeal of this faith, as of Christianity, was that its one God was more powerful than all the spirits that inhabited the world of the Korean peasant. At the same time, the new religion adopted some traditional shamanist elements familiar to the peasant and the lowborn. But above all, the movement was upliftingly egalitarian. Unlike Christianity, it did not propose that all are sinners, but rather that all are princes and sages, even the peasants. The *Tong-hak* activists called for social reform and an end to corruption, to strengthen the state against foreign powers. Uprisings began in 1862 and Choe was arrested and executed in 1864 for 'deluding the world and deceiving the people'.[94]

This was not the end of his movement, though, nor of troubles for the dynasty.

From the early part of the nineteenth century, western nations had sought contact with Korea. British trading vessels and warships had appeared off the Korean coast, French warships had also sought to deliver a diplomatic letter to the government, and some Koreans had been killed in an encounter with Russian vessels. Even though China and Japan had already opened their doors to the West, the Koreans were aware of the humiliation of their neighbours by these barbarian powers and were wary of any exchanges. A natural opening to the West was hindered by the fact that, as a tributary state, Korea's foreign policy was in Chinese hands. But Korean resistance to the outside had deeper causes. As the Confucianists who outdid the Chinese, Koreans thought they were superior and clung to their social traditions, which had no room for foreigners. The Japanese were seen as uncultured, and westerners, with their horrendously long noses, psychedelic hair colour and round eyes, were seen as barbarians and monsters. What could they offer but disease and discontent?[95]

Just how different the world of the Korean official and the westerner were a hundred years ago is captured in this description of an encounter between an American and a provincial governor in the city of Haeju:

A great wall of China seemed to separate us. My country, my calling, my appearance, were all mysteries to him. For example, why had I taken my hat off on entering, when Korean custom requires you to put it on if you will show respect? I tried to say that our country, being on the other side of the earth, had fallen into many customs the very opposite of those in Korea. 'The other side of the earth?' What did that mean? And at once we were into the perplexing question of the shape of matter in general. But, says the governor, Confucius says that the heavens are round and the earth square and flat, and here this foreign gentleman pretends the opposite; and a shock of nervousness took him that threatened violent protestations. The wall of China grew apace, till a servant brought in a table of food, and His Excellency asked me to partake, eyeing me closely the while to see whether I ate the food or the brass bowls and chopsticks; for Koreans hold that different degrees of spiritual being require different material for food, some eat metal, some wood, some grass, some air, while the purely human eats rice, pork, raw fish etc. The first spoonful of rice I took levelled that wall of China. The governor had unfailing proof that I was human, and he could afford to overlook minor differences on the question of the universe, seeing that we had in common this capacity for rice that made us fellow mortals.[96]

In the same year that the *Tong-hak* leader was executed, a new king, Kojong, took the throne, but as he was only twelve years old, effective power was exercised by his father, who was known as the *Taewon-gun*. Faced with internal rebellion and the spectre of foreign intrusion, he introduced a series of reforms designed to strengthen the authority of the throne, undermine the powerful *yangban*, and clean up the bureaucracy and the national defence. The *Taewon-gun* recruited foot soldiers from the lowest classes. Butchers were made into special units and armed with spears and swords. At this time, there were also some odd inventions, such as thirteen-layer bulletproof jackets that were so heavy that in the summer soldiers collapsed wearing them. Another was an apparent plan to build a zeppelin of sorts from feathers of cranes. The airship was never made, but the Korean cranes were almost hunted to extinction after the order went out to collect the feathers. The *Taewon-gun* believed that even trading with the West would lead to similar clashes as China had experienced. He slammed Korea's doors shut so firmly that the country was known to the West as the Hermit Kingdom.

But the viciousness of this policy brought on the kind of incidents he had sought to avoid. A third persecution against Catholicism resulted in the killing of nine French missionaries and some eight thousand Korean believers, and provoked a French retaliation. When the French spread rumours that they planned to kill a thousand Koreans for every martyred Frenchman, the populace panicked. The palace was reportedly besieged by hundreds of shamans offering to use their supernatural powers against the enemy. Seven warships anchored off the coast and seized part of Kanghwa Island before they were eventually repulsed.

In another incident, an American trading vessel had sailed up the river to Pyongyang and foolishly kidnapped a local military official to try to pressure the Koreans into talking about trade. The vessel was torched and its crew massacred.[97] In response to this, five American warships sailed into Korean waters intending to force the country to open its ports to trade. US marines captured some hillside forts, but they, too, were beaten back. An account of these battles records the bravery of Korean soldiers. The Americans were astounded to see wounded Koreans take their own lives rather than surrender. Some jumped from cliffs and others feigned death to be buried with the bodies of the dead. 'We were moved to tears when we saw them motioning us to stab them to death,' one officer wrote. 'We have never seen or heard of such tough and courageous fighting men. They were either the most patriotic soldiers in the world or imbued with a firm warrior spirit unknown to the western world.'[98] The impression from these accounts is of a fine fighting force with good communications, but poor weaponry. But there appears to have been an almost effete disinterest on the part of the throne, both in terms of communication with its troops and interest in the outcome of battle.

The anti-barbarians policy was popular with the Confucian purists. But it proved to be one of those unintended historic mistakes. The western powers had little interest in Korea, but these half-hearted attempts to open her up and secure influence did not go unnoticed by a more ambitious, would-be imperialist closer to home – Japan.

In 1873, the *Taewon-gun* was retired and King Kojong began to face the inevitable question of how to deal with the outside world. Japan pressured the throne into signing its first modern treaty, one which cleverly identified Korea and Japan as independent sovereign states, thereby undermining Chinese claims over Korea. The king sent officials to Japan and China to study modernisation. In the face of opposition from Confucian conservatives over any dealings with the West, Kojong asked the Chinese to mediate a treaty with America, which was signed in 1882. In the following year, the king is said to have 'danced with joy' when told that the first American diplomat had arrived in Korea.[99] The king had been wrongly informed that the wording of the agreement meant that the Americans would guarantee Korea's sovereign independence. Britain and Korea signed their treaty in 1883, followed by Germany, Italy, Russia, France and Austria-Hungary. At this time, too, the first Protestant missionaries arrived. Within a few years, they were to have tremendous impact on the Koreans.

Meanwhile, the throne faced domestic unrest. Many Neo-Confucian intellectuals viewed this opening with fundamentalist alarm. The Confucian system had not remained in place for so long simply because of vested interests and power politics. People believed in it. At the same time, there was an uprising by soldiers who had not been paid for over a year. In a complicated palace drama, the *Taewon-gun* secretly plotted with the rebels in a scheme against the queen, who had earlier engineered his downfall. The rebels killed a Japanese military official and burned the Japanese legation and, in the chaos, the weak-willed king brought his father back into authority. The Japanese responded by sending troops into Korea, which in turn prompted China to send troops of its own. The Chinese took the *Taewon-gun* back to China under arrest. Although the situation was defused, the foreign troops remained on Korean soil. With support from the queen, China became more deeply involved in Korean affairs. In 1884, a group of intellectuals called the Progressives, who favoured equality and modernisation along Japanese lines, launched an ill-fated coup with

Japanese support which was suppressed by Chinese troops. The two rival powers agreed to withdraw their troops, although the next decade saw much greater Chinese influence over Korean policy. Russia, meanwhile, was expanding its influence, a fact which alarmed the British government, which sent a naval force to occupy a strategic Korean island called Komun-do. As the sharks circled, the powerful queen and her Min clan took more and more control of state affairs. Corruption and incompetence increased.

These events once again saw the return of the *Tong-hak*. Under a new leader, Choe Shi-hyong, believers began to petition to clear the name of the martyred founder. Protests escalated into a crusade against official corruption and foreign influence and, in 1894, exploded into an armed peasant revolt. Both Japan and China sent troops to Korea. But the government and the *Tong-hak* called a truce and reforms were introduced. Japan and China then went to war and the *Tong-hak* took up arms again against Japan. They were defeated by the Japanese and their leaders executed. Thus ended the biggest ever peasant revolt in Korean history.

China, meanwhile, was out of the picture, having agreed in the peace with Japan to recognise the full independence of Korea after centuries of regarding it as a vassal. The Japanese cleverly persuaded the *Taewon-gun* to return to lead a new Japanese-directed government and pushed through a wide-ranging modernisation programme known as the Kabo Reforms.[100]

The reform script creates a picture of the backwardness of the society at the time. The changes included numerous measures to cement Korea's independence from China, including the use of the Korean script and teaching of Korean history. Other reforms sought to create a Japanese- (and British-) style constitutional monarchy with a cabinet leading the administration. One rule required officials to come to work in the morning. Normally, they just came in the afternoon, bringing their bamboo pipes with them. The upper class didn't actually work, and commerce was disdained, which may explain the sleepy atmosphere of old Korea. The system of *yangban* bureaucracy, in which holding office, for however short a period, was the priority of men of breeding, excelled in absurdity. In 1894, there were twenty mayors of Seoul, each in office for an average of two weeks.[101] The reformers also introduced modern monetary and banking systems. Taxes were to be paid in cash, not goods, and restrictions lifted on merchants in order to encourage the development of modern capitalism. In addition, a modern police force was introduced, government service exams were scrapped, torture was banned and modern courts introduced. Significantly, the legal basis for class distinction was abolished, slavery was outlawed, widows were allowed to remarry and minimum marriage ages of twenty for men and sixteen for women were set.

The Kabo Reforms were later scrapped as part of a rejection of Japanese influence. Nevertheless, the king introduced some modernising changes of his own, including the adoption of the western calendar, the establishment of some modern elementary schools and post offices. His most controversial decree required men to cut their topknot and wear their hair short like westerners. The king had his done by his minister of agriculture and commerce, who sobbed as he snipped.[102] The wailing of *yangban* echoed through the palace. How could they appear at their ancestors' graves with short hair? Mobs of Confucian purists attacked and killed several bureaucrats over this issue. In one village, the first man to have his hair cut was sentenced to death by suffocation by a clan tribunal. He was tied to a post and layers of sticky paper wrapped around his face. He blew and puffed at the paper until he was exhausted. Thinking he was dead, villagers walked away and his mother sneaked up and cut him loose.

Another important development was the beginnings of a recognisable legal system. Courts began to rely more on evidence and the testimony of witnesses. Also, government corruption, especially the selling of government offices, was punished. In an unusual case, a commoner successfully brought charges of power abuse against eight cabinet ministers. Although the court eventually ruled against the plaintiff, we see for the first time the application of justice regardless of rank, with high-ranking officials having to appear in court to be questioned by judges.

Japan had hoped to modernise Korea and bring it into its sphere of influence. When the influential Queen Min sought to harness Russian power to her cause against Japan, the Japanese had her murdered. This was followed with attacks on Japanese troops by guerrilla bands. During this crisis, the king and the crown prince fled the palace, which was under Japanese guard, disguised as court ladies, and made for the Russian legation where they lived for a year. Suddenly, Japan was out, and with them the reformers, and Russia was in. The Russians trained up several hundred young men to form a king's bodyguard. Among the trainees were thirty-eight *yangban* boys who were outnumbered by their servants, and who whined so much that they were allowed to go through some of the training on their servants' backs. From the sanctuary of the Russian legation, the beleaguered King Kojong declared Korea an empire with himself as emperor. It was a piece of surrealism that typified the crumbling of the dynasty. None of Kojong's subjects were impressed, least of all the young intellectuals of a group called the Independence Club. They favoured modernisation, and promoted national sovereignty, democratic rights and the limiting of royal power. The king eventually ordered the club suppressed, and with it died any turn-of-the-century hopes that Korea might become an independent constitutional monarchy.

Chapter Eight

THE BROKEN PEOPLE

When their efforts to gain influence in Korea through collaboration were rebuffed, the Japanese began planning a takeover. The flight of the Korean king to the Russian embassy intensified the rivalry with Russia, the other state which had imperialist designs on east Asia as China declined. The Russians had a secret military agreement with China, the rights to build the trans-Siberian railway through Manchuria, and leases on some Chinese ports. When, during the Boxer uprising in China in 1900, Russia moved troops into Manchuria, an alarmed Japan signed a treaty with Britain – which was motivated by its own fears of Russian expansion – to recognise Japanese interest in Korea. Japan attacked Russia in 1904, occupying Seoul at the same time, and surprised everyone by winning. The Americans, also concerned to check Russia, mediated the peace and acknowledged Japan's colonial interest over Korea. Thus over a short period, Japan had eclipsed China, defeated Russia and gained the acceptance of Britain and the United States for its designs on Korea.

In 1905, Japan made Korea a protectorate. When the king's ministers refused to sign the documents, Japanese soldiers went and got the seal from the foreign ministry and signed on their behalf. King Kojong officially declared the treaty void and tried to secure foreign diplomatic help against Japan, but it was too late. In 1907, he was pressured to abdicate and was succeeded by his son, Sunjong, who one historian has described as an 'imbecile'.[103] Several Koreans committed suicide and others joined guerrilla groups, led by *yangban* and augmented by soldiers from the disbanded Korean army. By Japanese figures, there were 1,500 clashes in 1908 alone and, in the biggest engagement, some 10,000 rebels marched on Seoul and were repulsed. Although they probably did not distinguish between the two

103

types, the Japanese authorities were dealing with criminal gangs at this time which posed as guerrillas. These 'fire bandits', as they were called, went around burning houses and robbing. A particular speciality was to go to the houses of widows, ask them politely to wash their dirty clothes, and then rape them. Some 17,600 guerrillas of varying types were killed between 1905 and the formal annexation of the country.

This annexation finally came in 1910, when the emperor Sunjong approved it and turned 14,700,000 Koreans into Japanese subjects. The Choson dynasty was over.

Although, of course, the Koreans experienced the arrival of their neighbours as an extremely aggressive usurpation, the Japanese were in many ways acting out of self-defence. By seeking membership of the imperialism club, they actually sought to avoid becoming its victim. They were latecomers as colonialists, and unusual in that they colonised their nearest neighbour and developed its industry, rather than making it simply a source of raw material and a market for its products. What this amounted to for the Koreans was a more bitter experience than they could have expected under any other power.

In Japan's takeover, many Koreans saw a positive opportunity for progress. There was also approval from many foreigners, not simply because the imperial powers had more important considerations than defending Korea, but because they either bought into the Japanese sense of mission to civilise Asia or at least thought it would modernise the country.

Unlike the Chinese, who from ancient times knew how to run a vassal state, and unlike the modern imperial powers who had learned from experience, the Japanese were new to colonial rule. The only practice they had had was with Taiwan, the Chinese island which became Japanese in 1895.

Japan had emerged into the modern world in the last three decades of the nineteenth century, through a revolutionary development programme called the Meiji Restoration, which had been imposed from above. The country had the longest ruling dynasty in the world. It had begun in 600 BC. For these reasons, the Japanese in western suits viewed Asia with a sense of superiority. But they lacked the philosophy for dealing with different peoples. Their methods were informed by a long anti-foreign tradition. In particular, the Christian concept of individual responsibility remained alien. In 1875, the authorities had taken a home-grown cult called Shinto and turned it into the state religion. It directed ancestor worship and other spiritual elements towards a central nationalistic statement – that the emperor was divine. In addition, a moral code called *bushido* was adapted to encourage acceptance of one's social lot and a vigorous self-discipline. As a martial code, it would soon find happy comradeship in the West's totalitarian camp and allowed for horrendous atrocities without disturbance of the conscience. Despite its appearance of sophisticated modernity, Japan was a corrupt and violent society. The military was a law unto itself and increasingly established its grip on power. The Koreans could guess what they were in for.

The Japanese masters approached the job of absorbing Korea with fundamentalist zeal and intruded deeply into every aspect of Korean society, with the modern advantages of the police state. The aim was to annihilate Korean culture and identity, and absorb the people into a greater Japan, as second-class citizens. Japanese became the official language. Korean was taught as a second language, but later even its use was forbidden. Later, too, Koreans were forced to abandon their names and adopt Japanese names.[104]

Seoul became known as Keijo (Kyongsong, in Korean). The colonial authorities destroyed 85 per cent of all the buildings in Kyongbok Palace,[105] the main royal residence, and erected their own government offices in front of the palace grounds with deliberate geomantic intent. Viewed from the air, this and the city hall building half a mile away were shaped to form the word 'Japan' in Chinese characters. The tallest buildings in the capital, such as the Chosun Hotel and the Bank of Korea, were all newly built by the Japanese.[106] There was a Japanese Shinto shrine on Namsan Hill in the city centre and monuments to Japanese heroes, including one built in the 1930s to three officials killed in a bomb attack by a Korean terrorist.

In order to justify their need to take over and civilise their neighbours, the Japanese convinced themselves that, despite being of the same race, the Koreans were actually hardly human. 'If you look closely,' said one member of parliament, 'they appear to be a bit vacant, their mouths open and their eyes dull, somehow lacking ... Indeed, to put it in the worst terms, one could even say that they are closer to the beasts than to human beings.'[107]

A Japanese travel writer, in a not untypical description, wrote that the seven major products of Korea were 'shit, tobacco, lice, *kisaeng*, tigers, pigs and flies.'[108] He was especially struck by Korean toilet habits and referred to Seoul as the 'shit capital of the world', for, allegedly, humans as well as their animals tended to relieve themselves wherever they felt like it.

The Japanese who lived on the peninsula considered the locals to be coarse and superstitious. Japanese residents were advised, for example, not to keep cats as pets. Not for the reason you might think. During an epidemic of scarlet fever in 1914, many residents lost their cats. They would find them, dead, in a pot under the wall of their house. Burying dead cats was just one of hundreds of Korean shamanistic spells to bring disease under control. Over a hundred Koreans were arrested for killing Japanese cats. Other practices were equally scary. A local newspaper reported that a 'doctor' tried to cure one Pak Cho-sa of an intestinal disease. He placed nine plates in a circle around the patient. 'After pouring oil into each of the plates, he set fire to the liquid. A quilt was placed on top of Pak's head and the burning contents of the plates were poured over the cotton fabric, causing it to catch fire. Members of the patient's family were then instructed to stand around him and press down on the smouldering quilt. After four hours of this, the quilt was removed, and Pak Cho-sa was found to have been burned to death.'[109]

Koreans began to be bombarded with such images of themselves. It was only a short step to the conclusion that their backwardness was the result of a natural inferiority. What had their slothful, dependent, superstitious and diseased ancestors ever produced that was worth preserving? With the Japanese control over modern education, young Koreans would lose touch with their heritage and settle into the Japanese assumptions. It is difficult to overemphasise the depth of this intellectual assault on the Korean mind. This was Korea's introduction to the real world, the civilised world of trains and telephones and great power that had hitherto passed them by. Coming into this world, they found their position – at the bottom. The majority of Koreans at this time were uneducated. There were of course sophisticated Koreans, but it was even harder for them to resist this negative view of their sorry nation.

Power in colonial Korea was in the hands of the military Governor-General. The bureaucracy was large and dominated by Japanese. Throughout period, Japanese occupied almost all the highest positions and even a majority of clerical jobs.[110] They lived as first-class citizens in Korea and enjoyed rights under Japanese law not extended to Korean subjects.

The country was divided administratively into provinces, counties, cities and townships. The Governor-General appointed the chiefs of these units. Officials, and even teachers, wore swords as symbols of their authority. In the first years of its rule, Japan conducted a nationwide survey of land ownership. Many small owners who failed to register lost their land. The state became the biggest landowner, with 40 per cent of the total. The Japanese also invested in road, rail and communications networks to serve the country's strategic interests.

The police had wide-ranging powers, including the right to make judgements and punish minor offences. Police corruption did not arrive with the Japanese. For a long time under the control of corrupt Choson dynasty officials, policemen learned to how to extort confessions and money from suspects or their families. A Japanese announcement that complaints could be lodged against corrupt police was at first welcomed, but this reform soon fell victim to corruption when police chiefs found that they could fire unpopular officers and pocket their salaries until they were replaced. A common form of corruption that continued until the modern period was payment by suspects' relatives to have them released. In some cases, men would offer their daughters as concubines or their sons as servants to police chiefs to spring a family member.

Half of the policemen were Koreans, usually from the lower classes and often with old scores to settle, who in common colonial fashion, frequently performed beyond expectation against suspects. Locals also co-operated in large numbers with the Kempeitai (thought police), informing against ideological offenders. During the hunt for guerrillas before the annexation, the Japanese tried to terrorise locals into turning in rebels. In one village, the Japanese allegedly shot some people, cut the bodies up, boiled the remains in pots, and displayed the gruesome soup to the villagers. Several suspected guerrillas were rounded up in one town and disembowelled. Elsewhere, suspects were buried up to their necks and then decapitated. The Japanese soldiers apparently had great fun doing this and treated it like sport.[111] In the first eight years of Japanese rule, over 200,000 natives were arrested as 'rebellious Koreans'. These people were not treated nicely. The police routinely tortured suspects to force confessions. One technique was called the 'crane' or 'aeroplane', and involved tying a suspect with his arms behind his back and hoisting him above the ground with a rope, whereupon he was beaten with sticks. Another was to pour water laced with hot pepper down a person's nose to make them choke.[112] Another common practice was to force a person to drink large amounts of water and then place a board across his stomach and jump on it. Another speciality was to push bamboo wedges up under a victim's toenails and fingernails. It took a special kind of commitment for people to continue in the independence movement knowing that this was their likely rite of passage. 'Once a person decides to sacrifice his life, he never changes,' independence activist Lee Myong-nyong told his grandson grimly.[113]

With the old upper class no longer in charge, the caste lines rapidly blurred. For example, over 90 per cent of those classified as butchers escaped the hereditary caste in the first two decades of the twentieth century. During the 1920s, the 33,000 or so remaining butchers started pushing for their rights, such as equal access to schooling for their children. They began answering back to commoners. Angry commoners took to sneaking into the offender's home and ripping his mouth as he slept. The police recorded numerous such incidents.[114] Despite many instances of being barred from schools, by the mid-1920s, some 40 per cent of butchers' children were in school, a much higher proportion than for other social groups.

One of the most significant front-lines of Korean transformation during the Japanese rule was the work of western Protestant missionaries, who had arrived in the 1880s shortly after their countries had established diplomatic relations, and were permitted to continue operating by the Japanese. In contrast to Japan, which had earlier rejected Christianity, in part because of internal disputes between missionaries, and China, because of Christian refusal to accommodate ancestor worship, Korea took to this new faith in large numbers. So much so, in fact, that Korea was rated as one of the miracles of growth in the world. In contrast to Catholicism a century earlier, Protestant denominations had an oiled path into Korea, despite opposition from Confucian scholars. Protestant Christianity was identified by the court of the fading dynasty with America, protection and modernity. Some missionaries became confidants of the king and queen, which may explain a wistfully naïve expectation of American backing against Japan.

Protestant missionaries also inspired, converted, and educated many of the reformist politicians. At the other end of the social scale they reached out to the lower orders with a love and care that ordinary Koreans had not experienced before. There is one extraordinary story of the conversion of an entire village, after a foreign woman was observed crying over the dead body of a cholera victim. Faith healing by Christians also accounted for significant conversions, as indeed did the modern healing by missionary doctors, and education by missionary teachers. But it was perhaps the loss of the nation which offered the most compelling impetus to accept the western faith. Not only had Confucianism failed the Koreans, but the western religion stood in opposition to the Japanese. Conversion was therefore acceptable both as a kind of penance for Korean failure, and as patriotic commitment to the future.

Until the eve of the Second World War, the churches remained the only institutions which were not subordinated to the Japanese. Combined with these favourable conditions, there were, among the Protestant missionaries, several figures whose commitment and leadership qualities played key roles. These missionaries, mostly American, but also British, Canadian and Australian, took the unusual step of formulating a shared strategy. Three key elements of this plan were non-competition between denominations, a decision to build churches with money from the local congregation, not from foreign missions, and a plan to hand over power as soon as possible to local pastors.

Despite good results in terms of numbers of conversions, many missionaries were frustrated by the lack of personal spirituality. One said Korea needed a 'mighty baptism of convicting and converting power' and that he wanted 'to see Korean sinners alarmed because of their sins.'[115] In 1907, such a mighty baptism came under unusual conditions. A wave of anti-foreign feeling, particularly anti-American, had swept through the Christian community over America's approval of Japan's occupation of Korea. A mood of repentance among missionaries over this and over more personal and organisational issues prompted a revival which billowed into the Korean congregations. The Great Revival, as it is known, began with Presbyterians in Pyongyang and swept uncontrollably through the entire country. Christians publicly confessed all manner of crimes, corruption and sins in paroxysms of mass emotion. Through this process, a shadow of guilt and self-hatred appears to have been removed. Many who went through this experience devoted themselves to the resistance to Japan and the development of a modern national identity.

Christians came to the forefront of the nationalist movement. What complicated matters for the Japanese was that, despite their suspicions, Christian churches themselves were not dedicated to political goals. Furthermore, they were supported by foreign countries which were, for now, Japan's allies. Therefore their suppression was not a simple matter. The first clash was not long coming. In 1912, 105 Christians were tried on charges of conspiracy to assassinate the Governor-General. On appeal, all but six were released. Despite the arrests and torture of individual Christians, this incident actually clarified some of the misperceptions of the role of missionary and church, and relations with the government improved.[116]

But it was in 1919 that the most significant anti-Japanese effort occurred. It began in the aftermath of the First World War with Koreans living overseas, who saw an opportunity for Korean freedom, after the American president, Woodrow Wilson, declared that all peoples had the right to self-determination.[117] The Koreans determined to bring their plight to world attention. Korean students in Tokyo issued a demand for independence. In Korea itself, our old friends the *Tong-haks*, who had renamed their religion *Chondo-gyo*, began to plan an independence appeal in alliance with Christian and Buddhist activists.

The plan was to use the cover of the funeral of the old emperor, Kojong, in March 1919, as a platform for nationwide protests and draw the otherwise non-political mourners into action. The Christians insisted that the demonstrations be non-violent and it was decided that a straightforward declaration of independence would be the best way to touch the international conscience.

On 1 March, the signatories met in a restaurant in Seoul and when the declaration was read out, turned themselves in to the police. The Japanese were taken completely by surprise as the Koreans paraded through Seoul, thrusting their hands into the air with exhilarating shouts of 'Long Live Independent Korea'. The police began hauling demonstrators off to jail and arresting Christian ministers. For the next three days there was calm. On 5 March, high school students were due back at school, but none turned up. At 9 a.m., hundreds of boys swarmed out of the shops and alleyways in front of the Seoul railway station, chanting for independence. Girls joined the march as it made its way through the city gate towards the palace. They got about half a mile before they were charged by police with drawn sabres and cut down.[118]

Thereafter, the demonstrations spiralled into a nationwide protest movement, the likes of which Korea had never seen before. Even the old *yangban* diehards, who had been bought off with offices by the Japanese, joined in. At this point, the Japanese administration showed its true colours, and weighed in with a vicious suppression. Peaceful demonstrators were shot, bayoneted, clubbed, arrested and tortured.

In some instances, Koreans fought back with vengeance and the violence escalated. In one village called Che-am in Kyong-gi province, Japanese police called the men to a meeting at the village church after the murder of a policeman. An eighty-eight-year-old widow, called Chun Dong-ne, once recalled for me what happened next: 'They said they wanted to officially apologise for having beaten a villager earlier. The men all went to the church. Then they nailed the door shut and set the church on fire and shot anyone who tried to climb out of the windows.' Twenty-three people died in this massacre, including her young husband.[119] In the following six months, there were as many as 7,500 killed and 45,000 arrested.[120]

Although the protests had been meticulously planned, they lacked leadership. In fact, the leaders were under arrest from day one. Koreans had hoped for a response from the major powers, but none came. Politically, the independence activists had misjudged the enemy's resolve, and overestimated the commitment of the major powers to their cause. Nevertheless, what was remarkable was the unity of the nationalists involved and the mass support behind the call for freedom. That alone has led many historians to consider that, if any moment marks the birth of modern Korea, this was it.

The uprising demonstrated more than a rejection of Japanese rule. It also demonstrated the rejection of monarchy. The royals were nowhere to be seen in the protests, except in the coffin which the organisers had used as cover. The crown prince had married a Japanese lady and lived most of his life in Tokyo. Revival of monarchy was dropped as an option for ever.

After the protests were subjugated, a new Governor-General, Admiral Saito Makoto, was appointed. A sophisticated diplomat, Saito gathered an experienced team and consulted with leading Koreans, and even with foreign missionaries, before launching an altogether more palatable and subtle rule under the catch-all 'Cultural Policy'. Moderate nationalists were permitted to form organisations and publish Korean newspapers, albeit under continuing censorship. Two modern leading dailies, the *Chosun Ilbo* and the *Dong-A Ilbo*, began in 1920 and became a magnet for young, patriotic intellectuals. Despite the Japanese assimilation plans, teaching of Korean was increased in schools and literacy increased markedly. Whipping was abolished as a punishment and some governmental responsibilities were decentralised. Policemen and officials no longer wore military uniforms and schools were built. There were also economic imperatives and investments were made to increase rice production for shipment to Japan.[121] Regulations were changed so that companies could be freely established without government approval.

At this time, the failure of the March the First Movement, as it became known, radicalised other nationalists, and the successful proletariat revolution in Russia soon drew the interest of Koreans. The Korean Communist Party was started in Shanghai in 1920. But factional infighting began almost immediately and, combined with police repression, limited the effectiveness of the left. Saito expanded the police, which became more sophisticated in gathering information, infiltrating and subverting opposition. As a consequence, during this period, moderate nationalists took a pragmatically gradualist approach towards independence. As the direct clash with Japan had failed, what was required was a methodical raising of the economic and cultural standards of the mass population and the development of future leaders.

Among the numerous organisations were two that enjoyed brief moments of nationwide support. One was a campaign to raise money to establish a university and the other, called the Korean Production Movement, which drew in entrepreneurs, was essentially a 'Buy Korean' drive. Both fizzled out due to infighting, corruption and attacks from radical nationalists. In particular, leftists held the view that business was itself a feature of imperialist oppression. With this argument, the ideological differences first broke surface which, despite efforts at unity, would cleave the nationalists into two broad camps, and, eventually, into separate countries. Sadly, this generation failed to create widespread popular support from ordinary Koreans, who continued their resistance more by sullen sloth than allegiance to any organisation. Although the left was fragmented, its vigorous resistance enabled it to be more deeply associated with the patriotic cause and explains its profound appeal in post-colonial Korea.

Shortly after the 1919 events, Britain was pushed by America and Canada to end its alliance with Japan. Increasingly, America appeared as the great foe of Japan, a perception which strengthened the military's grip and led east Asia down the violent path to war. Japan's exports plunged by 50 per cent during the global depression of 1929. The pressures of a growing population on limited arable land, unrelieved by emigration, provided impetus for expansion into China.[122] The once great Middle Kingdom now seemed ripe for the picking. Unlike Japan and like Korea, there was no modernising drive from above in China. The three-thousand-year-old imperial system presided over a chaotic and vast array of people, who despite the romance of Confucian ethics and glorious culture, lived in medieval backwardness. The Manchu dynasty had tumbled in 1911, its infant emperor Pu Yi bundled off the throne by a western-educated revolutionary called Sun Yat-sen. His republic divided into warring nationalists and communists, with the nationalists gaining the upper hand and alarming the Japanese. In 1931, Japan invaded Manchuria and created a new state under its control called Manchukuo.

A vast expanse, rich in untapped resources, Manchuria was linked up to Korea in the great Japanese development plan, grandly entitled the Greater East Asian Co-Prosperity Sphere. Under a new Governor-General, former Minister of War Minami Jiro, Koreans were now required to participate more fully in the development, and a more ruthless policy of forced assimilation was introduced.[123] The mass mobilisations which followed resulted in the uprooting of millions of Korean workers, an effort to obliterate Korean culture, and the effective destruction of the moderate nationalist leadership.

As the war against China intensified in the late 1930s, clashes increased with Korean communist guerrilla groups in Manchuria. The police dismantled moderate nationalist groups in Korea. Many radicals were broken by torture and paraded in public confessionals. At the same time, the expanding economy opened up opportunities for employment and careers that didn't exist before for Koreans. In this environment, many gave up their nationalist resistance and became open collaborators or collaborators by association. For this reason, the Korean elite which had remained on the peninsula lost credibility. The future leaders of both north and south Korea would be returning exiles.

In 1941, Japan attacked the United States and the world went to war. Koreans were drafted to help the Japanese war effort in huge numbers. From 1941 to 1945, for example, half a million Koreans were shipped to Japan. Some 250,000 Korean men were put to work in Japanese coal mines.[124] By 1944, 4 million Koreans were living overseas.[125] Organisations for mobilising workers were created and the dirty work of fulfilling quotas was done by Koreans. Such organisations also policed the workers. Thus Korean mobilised and spied on Korean.

An especially unpleasant feature of this time was the rounding up of unsuspecting young Korean women for work in military brothels. Many of these establishments were in front-line combat zones and women were required to endure large numbers of soldiers who, it is alleged, believed that sexual release in this fashion would enhance their performance in combat. These 'comfort' stations represented the institutionalising of the Japanese army's belief that a soldier had a right to rape. It is possible they were created in response to the outcry of the 1937 Rape of Nanking, when Japanese soldiers went on an orgy of rape and killing in the Chinese city.[126] The extreme anguish of these times was revealed in the 1990s, when Japan's wartime 'comfort women' became an international issue. Activists sought out and persuaded several elderly ladies to recount their terrible stories of brothels and day-long assaults by queues of soldiers. It is estimated that 150,000 Korean women and 50,000 Thais, Filipinas and other nationalities served in the brothels. Those who caught diseases were left untreated, and some were executed. Those who survived the war went on to suffer an anonymous life of loveless and lonely shame.[127] For modern Koreans, there is no better image for the barbarous experience of Japan's colonial rule of their country.

Korean men also served in more direct ways than manning its mines and factories. Most notoriously, they ran many of the prison camps, which is where thousands of allied soldiers, as POWs, first encountered them. This experience, which post-war Koreans are unaware of, directly contributed to the unproductive attitude of the Americans who took over the southern part of Korea from the Japanese, and regarded it as simply an extension of Japan, as Austria was of Germany. (Koreans were dumbfounded a few years ago when they learned that a veterans' group in Australia, which monitored names of Japanese companies and businessmen, doing business with Australia, for war criminals, also checked lists of Korean businessmen.)

Towards the end of the Japanese rule of Korea, local newspapers were closed and all types of associations were replaced with government-controlled federations. Protestant denominations were ordered to merge.

Use of Japanese language was expanded in schools to the point that not only was Korean study halted, but also all class instruction was to be conducted in Japanese. Pupils could receive corporal punishment for speaking Korean. Leaders of the Korean Language Society were tried in the 1940s for compiling a dictionary.

The authorities introduced the Japanese Shinto religion with a vengeance. Koreans were required to worship at Shinto shrines. This issue divided Christians into pragmatic and principled camps. Thousands of pastors and believers were arrested, thrashed and tormented by police torturers. Many continued to resist. Some died under torture, but many gave in.

But the ruling which caused the most widespread anguish, for it touched all Koreans, was a Japanese demand that they change their names. After this decree went out, all around the country, Koreans lined up outside police stations and government offices in comatose disbelief as they registered their new Japanese names. At schools, the new names were offered up to the emperor in Shinto ceremonies. Many of the elderly, in befuddled resistance, refused to choose and had names selected for them. For a people who could trace their male ancestry back centuries and whose fundamental sense of meaning in life derived from the imperative to continue their lineage, this was the final subjugation. For generations, a destitute Korean father above the slave caste had at least been able to bestow his name on his child. Now even that was taken away. Many Koreans submitted their new names for registration wearing black armbands and went afterwards to pray at their ancestral tombs. Parents begged their bewildered children to forgive them, and a new generation of nationalists discovered themselves in the crucible of their parents' misery.

In an autobiographical collection of stories, the writer Richard E. Kim describes how, as a young boy, he went with his father to register their new family name, Iwamoto:

> The long line of people is still standing outside, hunched and huddled, rubbing their ears and faces, stamping their feet in the snow. My father pauses for a moment on the steps, one arm around my shoulders, and says:
> 'Look.'
> Afraid, bewildered, and cold, I look up at his face and see tears in his eyes.

'Take a good look at all of this,' he whispers. 'Remember it. Don't ever forget this day.'[128]

The war ended in August 1945, when American planes dropped two nuclear bombs, obliterating the cities of Nagasaki and Hiroshima, and finally broke the Japanese will. Subjects in Japan, Korea and Taiwan heard the emperor's voice for the first time on radio, proclaiming that he was not a god and announcing the surrender. In Korea, flags that had been kept hidden appeared on the streets and crowds went wild in a jubilant celebration of freedom. Japanese citizens, and the collaborators who could, fled retribution. Korean families worried about their sons in the Japanese army, and mourned relatives among the thousands killed in the two bombed cities. But they got their names back. They eventually got their country back, too. But in two parts.

Chapter Nine

TWO WAYS TO BE KOREAN

The best-known fact about the Koreans is that they are a divided people. For a thousand years, they lived in a single state roughly along the same border with China. But in 1945, their peninsula was separated into two zones. The dividing line was drawn by two American officials at the 38th parallel as a convenient halfway point for the Soviet and American armies to meet and take the Japanese surrender.

As these liberators had opposing aims, they favoured rival figures among the returning exiles of the independence movement. From 1945 to 1948 there were various efforts at unity, including a proposed five-year US-Soviet trusteeship that was rejected by Koreans, and elections sponsored by the newly formed United Nations which were rejected by the communist North. These failures led to the inevitable creation, in the autumn of 1948, of two separate states, the pro-Soviet Democratic People's Republic of Korea in the North, and the pro-American Republic of Korea in the South.[129] In 1950, the North invaded the South in an attempt to unify under its terms, and failed, at terrible cost.

Even half a century later, the governments on both sides keep their people under strict controls and prevent any kind of exchange. Since the end of the Korean War in 1953, no people, letters, trucks, trains or goods of any kind have crossed the four-kilometre-wide demilitarised border zone (DMZ) that separates the two armies, except for one or two brief political gestures.[130] Only commandos, defectors, propaganda broadcasts, birds and bullets and, very occasionally, negotiators have crossed it. In the late 1980s two-way trade began, mostly through third countries, but some of it direct, by sea. In the late 1990s, in a breakthrough of sorts, south Korean tourists have been permitted to sail the few miles up the

116

east coast of north Korea on highly controlled trips to Kumgang mountain. But, still, at the DMZ, an eerie, surreal silence rules, broken by futile
propaganda. On a blustery day, the North's manic preaching is snatched
by the wind and only reaches the other side in unconnected phrases. The
south Koreans are more into music. One student who did his military service at a DMZ guard-post in the late 1980s said they used to have great
fun blasting Michael Jackson's *Thriller* album at full volume across to the
other side. A north Korean defector who had served as a soldier at the DMZ
on the northern side said he had been moved one winter by the haunting
sound of what he later learned were Christmas carols wafting over from
the southern side. Each side also has placed one or two large slogans on
the hill slopes, and in the fields, facing the other side. The North tells the
South it has built paradise. When I was visiting north Korea once, I read a
more appealing south Korean slogan through binoculars which reminded
northerners that every south Korean has a Hyundai car.

Could the Koreans have prevented their own division? This question is
not asked in Korea and the suggestion that they might bear some responsibility is not appreciated. Koreans are not accustomed to taking responsibility for their history. They feel, and rightly so, that they were helpless
pawns of superpower rivalry. As a German official would later nicely
comment, 'While we Germans were divided after the war because of our
sin, the Koreans were divided because of their innocence.'[131] Innocence
in politics is another word for weakness. And Korea's particular weakness
was, ironically, a result of the inability of its leaders to co-operate with
one another. In over twenty years of existence, a Korean Provisional Government, based in Shanghai, had never been recognised by any government, least of all those fighting Japan. It wasn't that the Korean
nationalists had no voice. The problem was they had too many. So many
rival organisations created a din at a time when the main powers were
committing millions of troops across the globe in the common cause, in
the fight for the survival of freedom and for huge geopolitical interests.
The Korean nationalists were so fractious and self-absorbed that they had
neither the good sense nor the ability to create a cohesive contribution
to the allied war effort, or offer a consistent, unified voice in allied
forums. The word 'Korean' became synonymous with factionalism even
in international communist circles.[132] Their disunity was a factor in their
division.

Nevertheless, it would have been possible for the conquering allies to
impose independence from above. In fact, immediate independence had
been suggested at a meeting of allied leaders in Cairo in 1943. But it was

ruled out in the face of objections from Britain, which didn't want its own colonies to get ideas about liberation. The next problem for the Koreans was that the Soviets were on the allied side and were offered half of Korea even though they played no role in the Pacific War. (The Soviet Union had declared war on Japan only a week before the capitulation.) The Americans and the Soviets came to take the Japanese surrender, and to set up a trusteeship as an interim step for Korea's independence at some undetermined point in the future.

An American Military Government was set up in the southern zone. In contrast to their occupation of Japan, for which they had planned for some years, the Americans were remarkably unprepared to administer the Koreans. There was a tendency to see them as low-class Japanese. They arrived on the peninsula to find that local 'people's committees', under the leadership of a moderate leftist called Yo Un-hyong, had already combined to form a Korean People's Republic. Although leftist-dominated, it was sufficiently broad to attract a conservative exile, Syngman Rhee, as its chairman. The AMG rather short-sightedly viewed many nationalists as pro-Soviet communists, and refused to accept the new republic and set about dismantling the people's committees. Even more short-sightedly, it sought Japanese advice on administration and hired many officials and policemen who had worked in the hated colonial bureaucracy.

In the North, the Soviets picked Kim Il-sung, a guerrilla leader who had fought in the Soviet army, from among the Korean communist factions and let him rule while they remained in the background. Within a few months, collaborators had been purged, and a sweeping land reform introduced that overturned the ancient landed structure once and for all. While this was going on, the communists sidelined moderate nationalists and began crushing religion, at first through united front tactics, and later more directly. The labour camps began filling up. Christians, ex-landowners, and committed anti-communists began moving to the South.

In south Korea, the years 1945–50 saw a chaotic and violent struggle between left and right for control. Before the opposing camps hardened, the ideological shades of grey suggest that much of the resistance could have been avoided had the Americans been better prepared to embrace the people's committees. Strikes and protests led to rebellion. The most extreme case was on Cheju Island, where communist-led rebels prompted an uprising in April 1948. Communists were trying to block United Nations-supervised general elections scheduled for May. As the rebels were mostly locals and the police trying to keep control had been pro-Japanese collaborators, rebels gained widespread support and were joined by some soldiers of a locally based regiment. They took over village after village, frequently being chased out by day and returning at night.

At this point, the authorities turned to the Northwest Youth Association, a 70,000-member group of anti-communist north Korean refugees.[133] A group of two hundred volunteers headed for the island, receiving some basic instruction on the two-day journey. Later several hundred more men were mobilised. These militias augmented the army and police units and suppressed the revolt with horrendous violence. Armed sometimes only with bamboo spears, they approached the chaotic guerrilla conflict, where it was impossible to distinguish friend and foe, civilian and combatant, with a terrifying rigour that would be later evidenced by Korean troops fighting in Vietnam. Entire households were wiped out and completely innocent victims selected for the most gruesome executions.

In one incident in 1948, a militia recaptured a village on the island's northern shore which had been occupied for several days by rebels. The commander lined villagers up on either side of the road. He faced one of the lines of peasants.

'I want you on this side to say that all these people on the other side collaborated with the communists,' he ordered.

'But they didn't,' some people objected.

'If you don't, you'll get what they're going to get,' the commander said. After a while, the villagers reluctantly gestured as they had been instructed. The commander ordered the fifty or so 'guilty' peasants to be taken away. A small boy was clinging to his mother as she was being led away and wouldn't let go.

'Ya! Run off or I'll shoot you, too,' the commander yelled, and the boy ran off down the road. The 'guilty' adults were marched off into a field and executed.

In this fashion, the island was pacified. It is claimed that over 30,000 people died, 10 per cent of the population, a terrible statistic that foreshadowed the carnage of the Korean War. The horror was buried. People never talked about it. Patrick McGlinchey, an Irish priest who settled on Cheju in 1954, and who recounted the above story of the villagers, said he heard of it only by chance, as the result of an argument.

'I'm driving along in a jeep with this fellow having this argument. I'm saying that people are basically good and motivated by love and he's saying people are selfish and motivated by survival,' he recalled. The other man was getting insistent. 'Then he stops the jeep and tells me this story. He had been a medic in the unit and witnessed the whole thing. In the end, he said dramatically that this field was where they were killed. It was all to make

the point about the small boy being more strongly motivated by his survival than his love for his mother. I was completely amazed and had forgotten all about the argument. But he says, "There, you see. Survival."
That's the only reason the story came up. As a way to prove his point.'

The most obvious explanation for the reluctance to talk about it was
fear of further reprisal. The anti-communist victors went on to rise in the
establishment and others remained on the island. The military commander, Song Yo-chan, later became a prime minister. The leader of the
first group of Northwest volunteers, Choi Chi-wan, became a national
assemblyman. A Northwest leader was made commander of the local regiment on the island and twenty-four other members joined the police and
settled on the island. Later, more refugees from the North were housed on
Cheju and they had a very real fear of communist subversion.[134] As well as
fear, guilt haunted the survivors, especially where they had been forced to
conspire with executioners in the way recounted above.

At this time, south Korea was an economic shambles. Bungled policies
had led to spiralling inflation, food shortages, and almost to economic
collapse.[135] The new republic in the South was not created amid celebration and expectation. Syngman Rhee, who had become the first president, was an elderly nationalist who had lived in America for decades and
who lacked the vision of economic growth. Around 70 per cent of the
industry built up by the Japanese was in north Korea. Half of the South's
energy had come from the North, which belligerently cut it off in May
1948.[136] The population grew over five years by 25 per cent, as millions of
Koreans returned home from Japan, or fled the communist North.

Per-capita income in south Korea in 1948 was $86. By this reckoning,
the United Nations rated Koreans on a par with Sudanese. It was reasonable to assume that fifteen or even fifty years later, these peoples would
still keep the same company on the UN statistics lists, that is, below Indi-
ans and Pakistanis.

'Korea can never attain a high standard of living,' wrote a US military
official in Seoul, giving the typical assessment. 'There are virtually no Koreans with the technical training and experience required to take advantage
of Korea's resources and effect an improvement over its rice-economy status.'[137] He reckoned that by 1949, when the occupying American forces
were to withdraw, the country would become a 'bull-cart economy'.

Many Americans thought that nature should be allowed to take its
course, and – when they pulled their forces out in 1949 and indicated
they did not intend to defend the South – it did. On 25 June 1950, the
stronger North invaded.[138]

The 1950–3 Korean War was the first major-power conflict since the Second World War and was feared at the time to represent the start of a Third World War between the communist and democratic camps. The north Koreans swept southwards, rolling over the lightly armed south Korean forces and taking Seoul in three days. They pushed on down to the south coast, 'liberating' towns and villages, organising supporters, executing opponents, and taking thousands of intellectuals, and others they considered useful to their cause, back north. The United Nations came to the rescue of south Korea. The first Americans arrived ten days after the initial attack. As they marched north to engage the communist forces, fleeing peasants stood to the side of the dirt roads and clapped. But the north Korean drive was relentless. The Americans and south Koreans were pushed back and soon all that remained of the Republic of Korea was the area around the port city of Pusan.

Men of the British Commonwealth 27th Brigade landed in Pusan in late August, and were soon followed by units from Australia, Belgium, Canada, Colombia, Ethiopia, France, Greece, Luxembourg, the Netherlands, New Zealand, the Philippines, Thailand and Turkey.[139] Korea became known to the outside world through famous battles, such as Bloody Ridge, Chosin Reservoir, Heartbreak Ridge, the Imjin River, the Iron Triangle, the Punch Bowl and the Pusan Perimeter. The most famous name of all was Inchon, scene of a bold, amphibious counterinvasion conceived by the UN forces' American commander, General Douglas MacArthur. Despite a 35-foot tide on the west coast at Inchon, MacArthur landed a massive invasion force which pounded its way to Seoul and dissected the north Korean army.

MacArthur's courage, rhetoric, and flair for dramatic PR made him so difficult to deal with that his own president eventually relieved him of command, but the legendary American soldier won the profound admiration of a generation of Koreans. When he retook Seoul, MacArthur staged a ceremony formally handing over control of the city to the Korean president, Syngman Rhee, in the bomb-damaged Capitol Building. 'By the grace of a merciful providence, our forces fighting under the standard of the greatest hope and inspiration of mankind, the United Nations, have liberated this ancient capital city of Korea,' he began. He ended by inviting the participants to say the Lord's Prayer. At that moment, bits of glass crashed to the floor from the building's broken glass dome. No one was hurt and, typically, MacArthur did not skip a beat in his prayer. With tears in his eyes, Rhee grabbed MacArthur's hand. 'We love you as the saviour of our race,' he said.[140] No phrase better sums up the feelings towards

Americans that lie in the hearts of south Koreans who experienced the war, all mixed in with their suffering, the shame at their own weakness and their resentment against authority and big powers.

UN and south Korean forces swept into north Korea, took Pyongyang and marched to the Yalu River. Chinese 'volunteers' then entered the war in massive numbers to rescue the defeated north Koreans and pushed the UN forces back again. Hundreds of thousands of refugees fled the advancing communists in the bitter winter weeks of 1950–1. After enemy soldiers were discovered infiltrating disguised as refugees, American planes strafed columns of fleeing peasants, killing hundreds. Vigilante squads from the villages on the refugee trail robbed the wealthy and killed suspected communists. The new south Korean army often fought courageously, but it also suffered from inexperience and corruption. Funds for the half-a-million-strong National Defence Corps were misappropriated and supplies never got through. That winter, several hundred recruits are thought to have died from starvation and thousands more suffered from exposure. Leaders of the Corps were tried and executed.[141] The refugees didn't stop until they reached Pusan, where they piled into squalid refugee camps and built shacks on the hillsides with stones and flattened drums.

Amid all this chaos, the south Koreans recovered their dignity and hope. Schools quickly resumed and officials and flag-waving schoolchildren turned out to welcome visiting foreign troopships. Perhaps the most telling symbol of their hopeful dependence was the construction along the airport road in Pusan of hoardings to conceal the squalor of the refugee camps from the view of visiting foreign officials. Officials didn't want to give foreigners, who held the key to their survival, feelings of disgust.

Amid the violence of the civil war and the reprisals as one side and then the other took control, any lingering ideas of Korean brotherhood disappeared. The perception among intellectuals of one united, victimised people had been honed by decades of Japanese oppression and was not easily changed. Many Koreans thought the communists were just another political party until their occupation of the South.

'I thought we were brothers and that we disagreed in our politics, but in our hearts shared the same love of the fatherland,' said Han Joon-myung, a Christian minister from the north Korean east-coast city of Wonsan. 'Actually, the communists began oppressing Christians as soon as they took power. Many from Pyongyang had already escaped. But in Wonsan, the atmosphere was different. I myself was not afraid of them because they were fellow countrymen. If they were Russians, we should be afraid, I thought, but we were the same people.'[142]

Han was to get a stark lesson in how nasty brothers can be to each other. A few days after the Korean War began, he was among several hundred intellectuals arrested and put into a prison barracks. In October 1950, when north Korean forces were in retreat, guards began taking prisoners away. Unknown to Han, they were being executed. At first they tied rocks to prisoners and threw them in the sea, but some bodies floated back up. They decided the next day that it would be more efficient to shoot them. They selected a tunnel in a hillside not far from the prison.

'They took us from our cells and tied our hands behind our backs. Four prisoners were tied together. I remember the other three with me. The young man on the left was called Kim Yung-nok. He was an electrical engineer. Next to him was an elderly doctor, called Oh Myong-nyang. Then me, and on my right, a tall farmer called Kang. We thought we were being relocated. After many hours waiting we were told to walk up the hill. The rows of prisoners were twenty steps apart. We'd walk a certain distance and then guards would tell us to stop, then we'd walk some more. I still didn't really understand what was happening and I still had no bad feeling towards the authorities. Actually, it was very cold, and I thought they were taking us to the cave for warmth.'

Eventually his line reached the entrance of the tunnel. It cut into the hill about six foot high and ten foot wide. Inside, an oil lamp lit up one alcove, where Han saw bodies in piles. A soldier in a navy-blue uniform was shooting the prisoners two rows ahead of Han. Another was reloading a gun. The next row stepped forward and knelt on the bodies of the previous line of victims and the soldier went behind them, shooting each person once in the back of the head.

'One-two-three-four. Like that. It was at that point that I realised the communists were not our brothers. I was suddenly shocked and afraid,' Han said.

Incredibly, Han survived to tell the tale of this loss of innocence, thanks to a bad leg. He couldn't kneel, and so he sprawled on the corpse below, which was still twitching.

'My mind was so clear. I could take everything in. In my heart I felt such anguish,' he said. 'Mr Kim fell forward. His face was kind of blown out. Then Dr Oh was shot and collapsed. At that moment, the head of a young schoolboy in front of me jerked up. "Look at that," the guard who was loading the gun said to the other one. They were a bit surprised. The other one stepped up, treading on my head and shot the boy again. Then he shot farmer Kang. The blood went all over me and he slumped down. The guard doing the reloading called for the next four to come. He'd shot the four bullets and forgotten about me.'

Another line of men climbed on top of them. After they were shot, the alcove was boarded up. Later, Han heard the noise of the executions being resumed. Some victims sang in loud, bold voices before they were shot. At the end, he heard women crying. They were the last to be shot. Then the mouth of the tunnel was blasted. Guards joked, telling their mates preparing the dynamite to be careful not to blow themselves up. Five others also survived the killing – two high school pupils, a young girl, a farmer, and a doctor. Two days later, chance American bombing of the area opened a small hole in the tunnel. One of the boys clambered out. The others, fearful that there were still communists around, stayed put. The following day, United Nations troops, hearing there had been a massacre, came and opened up the tunnel. They counted 289 bodies, including twenty-eight women and several children.[143]

The war ended with a truce in July 1953. It had been the bloodiest episode in Korean history. The statistics are staggering. As many as 3 million Koreans are believed to have died from causes related to the war. In addition, there were 900,000 Chinese dead and wounded. Over 33,000 Americans, 1000 British and 4000 other nationalities were killed. According to south Korean figures, 129,000 civilians were killed during the north Korean occupation of the South, 84,000 kidnapped, and 200,000 south Koreans press-ganged into the northern military.[144]

The economies of both sides were pulverised. The North was flattened by US bombing and industry everywhere was wrecked. Here is a human and economic damage assessment for south Korea: about 5 million people homeless, 300,000 women widowed, 100,000 children orphaned, millions of families separated; increased population pressure with the influx of 1 million north Korean refugees; tens of thousands of schools and other buildings destroyed; $3 billion (1953 rate) in damage, 43 per cent of manufacturing facilities and 50 per cent of mines destroyed or damaged; inflation accelerated as the currency in circulation increased from 71,383 million won at the end of 1949 to 650,153 million by 1953; wholesale price index (1947 = 100) grew from 334 in 1950 to 5951 in 1953 and the retail price index (1947 = 100) rose from 331 in 1950 to 4329 in 1953.[145]

After all this, the border had hardly changed.

But what had changed was that it now marked a division sealed in blood. In north Korea, Kim Il-sung managed to avoid being blamed for the whole war. A master at the art of turning disaster into victory, he actu-

ally strengthened his position. He claimed that America started the war
and thus presented himself as the hero who brought the great power to its
knees, begging for peace. Within the communist ranks, he blamed the
south Korean communists for having led him to believe there would be a
popular uprising in the South and had their leader executed (for being an
American spy). With Soviet and Chinese aid, he began to rebuild.

A measure of normality returned to the South. Barbers set up their
chairs amid the mud and rubble. Refugees from the North set up as market traders. Women cooked up soup and noodles in street-side shacks. But
life for so many was the daily struggle for food. Until the early 1960s,
peasants boiled grass and tree bark to make it through the spring when
the barley crop was harvested.[146] Each year, people died. Today older
Koreans still remember how they were constantly hungry. The common
greeting of 'Hello, did you sleep well last night?' changed to 'Have you
eaten rice today?' Through the 1950s President Rhee became increasingly
isolated and his regime grew more repressive. Management of the economy was hopelessly ignorant, short-sighted and corrupt. Beggars squat-
ted on street corners. In fact, a mentality of mendicancy pervaded all
levels, from the streets to the president, who rattled his can in front of
the American government.[147] Half of the government budget derived
from foreign aid. The United States pushed certain policies with its aid,
but its advice was often flawed, since American officials lacked experience
of the needs of a developing economy and, incredibly, were opposed to
national economic planning.[148] At the turn of the decade, per-capita
income was $80.[149]

Ever since the Korean War, the two rival governments have been locked
in a mortal combat. Almost half a century later there is still no peace. By
American estimates, north Korea has 1.2 million troops. South Korea has
over 600,000, which are augmented by 37,000 Americans in a combined
forces structure. All men have military experience and millions are eligible for call-up in war.

Over the years, north Korea has been far more belligerent. Despite the
failure of the war, it remained committed to forcible unification.[150] It has
made at least four attempts on the lives of south Korean presidents.[151]
Four invasion tunnels have been discovered under the DMZ and sixteen
more are believed to have been built. There have been numerous terrorist
and commando incidents. In 1987 two north Koreans planted a bomb on
a Korean airliner, killing everyone on board. North Korea has a twenty-
brigade elite special-operations force, the largest of its kind in the world,

125

and is believed to have biological and chemical weapons, and possibly the means to develop a nuclear capability.

Kim Il-sung is also believed to have sent numerous spies and several political agents to the South. In 1992, officials tried to put a figure on this activity, saying there may be as many as forty thousand northern agents operating in the South. It was admittedly a wild guess, calculated on the grounds that on any given day in south Korea, up to a thousand mysterious electronic signals were apparently being detected. (The official assumed that these noises were all coded broadcasts by spy cells reporting back to their masters in north Korea, and that each cell consisted of three people who were required to report twice a month.) If the real number was even one thousandth of this, the results from the North's political-subversion programme appear to have been limited. Although there have been surprising cases of north Koreans operating in the South, they all appear to be rather trivial. In 1996, newspapers reported that a Filipino Muslim called Mohammed Kansu, who taught Middle East Studies at Dan-guk University in Seoul, had been arrested as a north Korean spy. It turned out that his real name was Chung Soo-il and that he was a Chinese-Korean, who had gone to north Korea after experiencing discrimination in the Chinese diplomatic service (where he learned to speak Arabic). His alleged role was to be in place to be mobilised if the country became destabilised. He also allegedly faxed information out of the country. Assuming the facts of the case as reported by the Seoul government are true, it is not difficult to imagine that north Korea was proud of this spy before his capture. However, the top-secret material he was sending was apparently all publicly available information.

No agents appeared to have been in place in the city of Kwangju in 1980 to take advantage of a rebellion by citizens against martial law troops. But there are indications that Kim Il-sung tried to prepare for similar disturbances in the future after this event. In 1992, it was revealed that a top north Korean official had lived in Seoul under a false name throughout the 1980s and established chapters of the (north) Korea Workers' Party

South Korea used to send soldiers into north Korea, but is believed to have stopped these intelligence missions because so many agents were caught, and because the American intelligence over-flights of north Korea provided sufficient military information. The terrestrial missions were extremely risky ventures because north Korean society is too rigidly organised for agents to penetrate. There are claims that soldiers sentenced for serious crimes by military tribunals were given an option of undertaking these missions in return for their freedom.

Both countries have waged an intelligence war in third countries and are alleged to have kidnapped people from the other side or otherwise persuaded them to defect. A south Korean disappeared in the 1970s in Oslo, apparently after a taxi driver took him to the north Korean embassy by mistake. North Koreans are also believed to have kidnapped and possibly murdered Japanese citizens in order for agents to use their passports.[152] A young member of the north Korean elite in the 1980s, apparently intent on defecting to America, went to a south Korean embassy in Europe to ask how to get a US visa and was persuaded to go to Seoul. Sources also allege that south Korean soldiers used to go across the DMZ and kidnap villagers.

For many years, there was an equal trickle of defectors both ways, fewer than ten a year. Both sides publicised only incoming defections. In the 1990s, however, the numbers of northerners fleeing south has increased dramatically. These defectors provide useful propaganda, but they are not highly regarded, because they desert their families for what people suspect are selfish reasons. The remaining family members of people who defect to the South are invariably banished to the gulag. There have been some cases of entire families which have dramatically escaped to the South. No defectors have fired the southern imagination in the way that Solzhenitsyn and Sakharov inspired the West. Since 1996, thousands of starving north Koreans have fled into China. A few hundred have made it to the South. Prior to this exodus, there had been roughly seven hundred north Korean defectors to south Korea since the Korean War. However, reliable sources say that there may be as many as an additional four hundred unpublicised defections. These would include relatives of high-ranking north Koreans, people who were smart enough to request anonymity to protect their families from retribution, and people persuaded against their will.

Both governments have kept their citizenry in line with strict controls. North Korea's repression has been more excessive than that of the Japanese colonial state it claims to have freed its people from. For a Korean to profess an interest in the other side, or to back one of its policies for whatever logical reason, is considered treason. In the North, even showing an interest in a foreign country can be interpreted as intention to desert. An Hyuk and Kang Chul-hwan, two prisoners who defected to south Korea after their terms were over, said that they were in a prison camp in the 1980s with two language students who had been sentenced for expressing a desire to visit France.

North Korea may keep as many as 150,000 prisoners in its gulag. People may be classified as 'hostile' because they have relatives in south Korea. One north Korean history lecturer, who had burned his Workers' Party card for his own safety during the Korean War when the south Korean troops took over his town, was arrested for this crime after the war. Because of this and because some of his relatives had escaped, he was sent to a remote mountain village and had to work as a coal miner for the rest of his life.[153]

South Korea has always permitted more freedoms, but has been ruthless regarding north Korea. For decades, criticising government policy – even, in the 1970s, criticising American policy – was a crime. Suggesting alternative ideas about unification was interpreted as subversion. Tens of thousands of government critics have been labelled pro-communists under a national security law and jailed. South Korea has kept some men in solitary confinement for as long as forty years for refusing to formally declare they were not communists, giving the country the dubious distinction of having the longest-serving prisoners of conscience known to the world.[154]

What is the reason for such sustained severity? A lot of people must feel it is right and justified. I used to have lunch occasionally with a man who had been the head of the anti-communist section of the Defence Security Command, a military intelligence body that investigated anti-government suspects. He didn't keep a jar of human fingers on his desk. His justification for denying rights of suspects and withholding democracy generally was that too many rules and too much social freedom would have diminished his ability to do the job. It is remarkable the extent to which a person's profession fashions his outlook. To my mind, he was admitting to fear of failing in his job. My general impression from meeting many people with such views is that the real obstacle to democracy and decency is fear. It is difficult to appreciate the existence of fear, because it is not visible. It is a still, dark river over which people build their bridges. Fear of instability, chaos, collapse, fear for their own necks, fear of career failure, unemployment and humiliation. There is also fear of the unknown, for in an authoritarian culture, the idea of permitting individual freedom is a great unknown. Where there is fear, there is a kind of wartime morality in which violence is seen as justifiable force.

The two Korean governments have a reason to be afraid. Both have presented an option for the future of Korea, and only one will win.

North Korea's regime exists on the lie that it has built a Workers' Paradise, an ideal society. For years, there has been a slogan over a building in Pyongyang saying, 'We are happy'. The paranoid fear is that the lie will be exposed and the leaders strung up on the first telegraph pole. In the grip of such fear, it is perhaps natural to think that someone who defects really is a traitor for demonstrating that heaven isn't all it's cracked up to be. If someone reads *The Times* without permission, he is a spy because he may learn something about the outside world that challenges the lie. Indeed, a north Korean scholar did once tell me that he was struggling intellectually because he had been reading foreign press accounts of his country. 'The viewpoint is so different, but I cannot see where it is untrue,' he said. He could have been arrested if we had been overheard. Such is the fear of bugging, that he chose to tell me this when we were walking along a street.

South Korean paranoia is different. The fear has been that its people will swallow the northern lie, because it is not a complete lie. It's a half-truth. Incredible as this may seem to an outsider, the north Koreans had the better claim to legitimacy in the minds of Koreans. The Koreans' *han*, their resentment and sense of worthlessness, comes from historical acquiescence to greater power. Many intellectuals feel that, after being freed from Japanese rule, the south Koreans reverted to traditional attitudes of dependency, and willingly subordinated themselves to America as they had once done towards China. But, while the South was totally dependent on American handouts and troops for protection, the North developed its own version of communism, a nationalistic philosophy of self-reliance called *Juche*, which declared that the state would depend on outsiders for nothing. The 'truth' is more in the rhetoric and in the perception than in fact, which is why Kim Il-sung had to control information so tightly. In truth, north Korea as a state had been saved during the war by China and rebuilt with Soviet aid. It's just that it didn't let its people know. There is, for example, a Chinese war memorial in north Korea, but only Chinese visitors go to it. Ordinary north Koreans think that Kim Il-sung defeated the Americans and the south Korean 'puppets' on his own (not to mention liberating Korea from Japanese rule). But there is also substance. The North's way of getting outside support appeared to turn history around. It brilliantly played off its two allies, China and the Soviet Union, and got them competing to give aid, and thereby maintained a sense of independence.

During a lunch in 1994 with some foreign journalists and other visitors, Kim Il-sung explained *Juche*. 'It's anathema to me to follow others. We can learn from foreigners, of course,' he said. 'You must chew first. If it's agreeable you can swallow. If it's disagreeable, spit it out. East European countries got indigestion because they swallowed the Soviet Union. If it rained in Moscow, people put up their umbrellas in Berlin. You have to chew first. Then you eat it – in other words, you make it your own. Otherwise, you'll get sick.'[155]

In other words, don't let other people push you around. This is what Koreans had been waiting to hear. It was the therapy they needed. The reason Kim Il-sung was so threatening to south Korea was that he embodied this attitude even in his body language. A handsome man in his youth, Kim became rather fat and had a waddling walk. But as a public figure, he had a graciousness and an ease with the absolute power he wielded that made him come across like the kingly father figure. He filled that empty throne in the national psyche. He was one of the few guerrilla leaders who hadn't been corrupted or defeated, and he gave the sense that his first loyalty was to his country. Until the 1980s, when the rise of his son began to complicate north Korean feelings towards the personality cult of their ruler, people used to cry when they placed flowers at the foot of his statues on his birthday.[156] Those who were not victims of his brutal regime really loved him. The brutality was justified by many as unavoidable because they felt surrounded by enemies. Even many who were victims loved him, because they blamed lower officials for their persecution. All this was hidden from south Korean view.

Kim was also admired because he managed to do something that no Korean politician had been able to do. With great ruthlessness, he had quietened all the critical voices and melted down the myriad factions into one harmonious whole, thereby appealing to the traditional sense that lack of opposition indicated he had the mandate of heaven. This message was signalled with great Nazi-like ceremonies in which a million torch-bearing citizens marched in perfect goose-step, and acrobats and card flashers performed in perfect sync. These were not shown in south Korea either.

The irony is that south Korean leaders were also very independent-minded and difficult for foreign allies to work with. Syngman Rhee threatened for several years to 'March North'. But south Korea's strategy was to hitch its wagon to the United States. To this end, nationalistic feelings were suppressed to the point that south Korea, both its government and people, appeared to be the most pro-American of American allies. When anti-Americanism finally burst out in the 1980s, Americans and other foreigners were quite bewildered, wondering where it had come from.

Simply stated, being pro-American was what saved south Korea, and being pro-Soviet was what has led to the downfall of north Korea. The North stagnated under its communist system, and, in the 1990s when Soviet communism collapsed and it suffered massive food shortages, went into crisis. South Korea grew from a backward, corrupt dictatorship into a modern, industrial, democratic power. It was able to do this under the American wing. But a crucial factor was the leadership of Park Chung-hee.

PART THREE

Economy

Chapter Ten

THE SPECTACLE OF GROWTH

The 424-kilometre drive up the motorway from Pusan to Seoul takes about six hours. Heavy traffic, especially in the last 60 kilometres, and especially on a Sunday night when everyone is returning to Seoul after the weekend, can really slow you down. It is hard to appreciate, when you're driving along this permanently busy road, that most sensible people in 1968, when it was built, saw it as a complete waste of money. It only got done because it was the brainchild of the president, Park Chung-hee.

Park had started to develop the country's industry to provide the means for long-term defence against north Korea and to end the dependence on the United States. As part of this strategy, and under some US prodding, he had signed diplomatic relations with Japan, earning a useful $500 million in grants and loans, but offending the sensibilities of many Koreans, for whom the memories of occupation were still fresh. Students had protested so strongly that it almost brought the government down. Park saw that he needed good economic growth not just to build his nation, but to legitimise his regime. Pusan was the port nearest to Japan and key to the glorious future as a trading nation. The modern road was to strike diagonally across the length of the country, linking the south-eastern port with the industrial Seoul–Inchon region in the north-west. The World Bank had advised against it. The National Assembly had refused to approve it, thinking Park was going to bankrupt the country. Park ignored them.

There is a story that after a few months' work, the cement ran out. 'I don't care,' Park is alleged to have said. 'Finish it anyway.' It was done. Within three years, 80 per cent of the country's vehicles would be using the expressway and the area it serviced would be producing almost 70 per cent of GNP.

If the story of south Korea's remarkably rapid transition from agricultural backwater to modern industrialised state in one generation is recalled a millennium from now and reduced to a biblical-length verse or two, this slightly apocryphal episode may do.[157] It tells of a particular miracle that characterised the bigger miracle of growth. Like the biblical loaves and fishes, the cement was there somewhere. The miracle was that people were persuaded to produce it.

They were persuaded by a leader with a vision of development and the ability to push it through. It was Park who inspired, bullied, beat, cajoled and enticed Koreans out of the paddy fields and into the forefront of the industrial world. Author Mark Clifford has described him as an 'economic warrior'. He was 'a nation-builder with few peers in the modern world,' Clifford writes. 'None of the better-known national architects of the 20th-century – Ataturk, Nasser, or Lenin – have built a more durable and prosperous country than Park.'[158]

Over three decades, Korea's economy grew by an average of almost 9 per cent a year, from $2.3 billion in 1962 to $442 billion in 1997. Per capita income rose from $87 in 1962 to $9,511 in 1997.[159] By the 1990s, it had become the world's eleventh largest economy and thirteenth trading nation, and a major producer of ships, steel, electronics and cars. Its huge conglomerates had gone multinational and joined the ranks of the world's biggest businesses. As a measure of the changes, in 1962, there were 30,800 registered vehicles in the country. By 1997, there were 10,413,427, almost all of them Korean-made. On major national holidays, when people drive out to the countryside to pay their respects at ancestral tombs, these vehicles all seem to go out at once. The Seoul–Pusan expressway and the other broad, modern motorways which now link all the major cities of this country, where people still remember army jeeps bouncing along potholed tracks and peasants slapping their lumbering oxen, get virtually gridlocked.

Park ruled from 1961 until his assassination in 1979. He is a towering figure in the Korean story. Yet, if we can identify a fatal flaw, it was that he appeared to make economic growth itself the goal of everything that he did, and in doing so, missed the lesson that had been learned already by human beings elsewhere and was in evidence in more developed states to be borrowed. That is that the goal of decent government is happiness and a civilised life for its people and that economics is a means to this end, not an end in itself. As a result of this shortcoming, even in developed Korea today, there is a harshness. It is a state which bulldozes ancient monuments, removes entire hills, and fails to restrain developers for the broader good of making life that bit more green and pleasant. An almost brutal obsession with economy still remains with Koreans.

Like Rhee before him, Park came to believe that the nation couldn't survive without him, and altered the constitution and rigged elections so that he could stay in power. In the end, he was shot at the dinner table by his own intelligence chief. Despite his aggressive suppression of labour unions and political dissidents, he is missed today by many Koreans, who feel that he would know how to get the nation through its current economic crisis.

He was the son of a *Tong-hak* rebel who had been pardoned in an amnesty and had become a subsistence farmer.[160] His struggle began early, when his forty-five-year-old mother tried to abort him, because she already had too many children. She drank raw soybean sauce and willow soup to try to poison him, tied a belt around her belly to constrict him, and even jumped off a wall. He survived this pre-birth battering.[161] Park did well at school and became a teacher before joining the army. He came top in his class at the Japanese Manchukuo Academy and went to the elite Tokyo Military Academy.[162] After his graduation in 1944, he was commissioned a lieutenant in the Japanese-controlled Manchukuo army.

This Japanese experience was a vital component in the character of Park's future rule. Not only was he exposed to Japanese planning, but he and his fellow Korean officers were imbued with the Japanese attitude of placing the interests of the group and nation before personal or family interest. 'As a group they had scant regard for the intricacies of etiquette, which all too often limited action in Korea,' Clifford writes. 'They also placed much less importance on the family and more importance on the organisation – both the nation and the corporation. In this sense they were much less typically Korean than the generations that preceded and followed them. It is hard to over-emphasise their importance in Korean development.'[163]

Despite the Japanese background, Park was not seen as having been a collaborator. After his older brother was killed by police in 1946 during a communist-led riot in Taegu, Park sided with the political left. He saw it as more organised, patriotic and less corrupt than the right. In 1948, he led a communist cell in the army and was sentenced to death for his part in a revolt of junior officers. The sentence was commuted to fifteen years and he was later pardoned due to his co-operation with investigators. He was promoted to brigadier-general during the Korean War and major-general in 1958. Park had a strong dislike of the Rhee government, which he felt was corrupt and overdependent on the United States. The Kennedy administration knew enough about his history to worry after his coup that he may have still been a communist. The local press gave him a Russian-sounding nickname, calling him 'Parkov' (enjoying a press freedom that was later curtailed).

'Park Chung-hee was never an ideological communist,' says journalist Cho Gab-je. 'But he was an emotional communist because of his mind for independence. He thought that Japanese imperialism had been replaced by American imperialism. He was a very independently-minded and practical person. His basic way of thinking was that you can travel as far as your power allows you. Power is the most important thing, not empty words. He endured the humiliation [of dependency] and wanted to build up Korean power in order that we could be independent from both Japan and the United States.' In other words, *Juche* by a more subtle route than Kim Il-sung's.

Immediately after taking power, he launched an anti-corruption campaign, rounding up the rich, centralising economic planning and generally making it clear who was the boss. Several wealthy businessmen were arrested, but most were let off provided that they set up companies in certain designated industries. Rather than suppress businessmen, as the leftist within him may have wished, Park sought to harness their profit-hunting abilities to the cause of national growth. Thus, as economist Alice Amsden notes, within days of his coup 'an alliance had been formed between business and government that laid the basis for subsequent industrialisation.'[164] Bankers, however, were not so favoured. Banks were nationalised. As we shall see later, this was a crucial factor in the centrally planned growth. Failure to adjust later and permit banks their independence led inevitably to the financial crisis in 1997.

In 1962, Park launched his first five-year plan. No one was impressed. Burma and the Philippines were seen as the promising Asian economies of the day. The prevailing forecast for Korea was gloom. During that first five years, annual GNP growth averaged 8.3 per cent, exceeding the planners' own forecasts. Exporting was the priority and would become a patriotic duty. The mantra of growth soon became 'export good, import bad'. Companies were given export targets by bureaucrats. Firms that fulfilled gained preferential credits, tax benefits, and the grateful support of bureaucrats, who were being held responsible by the all-powerful Blue House for the results. Firms that failed to meet their targets could get into trouble and even find themselves under orders to be taken over. During the second plan annual GNP growth averaged 11.4 per cent.

In the early 1970s, Park launched a major drive to build up heavy and chemical industries. Around the same time, he also started the Saemaul

(New Village) Movement which, through a combination of self-help projects and government funding, sought to modernise agriculture and raise rural living standards. This programme began with a cement surplus in 1970. Park ordered that every village be given 335 free bags. The following year, villages which were deemed to have used them well (about half), were given another five hundred bags and a ton of steel. Park wrote out an eleven-point memo containing such wisdom as, 'Projects forced upon villagers by the government are doomed to fail,' which became the basis for the Saemaul Movement which later spread to cities. Although a self-help movement, Saemaul appeared to Park's critics to be highly ideological.

Few believed the development would last. The north Koreans denied it was happening and, to convince themselves, stopped releasing their economic statistics in 1965 when it appeared that the South was overtaking them.[165] I once heard a wonderful story illustrating north Korean denial. It was during the first ever North–South talks in Seoul in the early 1970s. The southern delegation was led by Lee Bum-suk, a man of rare humour. (A fluent English-speaker, Lee often cracked jokes about his own name. Once at a press meeting, a foreign journalist politely pronounced his name in full with the correct Korean pronunciation – 'Ee bomb sock.' 'Just call me bum-suck,' Lee said.) Lee was in a car coming from the border point of Panmunjom with the head of the north Korean delegation. They drove into Seoul, and the north Korean got his first look at the city, which had been rebuilt since the war and was bursting with construction and traffic, a bit different from the bombed-out Korean War pictures and streets of beggars, prostitutes and American GIs of north Korean propaganda. The north Korean was not fooled. He could tell by the flowers planted along the roadside even before they reached the city that the South's propaganda machine was in overdrive.

'We're not stupid, you know. It's obvious you've ordered all the cars in the country to be brought into Seoul to fool us,' he said.

'Well, you've rumbled that one,' Lee deadpanned. 'But that was the easy part. The hard bit was moving in all the buildings.'[166]

Of course, the propaganda machine was in full swing. Houses along the route from Panmunjom to Seoul were bigger and better. Obviously the cars carrying the north Korean officials did not swing through the red-light areas, nor the poor districts, nor past the huge American military base near the centre of the city. These were features, but no longer the illustrative features, of what was really happening in south Korea. After a decade of Park's rule, the country was definitely on the move.

Through the 1970s and '80s, as job opportunities expanded, people poured into the cities. They worked hard and invested in the education of their children. They saved, too. South Korea's savings rate is 35 per cent. In contrast to the ideologues in the North, their leaders were more pragmatic than theoretical. Park and the people around him did what they had to do to deal with the obstacles to growth. Thus the explanation for the course of Korean development is often best made with reference to the obstacles it faced. A shortage of foreign currency led logically to an emphasis on exports. The absence of natural resources led to a concentration on industrial products. Changing patterns of competitiveness and the needs of nation-building led to a natural progression of these products from textiles, to ships and iron and steel, to electronics and automobiles. In this process, Park crushed dissent, ruined businessmen who did not co-operate, and pushed workers to endure long hours.

Park understood the importance of the American alliance for Korea's growth. Indeed, the rise of south Korea may be viewed, without offence to Koreans, as an American success story, too. After its initial bungling, including its responsibility for having divided the country, the US government stood by its ally, providing a security shield against possible renewed conflict with north Korea, and a market for Korean products. There have been tensions and difficulties, but the benefit to Korea was that it was both in American strategic interests and a natural consequence of American values as a nation born in opposition to imperialism, that its client state grow economically and politically from near-total dependency to equal partnership. America did not start the growth. But it provided a continued security umbrella that enabled it to happen. It also demonstrated by its own wealth and freedom what Korea, too, could become.

But America was no China. It did not offer permanency to a little brother. Indeed, the withdrawal from Vietnam demonstrated the relative fickleness to the east Asian mind of a country whose government changed every four years, instead of every four hundred years. Park knew that he had to build his own industrial base, and resist or ignore the Americans when they appeared to stand in the way. The Koreans' growth was of their own making. America was the market, the model and the matron.

The developed West in general was crucial to the Koreans for its technology. Korean growth was possible because Korean workers were cheap and disciplined, and educated enough to learn how to use or copy foreign machines (often from sneak photographs taken by managers visiting factories in foreign countries). An obvious, but often overlooked, point is that Korea and others have been able to develop so much more rapidly than western states due to the fact that other countries had already pioneered the path. The development of Korea and the other Asian Tigers has been so impressive that it is easy to go over the top talking about it. There is a widespread belief in a coming Asia-Pacific Age and the decline of the West. Its proponents essentially make an argument about ethics, contrasting moral decay and family breakdown in western society with the strong family ethic and emphasis on harmony and learning in the Confucian part of the world. They point to the economic rise of Asia as evidence.

I'm not sure if I can be objective about this prediction about my own decadence and decline. I find it hard not to dismiss it as geriatric twaddle. Certainly, the rise of Asian economies, and especially the rise of China with its enormous population, is going to change the landscape in the next few decades. But it does not follow that this amounts to a tilting of scales as if there is only so much development to go round. The determinant of economic success in the information age is far more likely to be sound business culture than cultural geography. Furthermore, the ethical argument is flawed. One could just as easily compare the strong Christian values of so many westerners with the moral relativity in corrupt Asia and make the opposite case. It strikes me that what the Asian capitalist states are doing is not tilting the global scales, but balancing them by catching up with the developed West. Once they've caught up, they find themselves dealing with the same economic issues as other developed states. This is in fact Japan's experience. The lead runner of Asian economies since the Second World War, Japan has had the slowest rate of growth among the world's developed states in the 1990s, while American companies and technology are fuelling global change. The western social problems that look so ugly to many Pacific Rim-ists may be the warts of post-industrial society, not just western culture. Japan is facing such post-industrial issues. The Koreans are beginning to face questions which lay buried or ignored before. Perhaps, for all of us, it's part of growing up.

After Park, another military coup-maker, Chun Doo-hwan, took over after a brief period of uncertain civilian rule. Chun continued the top-down management style of Korea Inc. after allowing himself to be tutored in economies by two brilliant advisers.[167] The economy boomed during his 1981–8 rule. However, by continuing Park's system, Chun began a tradition of postponing essential reform that continued until the near-collapse of 1997.

South Korea's industry should have been restructured or reformed in the late 1970s or early 1980s in keeping with the natural shift from labour-intensive to capital-intensive. Chun failed to do this because he did not want the risk of social turmoil. He came to power through a brutal suppression of pro-democracy protesters and did not want to provoke unions and ordinary citizens into anti-government comradeship with students. So he continued the Park tradition of suppressing wages and growth through exports. Another failure was that his administration's concern to prevent inflation lay behind an unwillingness to invest in social infrastructure, and build the ports, roads and rail connections that were needed. As a result, in the 1990s, transport costs (as well as labour costs) rose dramatically, pushing up the price of Korean products and eroding the nation's price competitiveness.

In 1988, when Chun's successor, the democratically elected Roh Tae-woo, opened the Summer Olympics in Seoul, the rest of the world had its first good look at modern Korea. Although western correspondents had been reporting on the economic changes for years, the greater emphasis had been on the absence of political development. Images of student protests and labour unrest and the 'dark side of development' conveyed the sense of a still backward nation. The Olympic Games brought in the largest influx of foreigners since the Korean War and most of them, athletes, officials and sports writers, had little interest in political demonstrations and sweatshops. To them, the modern stadiums and facilities and the ability of the Koreans to organise what at the time was generally recognised as the best Games to date, was nothing short of astounding, compared with what they had been led to expect. This was a developed state as far as most were concerned.

In many ways, this event marked the moment of south Korea's ascendancy over north Korea, in the minds of all Koreans. Southerners continued to be paranoid beyond a reasonable level of fear about the North, but the contest was over in terms of which system would win. The telling measure of this was the decision by the North's east European allies to participate, ending a run of Games marred by boycotts (Moscow in 1980 and Los Angeles in 1984).[168] The Chinese, who were participating for the first time, refused to join a north Korean boycott and got a stirring welcome when they entered the Chamshil Olympic Stadium in Seoul.

There was more than sports and symbolism in the east bloc decision. Beijing had already developed a significant trade with Seoul and other states were taking a particular interest in how south Korea had grown so remarkably under strong authoritarian government. In 1989, several Soviet journalists visited south Korea to get a closer look. One of the tours was around a Hyundai Motor Company plant. An American in the group remembers the reaction of the Soviets.

We were watching robots welding car bodies. Unattended mechanical arms were flailing around, touching down in precise spots as the cars moved along the belt. Zapping noises punctuated each tap of a robotic index finger and sparks were flying everywhere.

This tour came several days after a week of witnessing technological miracle after miracle, everything from computerised steel processing and cold fusion research to the high-speed 'talking' elevators in our hotel.

Natalya Yakovleva, North American Editor for the now defunct Novosti Press Agency, watched in silence for a long time. Eventually she emitted a barely audible sigh, but one that had been building up for a week. 'Why is it we can't do something like this?' she said.

'Private ownership,' I replied using the shorthand phraseology that had developed in our friendship and discussions over the previous couple of years.

'Never,' she said. 'Private ownership violates one of the basic tenets of socialism.'

'Well,' I said quietly, 'you can have basic tenets of socialism or you can have cars that weld themselves,' and added in what I hoped would be received as a respectful tone, 'but you can't have both.'

She looked at my eyes for an overlong moment – like you do when you're about to say something – then looked back at the spastic dance and light show, supervised by one lone worker in a control booth. Then she turned away.[169]

Within four years, virtually all socialist and former socialist states had developed full diplomatic relations with Seoul.

In the mid-1980s, the big Korean companies started investing overseas. Labour-intensive industries such as footwear and textiles were suffering, and sought to shift production to countries where workers were cheaper. At the same time, anti-dumping duties and fears that protectionism would shut Korean products, especially electronics, out of developed markets prompted big firms to set up operations in Europe and North America. Companies were additionally attracted to Britain and other European countries which offered good incentives. In the 1990s, the biggest conglomerates have been seeking to enter growing markets, producing locally and providing jobs. Daewoo's car and electronics affiliates, for example, are in Poland, India, Burma, Vietnam, Malaysia and Ukraine.

The Koreans have received a mixed reception overseas. In many ways, they are very highly regarded, and certainly the prospect of investment by Samsung, Hyundai or one of the other large conglomerates, is extremely attractive for developed and developing countries. The various British agencies, such as Locate in Scotland and the Welsh Development Agency, are active in Korea promoting their regions, for example.

On the other hand, in business and on the shop floor, the Koreans have not always been appreciated. One problem has been corruption. To survive in business in Korea, it has been necessary for companies to make payments to government officials and political parties. Companies also need to be creatively ruthless to win contracts. Such behaviour does not go down well in developed countries.

Another problem is treatment of workers. In Korean society, disputes are usually solved by force. A manager may assert his supremacy by making threats and shouting. Many of the foreign workers, who came from poorer countries to Korea for labouring jobs, often illegally, complain of physical abuse. There was a case in China of a strike at a Korean-owned firm after the boss, a woman, ordered all the Chinese workers down on their knees in front of her in an effort to show them who was in charge.

Korean managers do not do this with blue-collar workers in developed countries. In fact, here they are often appreciated for their earthiness and warmth and willingness to become involved with workers. In developed countries the difficulties are often between Korean managers and white-collar workers. A manager may be very warm and attentive to the people on the shop floor, but try to assert himself with his middle managers in ways that are perplexing and hurtful.

I heard of one case in Britain, for example, of a Korean company president who asked a senior British executive to do a market survey. When the report was presented to him, he declared it to be rubbish and threw it to the floor without even looking at it. The person telling me this story was completely bewildered by what struck him as rather brutish behaviour. I suspected that what was really happening here was something else. In Korean companies, you follow your bosses' orders. Koreans are not encouraged to speak their minds, with the result that meetings are not characterised by lively discussion on issues. They tend to be one-way affairs. If the company president was faced with western staff who were used to objecting to ideas, even in a polite British way, and throwing counter-proposals around, he may have found it extremely hurtful and felt he was being undermined. One solution would have been to use force to reassert himself by, say, commissioning a study and then throwing it in the bin in front of its author.

Chapter Eleven

CONGLOMERATES

T he predominance of huge conglomerates is the most notable and at the same time unusual feature of the Korean economy.

Some, like Samsung and LG (formerly Lucky-Goldstar), began during the Japanese rule at a time when Japanese business was dominated by large family-held conglomerates called *zaibatsu*.[170] More were born after the Second World War, when the assets of Japanese companies operating in Korea were confiscated and sold off at exceptionally favourable terms to Korean businessmen. Others, such as Daewoo, began in the 1960s.

At first, Park Chung-hee actively supported certain companies, but these almost all failed.[171] Rather than back his favourites, he more generally created an environment in which creative and energetic entrepreneurs could succeed. In a sense, Park strapped a rocket to these businesses but it was up to the tycoons to light their own fuse. The broad measure of success was performance in export markets. Many either never took off or dropped to earth. Those that succeeded went into orbit and are the multibillion-dollar corporations that are internationally known today.

Park wanted firms that could compete internationally with the Japanese. He thought that, as Koreans were not hard workers, and, as businessmen and politicians were corrupt, a few loyal and capable lieutenants would be more effective than the vast army of small and medium businessmen. There was a risk. Large, powerful groups could become power bases for ambitious tycoons to challenge his authority. It was precisely this fear that was behind Chiang Kai-shek's unwillingness to foster large firms in Taiwan. But Park Chung-hee thought he could control the large conglomerates, or *chaebol*, as they are called in Korean. (In 1992, the political establishment was directly challenged by big business, when the Hyundai founder, Chung Ju-yung, formed a party and ran for the presidency.)[172]

Going the Japanese way also posed a risk of another kind. The Korean business culture is characterised by an extremely low level of trust between people who are not of the same family. From this point of view, it would have been more natural to foster small- and medium-size family firms, and for the state to create the large corporations in sectors where size is necessary.

The scholar Francis Fukuyama has introduced this notion of trust as an underlying factor in business success.[173] He notes that Japanese, for example, can do business more easily with, say, Americans, than they can with their neighbours and cultural cousins, the Chinese. The point is that in some countries, rational and fair legal systems and business practices underlying economic behaviour work because they are underpinned by a high level of trust between people. This trust may be strengthened by democracy and good, fairly enforced laws, but ultimately it derives from cultural factors. In other countries, trust is very low. Germany, Japan and Britain, and some parts of America are examples of 'high-trust' business environments, while Taiwan, China, France and Italy are 'low-trust.' In high-trust societies, you see businesses ranging from small family firms to huge conglomerates that endure through several generations of management. In low-trust societies, most businesses are small, family-run affairs. These are lucky to survive through the third generation because young owners seldom have the same interest as their grandfathers, and the family can't make the leap of trust to introduce professional non-family members into management. Such societies can develop economically when the state steps in and creates big corporations at the other end of the business spectrum.

For Fukuyama, Korea is an anomaly. It has massive corporations and a highly concentrated industrial structure just like a high-trust society. But it has a low-trust culture. What is unusual is that the state has consciously promoted gigantic conglomerates as a development strategy. 'The Korean case shows ... how a resolute and competent state can shape industrial structure and overcome long-standing cultural propensities,' Fukuyama observes.[174]

The Korean government has controlled companies through a complex licensing system, through subsidies, and protection in the domestic market from foreign competition. But the key lever of control was the restriction on the financial sector. The *chaebol* were forbidden to own more than an 8 per cent share in a bank. In this regard, the Korean system is very different from that of the Japanese business networks which tended to grow up around a bank. Korean businessmen looking to borrow money to start or expand their businesses had to go to state-directed banks and get government approval for loans. Government approval was also needed for overseas loans. In this way, finance was directed into productive nation-building endeavours like shipbuilding and steel, rather than restaurants and home loans. The bankers did not have to take responsibility for bad loans because it was government that had approved them and government that would bail them out, company and bank.

The mechanism of government control of the banks served as a whip, for the availability of credit led companies to go boldly into completely unconnected types of business. But it was also a restraining leash. There was more than one hand on the leash. The presidential Blue House yanked when it was displeased. For example, credit was stopped to the Kukje Group, causing its collapse in 1985, in part because it was known to have provided funds to the parliamentary opposition party and to have not provided sufficiently large under-the-table donations to the Blue House. The other hand was that of the economic planners in the bureaucracy who favoured pushing the *chaebol* out to the mercies of market forces. The Kukje Group was bankrupt and poorly managed. Letting it go would send a signal to the others to shape up.

Big companies looking to finance non-approved projects, and small companies which were unable to secure short-term funding, could go to the unofficial curb market. Money here was often managed by loan sharks or representatives of *gye*, associations of small lenders. Clever operators, especially in the distribution business, taking immediate payment from clients but delaying payment to their own suppliers, could also take advantage of this lucrative business. Interest rates were at one point as high as 4 per cent a month. Many wholesalers could profit more from putting their client's payment into a high-interest three-month deposit than from their actual margin on the sale of a product. The scale of this unofficial market was not easy to guess, but has been estimated to have accounted for over one-third of total credit.

It is important to appreciate that the purpose of Korean companies has until now been different from the purpose of western companies. Unlike western companies, whose *raison d'être* is to increase the wealth of their shareholders, Korean firms existed initially for nation-building. Thus Korea appeared to be a capitalist country on the surface, whereas on the inside its practices and attitudes made it appear much more socialist. In fact, it could be described in our century of failed experiments, as one of the world's most successful centrally planned economies. (The closest sensation I have ever had of a workers' paradise has been in the cities of Ulsan and Pohang, which are so dominated by their resident *chaebol* – Hyundai and the Pohang Iron and Steel Company (POSCO) respectively – that they strike the visitor as the kind of fiefdoms that Marxist planners in communist countries could only ever dream about.)

As the country developed, this purpose of the company became somewhat confused. For as long as Korea lacked a social welfare system, it was the unofficial duty of big business to absorb the huge numbers entering the labour market. *Chaebol* were given quotas of students to employ. Labour laws made it almost impossible to fire workers and the government set pay guidelines that saw a dramatic rise in labour costs in the second half of the 1980s. At the same time, the stock market was set up in imitation of the Anglo-American system, but without any protection of the small stockholders. Owners started floating their companies, but still conceived of them as their own. People who bought shares were seen as gamblers without any rights, rather than co-owners.

The main feature of the *chaebol* is the concentration of ownership by the chairman, his family, and by subsidiary companies. Ownership by chairmen and their families has dropped in recent years and in 1996 was around 13 per cent for the top thirty conglomerates. But total internal holdings, which includes cross-ownership by subsidiaries, has remained consistent for years at around 45 per cent.[175] In 1994, Hyundai had the largest percentage of family-owned equity (61.3 per cent). Among these shareholders are four sons and two nephews of the founder who are senior Hyundai executives, and another son who left the group to go into politics. (Two other sons who were also Hyundai executives have died.) A little under one-third of *chaebol* subsidiaries were listed by 1994, but almost two-thirds of equity was public. This first figure has not changed so much. However, the public offering of corporate stocks continues to grow as owners are no longer able to internally finance their expanding businesses.

The *chaebol* have a large number of subsidiary companies, spread over a wide range. In 1997, the top thirty groups had 804 affiliates. The Daewoo Group, for example, has thirty-seven companies. Its firms are in trading, construction, hotel management, machinery, shipbuilding, cars, car parts, electronics, securities and fund management. From the early 1980s, Daewoo began investing overseas. As of June 1997, it had 454 overseas subsidiaries and branch offices and 250,000 employees worldwide. Total sales in 1996 were $65 billion, giving it twenty-fourth place in *Fortune* magazine's Global 500.

Given their access to the top graduates, to political power, and finance, these *chaebol* firms usually dominate the local markets they enter. Thus, almost all large firms in Korea are subsidiaries of *chaebol*.

The *chaebol* are viewed with great ambivalence by Koreans. On one hand, they are credited with having built the country and directly provided employment opportunities for millions. On the other hand, they are resented. Their corrupt collusion with politicians, speculation in real estate, and domination of the local markets create an impression of capitalist greed and murky hands controlling the country. Corruption, unfairness and powerlessness are general complaints of Koreans about their authoritarian culture. The *chaebol* are in some ways a visible and convenient target for this much broader negativity. Mindful of this, government, an even bigger target, has sought to deflect some of the negativity from itself by addressing the '*chaebol* problem'. Governments have repeatedly declared they would rein in the conglomerates, but haven't, or couldn't. By the 1980s, the *chaebol* had turned into monsters which outgrew the government's ability to control them. Combined sales of the top thirty groups were equivalent to 87 per cent of GNP. Government could not prevent them from all diving into competing sectors and creating overcapacity.

Small companies have plenty of reasons to dislike big ones. As the tree of Hyundai and others rose under Park, other saplings withered in their shade. Seven small shipbuilders were overlooked, and some went bankrupt, as a result of the massive funding of the Hyundai yards. In steel, POSCO was favoured and small steel mills which had been in business since the Japanese occupation were ignored. In cement, the Ssangyong Group, whose founder was in Park's ruling party, eclipsed a more experienced rival, the Tongyang Corporation. In machinery, a large number of smaller and older companies lost out to Hyundai, Samsung and Daewoo.[176]

One unusual aspect of business relations in Korea is the extent to which the big conglomerates mistreat their suppliers. Unlike the Japanese conglomerates, which tend to cultivate relations with suppliers and see them as integral to their network, the Koreans take a rather abusive attitude. Prospective suppliers are treated like supplicants. Once they win a contract, the real abuse starts. Fees may be reduced, and payment delayed. Suppliers are invariably paid with a promissory note, a kind of cheque which the recipient can't cash for three or six months.[177] When the unofficial loan market was active up until the late 1980s, a company could lend this money it was holding back from suppliers at 30 per cent interest. Thus abusing suppliers is not just a consequence of culture. It happened because it could be extremely lucrative. Printers, who are an example of suppliers who supply suppliers at the end of the chain, seemed to be a highly abused business caste and have a high rate of bankruptcy.

The 'little guy' expects to be abused. One small company spent years developing a continuous variance, or gear-less, transmission for cars. (Big international firms have been working on this for decades and have not come up with a commercially viable product.) Two Korean inventors put their prototype into a Hyundai Stellar. I had a go in this car. The sensation of going from 0 to 50 m.p.h. without changing gears and without the revs going up was quite unusual. (A slight problem was that it had no reverse gear, so it still needed some work.) The inventors were invited by a leading *chaebol* to use their facilities under a deal by which the *chaebol* would have first refusal on buying the final product. After a few months, the inventors discovered that the *chaebol* had registered a near-identical patent. The *chaebol*'s engineers had been unscrewing the product at night and copying it.

This kind of arrogant abuse is common because employees of large groups feel they are superior to people who work for small companies. Employees of small companies often agree with them. Dumping on those under you is the pattern and it comes of course from the top. There, at the dizzy heights of *chaebol* chairmanship we find an atmosphere of power which the ordinary western person on the street would find very peculiar. Despite the peasant background of many *chaebol* chiefs – or perhaps because of it – the environment around them when you visit their offices can feel like that surrounding Yul Brynner in *The King and I*, where the ordinary mortals were not allowed to have their heads higher than the king, even when he was sitting down. Obviously people are nervous around bosses everywhere and many western companies have a pretty fearful authoritarian culture. But Koreans seem excessive. In some companies, even the top executives stand to attention when the chairman walks in. In many ways, the boss is like a big baby with a tie on. To get him to approve an idea, you may have to present it in such a way that he can pretend he was the one who thought of it. Such tiptoeing around bosses also happens because they seem to be flipping out, or crushing you, all the time. I used to have an office on the same floor as the top executives of the Dainong Group. On the first day back from new year holidays, the big boss would assemble his staff and yell at them for half an hour. 'It's just a pep talk,' my secretary would tell me. It sounded more like the regimental sergeant major on a bad day. The yelling is a feature of a top-down management style under which middle managers are denied the freedom to fully exercise their common sense and creativity. There were surely other factors, but from my recollection of the new year barking sessions, it did not surprise me when, some years later, that this group's flagship company, the Midopa Department Store, went bankrupt.

I once got quite friendly with the brother of one *chaebol* chairman. He was given the presidency of one affiliate, although he was not really into business at all. Once you reached the executive floor, there was a hushed quiet. People spoke in low voices and padded around on thick carpeted floors. His office was a place where work didn't get done, at least not work in the sense that we know it. The bookcases contained a decorative set of reference books, probably bought by a secretary and never opened, and the desk was clear, with no evidence of paperwork. I'd always find him sitting in one of the armchairs. He liked to chat about politics to practise his English and he'd tell me how the political parties were always after him for donations. Before we went for lunch, he would press a button, then stand up and say, 'Let's go. Is Chinese OK?' He then transformed from a casual, rather artistic, character into the corporate general, and march out of the office. The secretaries would already be standing to attention and an aide would be holding open a private elevator. I would follow, and acknowledge the aides, and wink at secretaries, pretending to be a democrat but enjoying the role as the boss's foreign pal. We were ushered down the elevator, and at the bottom, the driver was waiting to whisk us off to a posh local hotel where a table lay prepared in one of the private rooms of the Chinese restaurant.

'Why do you bother with all this?' I asked him after he confided that he'd rather be playing music than doing business. 'I mean, the staff just being paid to hang around you and all the standing to attention?'

'I know,' he said. 'If I didn't do it, they wouldn't take me seriously.'

That was certainly true. Nothing dilutes authority more than fraternising with the troops in the wrong way. I can think of only one boss that I came across who behaved as if people were all equals. He had been a scholar, and had spent years in America, which may have explained it. He would actually chat with secretaries as equals. Seeing a Korean man in a senior position like this, even I found it to reflect weakness and inexperience in business. He was replaced after a while and returned to academia.

Many of the first generation of *chaebol* leaders are truly charismatic achievers. The undoubted champion of them all is Chung Ju-yung, the founder of the Hyundai Group.[178] A peasant from north Korea, Chung left school at the age of fourteen and began doing odd jobs on building sites. After a stint as a dock worker in Inchon, he moved to Seoul, where he got a job delivering rice. Soon he had his own business, but it collapsed when the government introduced rationing. Then he went into car repairs. His first workshop burned down and he started again. After independence in 1945, he opened another garage, called the Hyundai Auto Repair Company.[179]

Five years later he started the Hyundai Construction Company. Thanks to his brother, In-yung, who spoke English and had good relations with US military engineers, Chung won contracts to build facilities for the US army. Hyundai also won major government contracts. Although a tough boss, Chung was not aloof. He used to roll his sleeves up and work on sites with his men and, for relaxation, would challenge them to wrestling bouts. In the 1970s, Hyundai was chosen by President Park to build a large shipyard and to spearhead the expansion of Korean construction companies to the Middle East. Later, Chung took his group into electronics and car manufacturing. The scale of these operations was breathtaking from the start. The Ulsan shipyard was the biggest in the world, but it was being built by a company with no experience in shipbuilding. The first ship was built at Ulsan while the yard itself was still under construction. In order to get progress payment, the Hyundai workers spot-welded the keel and invited international certifiers in to approve it. Later they completed the welding.[180]

The typical Hyundai worker is popularly seen as being something of a construction-site foreman. 'They're very pushy, energetic, masculine, vulgar and rude. Once they embark on a project they do it no matter what,' says Lee Kyu-uck, president of the Korea Institute for Industrial Economics and Trade and an expert on the *chaebol*. 'Samsung people, in contrast, are seen as gentleman-like, shrewd, calculating, but not so cold-blooded. These qualities come from the first generation.'

Until the late 1980s, Hyundai was the more highly regarded of the two biggest groups. 'Samsung started in textiles and sugar,' says Lee. 'People feel it skimmed the cream off the economy, whereas Hyundai was seen as a real nation-builder.'

Chung survived the arrival of a new military dictator, Chun Doo-hwan, in 1980. Like other *chaebol*, Hyundai paid millions to the presidential Blue House in political donations. Among other donations to the national cause, Hyundai also funded Seoul's successful bid in 1981 for the 1988 Olympics. In the later part of the decade, Chung led the charge of Korean business into Russia and China. In 1989, he became the first south Korean businessman to visit north Korea. He returned to his home village with a convoy of vehicles bearing gifts. When he stepped down as honorary chairman in 1991 at the age of seventy-five and launched his bid for the presidency, his younger brother, Se-yung, took over. Hyundai is now run by Chung Ju-yung's second son, Mong-koo.

Another business figure who went more successfully into politics was Park Tae-joon, the man who developed the country's steel industry. An officer in the Korean army, he inherited some aspects of an American management training with its emphasis on rationality and efficiency. As an aide to Park Chung-hee, Park Tae-joon (no relative) was put in charge of the plan to develop a steel industry.[181] After being turned down for World Bank and US Exim Bank loans, he used personal connections in Japan and an argument that the Japanese were honour-bound to atone for the occupation by helping the Koreans. He got the loans he needed in 1969. By the mid-1980s, his Pohang Iron and Steel Company (POSCO) had turned the small fishing village of Pohang into the world's single biggest steel-production plant. Ten years later, after new plant openings, POSCO had become the world's biggest steelmaker after the Japanese company, Nippon Steel. Originally conceived for weapons manufacturing, the Korean steel business soon began to make a name for itself. Much of its product was taken a few miles round the coast to Ulsan, another small fishing hamlet which had become the site for the huge Hyundai shipyards and car factory.

Park Tae-joon had the same single-minded capacity for hard work as Chung, but instead of being a cutter of corners, he was a perfectionist. He later became a leading political figure. He opposed the nomination of Kim Young-sam as the then-ruling party's presidential candidate for the 1992 presidential election and wisely moved to Japan after Kim won to avoid retribution. He returned to politics in 1997, as an ally of Kim Dae-jung, who became the president in 1998.

Another phenomenal hard-worker is Kim Woo-choong, the founding chairman of the Daewoo Group. Unlike Hyundai's Chung, whose sons were parachuted into top positions, Kim could not be accused of nepotism. He could be accused of neglect, though, along with a million other Korean men of his generation. Kim was a fifteen-hours-a-day, seven-days-a-week man for about three decades. He is said to have taken his first day off work in 1990, at age fifty-four, after his son was killed in a car crash.

Like so many of the leaders in modern Korea, Kim was poor. His family story illustrates the combination of suffering and solidarity that lies behind so many successful Koreans. When he was a boy during the Korean War, Kim's father was dragged off by north Korean soldiers and never seen again. Still in his early teens, he became the breadwinner, selling newspapers. He used to have to make a certain amount each day to meet the family's basic costs and he wouldn't come home till he'd made it. His mother and younger brothers waited till he got home before they had dinner. 'I was so happy, and we really enjoyed those meals,' he wrote.[182] Sometimes they would already be asleep when he got home. On those occasions, he realised that there had been only enough rice for one bowl and that they had saved it for him. His mother would fib and say they had already eaten. He would fib and say he had eaten out that night. 'We were obviously lying to each other and we both knew it,' he wrote. 'We were materially poor, but rich in heart.'

On the paper round, he competed with others boys, trying to poach each other's customers. He learned that he could outdo his rivals by running around his route, delivering the newspapers and returning later for payment. This kind of street-smart mentality is typical of Korea's tycoons. Once Kim went to Singapore with fabric samples from Hong Kong and Vietnam. He claimed the samples were Korean made, got $300,000 worth of orders, went home and had the clothes copied and made.[183] He broke into the US market after he had bought a range of American shirts and had them taken apart stitch by stitch and copied.

Daewoo ('Great Universe') began as a trading company with a $5000 loan in 1967. Three years later, it had export sales of $4 million. Kim expanded from selling into manufacturing textiles. He soon gained the attention of Park Chung-hee, who had been a pupil of Kim's father at Taegu Normal School. With his political connections and energetic business sense, Kim began to expand into cosmetics, shipbuilding, construction, electronics, automobiles and other sectors. He did this by taking over existing companies, often at the government's request, rather than starting new businesses in the Hyundai style.

Kim Woo-choong was something of an upstart among the older *chaebol* chiefs in the 1960s and 1970s. He is also unusual in that he neither drinks nor smokes and has little time for formality. Indeed, he is reputed to be almost vulgar in his eating habits, slurping his noodles at breakneck speed and finishing before the others at the table have got through the toasts. These bad manners reportedly upset the north Korean leader, Kim Jong-il, when the Daewoo chief visited Pyongyang for business talks.[184] They also created a bad taste once in Italy, where he apparently offended some Italian businessmen who had prepared a sumptuous meal that he endured for about ten minutes.[185]

In the end, though, you have to ask yourself what it is exactly that these legendary tycoons are so good at. In 1999, the Daewoo giant is teetering on the edge of a nation-rattling bankruptcy. It has 57 trillion Won in debts (which is around 30 billion sterling, give or take a few billion), more than the external debt of Malaysia.

Chapter Twelve

MISMANAGING

One western consumer goods company was for years frustrated and perplexed by its Korean partner's apparent lack of concern about its lacklustre performance.[186] Every time the western partner proposed assistance, the Korean company resisted. As the proposals were coming from the foreign managers assigned to Seoul, the Korean partner just sucked his teeth and waited until they were rotated out. 'You'll be here three years, we've been here four thousand years,' one was told. The source of the difficulty was that the Korean company was an affiliate of a *chaebol* and was not trying to achieve individual efficiency. Its profits were being transferred, in ways that were obscured from the partner, to help out other affiliates in the *chaebol*. Eventually, the foreign company decided to buy out the Korean partner. When foreign auditors went in to assess the value of the Korean company, they were astounded to find a vault with $5 million dollars worth of Korean Won that was off the books. The money was used for under-the-table payments. All suppliers were paid in cash and fictitious amounts were entered into the books. The new foreign manager who took over found a warehouse full of chairs, which had been bought from a company owned by the previous chairman's uncle. There was a yard with thousands of pieces of equipment lying around, testimony to the tendency of Korean companies to replace, rather than repair, damaged parts. 'We refurbished them, wrapped them in plastic and sold them to dealers,' the manager said. The former company president had a huge luxurious office at one plant which he visited only once a month, while workers on the shop floor operated in semi-darkness as lights were switched off during the day to save money.

These kinds of inefficiencies appear to be normal with affiliates of large conglomerates, which are only half as productive as American companies.[187]

153

'*Chaebol* typically are involved in a range of different business activities and by their structure lack focus,' says James Harting, the Coca-Cola Korea Company president. For many years, Coca-Cola has made its own concentrates in Korea and sold them to four local companies, which bottled and distributed the drinks under licence in four separate regions of the country. The bottling firms were all publicly listed companies and affiliates of *chaebol*.[188] As a simple example of the problems associated with such partnerships, the bottling firms bought their bottles and cans from their own affiliates, and at high prices, a common technique for both reducing profit and helping out a sister company. In 1997, the American company restructured its business in Korea after several years of frustration with local bottling partners. It set up its own bottling company and bought the assets of its Korean bottlers. Haggling over the value of assets got acrimonious and saw some serious brinkmanship. Harting had death threats from labour unions during this time and hired bodyguards for his western directors.

'We took a western approach,' he says. 'We had meetings and then walked out of them if things didn't go well. This really shocked them. With one bottler, I had to go from a final meeting to the airport. We'd already agreed but when we finally came to sign, they wanted to re-debate the details. It was like an agreement was never a final agreement. I said, if you don't sign now, there's no offer. No deal. You keep your assets. I really had to go, so I got my coat and picked up my briefcase and still they said nothing. I walked to the door and put my hand on the doorknob, and the company president said, "OK, give me the paper." It was a $60 million gamble. They had a real emotional attachment to their identity as the Coca-Cola bottler. There was a major wringing of hands, sucking of teeth, and tears. "What's going to become of us now?" they said. What was so frustrating for me was that we had been telling them all along that we would really help them if they would just show willingness to improve the business. We really wanted to keep them as bottlers. But they didn't see it.

It turned out that the bottling companies were labouring under heavy debts. In this they were not so different from most Korean firms. To what extent an individual company is struggling with debt has always been impossible to fathom because of the way companies keep their accounts. It is standard practice for Korean companies to keep three different sets of books, one for external reporting, one for the tax authorities, and one for internal management reporting. This last set of accounts is secret and is the basis for management decision-making. It is sometimes claimed that big *chaebol* keep a fourth set for the chairman's eyes only. Accountants say this is unlikely to be a full and separate set because it takes ten people to maintain a set of books. It's more likely that the chairman will keep certain information from his executives.

Corporate finance officers are frequently kept out of the financial loop. In Korean Air, one accountant said, there is a whole department responsible for purchasing airlines. They do all the preparatory work and then pass it on to senior management. After that, this department never actually gets to see the price that is paid for an aircraft. In construction companies, there is similar obscurity. One department negotiates contracts but the chairman finalises them. No one gets to see the final amounts. In such deals, particularly in construction and shipbuilding, the two companies' chairmen may agree on a price that is higher than the market value, and split the difference. Until quite recently, a company president could get as much as 20 million Won from his staff, sign a chit saying he had received it, and then spend it on what he wanted. Owners used company money to buy stock. These abuses have been outlawed, but entertainment and ad hoc bribery expenses are sanctioned as 'confidential expenses' and tax authorities do not require that details be revealed.

The set of books for the tax authorities is somewhat superfluous because Korean companies normally meet with tax officials and negotiate how much they'll pay. The amount is usually based on government needs and last year's amount. This is possible because the tax law is actually very vague, in a way which allows tax officials wide powers of interpretation. An unbidden tax audit is invariably aggressive, because tax officials can easily find that you haven't paid enough. At the Seoul Foreign Correspondents' Club, we were audited once. The Club secretary became very alarmed when the tax officials doing it suggested that the 10 per cent service charge that we levied on food should be paid to the Club's restaurant staff. If applied retroactively, this would have bankrupted the Club. As the president at the time, I was legally responsible for this and could have been in trouble if the reason behind the audit had been government displeasure with the foreign press. On advice, I went to meet the director of the Office of National Tax Administration. We supped ginseng tea for half an hour and chatted about politics without referring to our 'little problem'. Then he called in the man who was responsible for doing the Club and berated him in front of me. From my limited Korean, it struck me that he was making a show of having discovered some error in the man's thinking, possibly that this service charge thing didn't apply to non-profit organisations like ours. The man bowed and disappeared. 'It's OK,' the director said to me with a smile.

The tax office is often referred to by journalists as the Blue House's 'pit bull'. It is normally restrained, but when unleashed, you know it will bite.

Foreign companies and wealthy individuals have been audited as a way of signalling government dislike of imports, especially of 'luxury goods', such as cars. Local companies get audited for political reasons. Once when the *Segye Ilbo* newspaper broke a story about a businessman who had paid huge bribes to top administration officials to be allowed to build on a green belt, a health-drinks company owned by the same *chaebol*, the Tongil Group, was audited. The company requested an in-camera ruling, which meant that it would not suffer PR damage from publicity, but at the same time would not be able to appeal. The final bill was around $4 million. Group executives pressured the newspaper not to break anti-government stories again.

All the accounting problems are compounded by the fact that the *chaebol* do not keep group-wide, or consolidated, accounts that show the dealing between affiliates. In other words, you cannot see the picture of a group's total debt because transfer prices can be manipulated. Companies listed on the Korea Stock Exchange are required to produce consolidated accounts, but usually a *chaebol* may have only a few of its affiliates listed. A comparison between the two types of accounts for some major *chaebol* affiliates in 1996 showed an average discrepancy of 37 per cent in the figures for profits and debt.[189] By one reckoning, the internal debt carried by corporate Korea – in other words debt owed to Korean banks by Korean companies – was roughly US$350 billion in 1997.[190]

No one in the chain in Korean companies has really had to manage the finances. The CEOs and chief financial officers of Korean companies don't have the financial management skills of their western counterparts because it is not financial health that determines whether they get loans. The important determinant is sales volume.

'In Korea, we have this focus on volume. This is typical of our character. We like to show off. The contents inside don't matter,' the vice-president of one *chaebol* affiliate said.[191] 'When you want to borrow money, you have to present financial statements to the bank. But the first number they look at is sales volume, not profit. So as a company, we never permit our sales volume to go down. If sales do not increase, you cannot borrow money, and you have to give up. If you've actually made less in sales one year, you have to lie or find some way to manipulate the numbers. Almost every company will record sales growth of ten to twenty per cent a year. Ninety-nine per cent of Korean companies are growing by sales volume. This means there must be something wrong. The problem here is the way the banks evaluate us. Why do they do it like this? I don't know to be honest. In the seventies it was necessary to reward the growth in quantity. But once you reach a certain volume, you have to shift from quantity to quality. But we have never made the transition.'

As a result of this type of credit analysis, unsteady companies get loans and then borrow more to pay the interest. The debt which most groups carry is staggering. The vice-president said that his company had outstanding loans with interest ranging from 0 to as much as 45 per cent. Sometimes money is borrowed for just twenty-four hours, he said.

Hitherto, the booming economy had made it possible for companies and banks to keep peddling like fury and repay their debts. When they got into trouble, there was always the promise of a government bail-out. But in 1996 and 1997, the government appeared to be increasingly less willing or able to step in. Bad loans were reckoned in 1996 to account for 8 per cent of all lending, around $24 billion, which was roughly the value of the banks' total equity capital.[192] There were record bankruptcies of small companies and some notable collapses of large businesses, such as Hanbo, a steel giant, and Kia Motors. Hanbo had debts of almost $6 billion. In December, 1997, the twelfth biggest *chaebol*, Halla, foundered under debts of $5.3 billion. As a measure of how much the system, rather than the individual management, is seen by business leaders as the source of the problem, of the eight *chaebol* which went bankrupt in 1997, only one chairman, Chung In-yung of Halla (and brother of the Hyundai founder), delivered an apology for poor management, a public gesture that is common in Japan.

'Everyone knew the problem,' said the vice-president. 'But bankers are very weak. They can't say no. If I am a government official and you are my friend in business and I ask a banker to take care of you, he will lend you money unconditionally. In return, you support me, the government official, financially. The politicians have said we must change this system, but they themselves are dependent on it. They are not going to shoot a bullet which will bounce back and kill them.'

Despite the rapid peddling of their conglomerates, Koreans were riding high, conceiving of themselves as a developed country, a proud member of the OECD. Then in late 1997, they suddenly found themselves in a huge financial crisis. The currency plunged, the stock market nose-dived to a ten-year low, and the massive conglomerates faced collapse. At the time the country's total foreign currency debt was $153 billion with just over 50 per cent of it due in under a year.[193] Because Japanese banks held a significant portion of Korean debt, a collapse threatened an already unstable Japanese banking system which in turn alarmed western economies. The International Monetary Fund stepped in with a $58 billion loan, its largest-ever bail-out of a country. But the money came with conditions that require Korea to clean up its act.

This crisis was perhaps inevitable given the failure of the Korean economy to adjust to changes in the last decade. Korea had the fastest rise of wage rates of any other developed country in the last ten years. At the same time, there was increasing competition from newly industrialising countries like China and Thailand. Korea was unable to compete with the more highly developed economies. As a measure of this 'sandwich' situation, as it was often called, the trade deficit widened through the 1990s. Bureaucratic efforts to squelch imports of luxury items, which made up a small fraction of imports anyway, angered trading partners and reflected the continuing unwillingness to release control. The weakness of the system, and particularly the banking system, was the result of the failure to let market forces play a fuller role. Private banks should have been permitted years before to take over the job of allocating credit from government bureaucrats.

The crisis was triggered by Korean merchant banks. These are not merchant banks in the British sense, but are short-term lenders. They began as loan sharks who, in the early 1970s, had been ordered to write off debts that *chaebol* had run up with them. In exchange they were allowed to set up officially as short-term finance companies. These flourished until the mid-1990s when they were given a choice of becoming commercial banks or short-term lenders. This latter group are the merchant banks. Most of them deal in three-month commercial papers issued mostly by big companies. These banks were leveraged up on average ten times. In other words, a bank might start with $100 million capital, borrow $1 billion, and then lend $1.1 billion. Thus they tried to grow, just as the *chaebol* had, by piling on more debt. They went overseas and invested in south-east Asian currency. When these currencies collapsed in 1997, the merchant banks were left unable to pay their debts.

The central bank started depositing foreign currency in the merchant banks and foolishly tried to hide the problem. Once word got out, international investors started withdrawing their money from Korea, and as a result the exchange rate went haywire. Then there was further panic. Rather than let the foreign exchange market fluctuate, the central bank tried to prop up the Won artificially and started selling dollars in its reserves at the prompting of the finance ministry. It reportedly depleted its reserves by 30 per cent ($10 billion). The Won halved its value in a matter of weeks. By the end of the year, banks had completely stopped giving new loans, even to healthy companies. Even good small businesses began going under because they couldn't afford the 13–18 per cent monthly interest rates being offered by loan sharks, who had mushroomed in Seoul behind doors with signs on them like 'Mountaineering Association'.[194] An increasing number of men were leaving home as usual in their suits, but going off to the mountains where they kept hiking gear in lockers: white-collar workers concealing the fact, sometimes even from their families, that they were out of work. You could also see them in cinemas, coffee shops and saunas.

Just how severe the crisis was became quickly apparent. The following statistics for January 1998 all represent the biggest monthly drop ever recorded (compared with previous Januaries): industrial production fell 10.3 per cent, total manufacturing shipments fell 7.2 per cent, domestic manufacturing shipments fell 20.6 per cent, consumer durable goods shipments fell 23.2 per cent, consumer non-durable goods shipments fell 17 per cent, machinery imports fell 47.3 per cent. Other records: the composite leading index fell 3 per cent (month-on-month), the composite concurrent index fell 3.5 per cent, and capacity utilisation fell to 68.3, the lowest level ever recorded.[195]

As they entered what they referred to as the 'IMF era', Koreans went through the gamut of emotions: at first there was a kind of denial, and wounded pride that the country was asking for foreign help. There were angry accusations – it was Kim Young-sam government's fault. There was even a proposal to hold hearings and identify which bureaucrats to blame. No, it was all the conglomerate's fault. No, it was a foreign plot. (This, most notably, from the head of one of the largest business groups, who alleged that industrialised countries had, before the crisis, already finished 'working out a programme to punish the Korea Inc. and waited until the time was ripe'.)

Then people rallied round in a way that shows why Koreans are so lovable and annoying at the same time. Tens of thousands got caught up in a gold-selling fever launched by KBS TV and the Korea Housing and Commercial Bank to raise dollars to help repay the IMF loans. People queued up to either donate or sell their gold after experts had announced there was an estimated $20 billion worth kept in Korean homes. This was a gesture from the old days, an indication of how pliable and easily mobilised the Koreans still are. Many felt that it was a pathetic gesture made out of a kind of denial. But, nevertheless, you couldn't help getting a lump in your throat at the sight of young couples handing in their wedding rings and old ladies handing in items of tremendous personal significance with the feeling that they were helping save their country. (As a result of this campaign, the international price of gold dropped to the lowest in eighteen years.) People felt they had to do their bit. People stopped drinking coffee because it is imported. In the Ministry of Defence publishing house, for example, secretaries offered visitors local teas (*uri cha*, meaning 'our tear') instead of coffee and explained it was 'because of the IMF'.

The blessing in thin disguise here is that the shock of the collapse has forced the government to make, and public opinion to accept, the structural changes that should have been made ten years earlier. In early 1998, laws were passed to permit companies to lay workers off for the purpose of downsizing. Just in case there's a reluctance in the implementation, the IMF has made these labour changes, as well as transparent accounting, conditions for receiving more loans.

As one banker had put it, 'a monk cannot cut his own hair'. Now he's getting some help. But it is only a mirror. The Koreans still have to do their own cutting.

The economic crisis was a consequence of a fragile banking system and heavy *chaebol* debts. Despite the fact that they are the cause, the business groups themselves are extremely reluctant to restructure. They feel threatened by the new government of Kim Dae-jung because they fear he will not permit banks to lend them more money. As this fear indicates, they still believe that the government will continue to control the banks. Breaking out of this mindset is monumentally difficult. The Koreans have very collective social values and have not been prepared through their education system for the free market. Decision-making has not been rational. Rather it has been based on personal connections and loyalties. The market reforms that are needed would break up this pattern of relations, both among decision-makers and between a paternalistic company and its workers, and place people in a new pattern of relationships that typify the free-market system. The process is very hard to accept.

If one takes a long historical look at Koreans, we can see that they have excelled at imitation. This is not meant as negatively as it may seem. They have borrowed foreign systems – for example, Confucianism, Christianity, communism, capitalism – and in each case developed the most extreme and successful version of that system, often outdoing their mentors. One possible explanation that presents itself to this western mind for this is that Korea has, in order to survive, adopted an inferior role and is driven to excess by a kind of guilt or denial of this fact. However, an east Asian explanation may be that zeal began with Confucianism and subsequently was a consequence of the deep rooting of that religion's basic tenet – filial piety – into the Korean mind. Korea wishes to be the perfect child. Whatever the explanation, Korea at the end of the twentieth century is a nation that must grow up, come out of denial, take responsibility for its history, and submit to the surgery it knows it needs.

If it does this, we may see the country developing in a service direction, and characterised by small and medium companies led by its many gifted entrepreneurs. In this picture, a few large companies would remain and a lot of industry would be owned by foreigners, seeking to use Korea as an export base to the region. Right now, this prediction would raise terrible fears of national disintegration and foreign control. But fears never evaporate until they are faced.

If the country fails to take the necessary steps, it is possible to imagine it lurching along, but we may safely say that it has reached its ceiling. If the 1997 collapse had not occurred, I expect I would have been suggesting that a change in the north Korean situation may create an opportunity for another decade or two of Parkian-style development. As it is, I would now suggest that if south Korea fails to adjust properly, it may not be able to handle reunification.

Until now, Koreans have demonstrated a remarkable resilience and ability to shrug off suffering and move forward. At this point, though, they need more than resilience. They cannot barge their way through their economic difficulties. What is needed is rational corporate governance, financial transparency, and accountability, sustained by a system of government that is fair, transparent and accountable. Until now, although it has been authoritarian and corrupt, as we shall see in later chapters, it has worked because its leaders could provide. Now it no longer works.

The current president, Kim Dae-jung, needs to both adjust the economic system to the needs of the free market and create moral leadership which engenders trust in that system.

Chapter Thirteen

FOREIGN BUSINESS

Korean business is stacked against the foreigner. Because national development has been a process of catching up with developed countries, it has involved imitation, not innovation. This means that foreign companies have been deemed useful for as long as their technology is needed. While making money out of foreigners – i.e. exporting – was considered virtuous, there was a collective revulsion at the notion that foreigners should be making profits in Korea.

One of the worst manifestations of this attitude in recent years involved the American company, Amway. This highly successful company is no stranger to controversy. Its multilevel marketing method of distribution has been frequently attacked in other countries and it is often associated with dishonest and predatory 'pyramid' companies. Amway gained approval to enter the Korean market in 1991 after a request by the then-US President, George Bush, during an official visit. Multilevel marketing, whereby independent salespeople receive commission on the sales of other salespeople whom they recruit, was perfectly suited to Koreans. Distributors could operate independently and avoid the stifling hierarchy of a normal company, and, secondly, they could recruit and sell through their large circle of family and acquaintances. Seventy per cent of the distributors were women. Amway threatened the established order of the conglomerates which controlled the distribution and labour markets. Early success with its soap and detergent products led to attacks in the media and bureaucratic delays, especially in customs clearance of key product components, which were prompted in part by business rivals.

Two years later, prosecutors began investigating pyramid sales. Two American executives of Amway and several Korean staff were held in jail and interrogated by prosecutors for allegedly infringing rules on distributor training. The company president, David Ussery, was kept behind bars for nine days with his hands often bound. 'I wasn't badly treated, but the Korean staff were knocked about a bit,' he said. The company was later found guilty of violating a provision in the law that was later revoked. By 1996, Amway's annual sales represented almost 40 per cent of sales in the multilevel-marketing sector. This last statistic, market share, is the real issue for Korean firms. In 1997, the Korea Soap and Detergents Association, a grouping of eighteen rival companies, launched an attack. It took out advertisements alleging that one Amway product was a major cause of water pollution. The National Council of Consumer Protection Organisations, which is funded mostly by the government and *chaebol*, formed an anti-Amway committee. Reporters who included Amway's position in their stories got angry calls from these organisations accusing them of taking bribes from the American company. As a result, during the year, sales dropped by 64 per cent and half of the 140,000 distributors stopped working. The company hit back, taking advantage of a climate that was less anti-foreign than five years earlier. The Fair Trade Commission ruled against the Korea Soap and Detergents Association, which was forced to apologise.[196]

Given this type of treatment, it is hardly any wonder that Korea began to be described as Asia's graveyard for foreign investment. 'Foreign companies are just tolerated as a necessary evil,' said one businessman bitterly at the time of the first Amway incident. 'We are getting fed up with the attitude. The Chinese, by contrast, are very welcoming.' Indeed, in 1993 alone, China attracted $27.5 billion in direct foreign investment, more than Korea had done in forty years. Other Asian countries, like Singapore, Malaysia and Indonesia, were attracting much more than Korea. Gradual easing of restrictions meant that Korea managed to gain over $2 billion of direct foreign investment in one year for the first time in 1995, several years later than it should have.

The anti-foreign attitudes have eased somewhat in the late 1990s. But there are other difficulties of doing business with Korean companies. Their management system is not easy to understand, and there is no real body of knowledge to study. In old Korea, commerce was something that the lower classes and scoundrels engaged in. There were no large-scale non-business organisations where Koreans could learn how to manage large numbers of people in complex tasks. During the Japanese period, Koreans were in low positions and gained little actual management experience. After the Second

World War and the ousting of the Japanese rulers, Koreans began studying American management principles.

Koreans learned directly from the experience of working with Americans, who were great teachers and examples of professionalism for so many of the political, academic and business leaders who were key in the country's development. Their greatest influence was on the military. Officers were trained in American management practices. During the period of military-backed rule, hundreds of these officers took executive posts in state-run companies and organisations. Americans were looked up to because they were more powerful, wealthier, more free, and better organised. Until recently, they were also a lot taller. They displayed their authority very differently. Individual Americans in powerful positions are often so untypical of the Korean (or even the European) idea of leaders, and seem to many Koreans who deal with them to combine professionalism and informality in a way that is at once engaging and confusing, for it is so distinct. The Korean management style often seems to be the exact opposite of the American, highly formal and not always so competent.

In the late 1980s, the US military introduced Korean officers to simulated war games. At first, the Korean generals were so reluctant to participate that the American commander himself had to sit down at the console and jolly them along, 'It was "Uh-oh, General Kim, you just blew up your own side. Hahaha. Never mind,"' an American official said. 'Once they realised they were not going to be criticised for making mistakes, they learned so fast they became better than our guys. Those Koreans are so focused.'

In college, Koreans study American management principles, and have grown up believing that Korean principles either don't exist or don't amount to much. For this reason there is often an unusual discrepancy between the principles that managers think they are adhering to and those that actually are at work. In hiring, for example, this discrepancy becomes apparent. For a western interviewee, it is important to be articulate in order to convey a sense of competence. But Korean companies don't always like such people. It is expected that they will lack loyalty and not get on so well with others. A government office once invited an American to sit on a panel interviewing applicants for a bilingual secretary-receptionist job. The successful candidate would be dealing with foreign business visitors. She had to be presentable and speak good English. Among the candidates, five were shy young women who mumbled demurely in answer to questions. Such displays of deference brought out a paternal affection in the men on the panel, who prodded away with various questions, more as a formality than anything else, and ended up by inviting the candidate to answer a question in English from the American. The sixth candidate was altogether different. An attractive former air hostess, she spoke excellent English and volunteered English answers for the benefit of the foreign panellist.

'What is your opinion?' the chairman of the panel asked after the last interview.

'I think there is no question,' the American said. 'This last one is the obvious choice.' There was a silence during which he was permitted without assistance to realise that his was the minority opinion. The chairman sucked inwardly through his teeth.

'Yes. She is clearly capable,' he said. 'But we are afraid that she would not harmonise well.' There was no more discussion. The air hostess didn't get the job because it was thought that other secretaries in the organisation would be jealous of her abilities. Harmony between the secretaries was more important than their individual abilities. Thus, there was a mix of the American focus on the narrow boundaries of the job requirements, which the panellists thought they were following, and Korean reality in which personal relations take precedence over competence.

The current 'IMF crisis' leading to restructuring of the conglomerates is bound to have a profound effect on corporate management and Korean society, but just how remains to be seen. Workers once took for granted that their jobs were secure. In return companies expected loyalty. Now these agreements are being broken.

This is deeply disturbing for the present generation whose notions of management begin with the pattern of familial relations. In many ways the *chaebol* chairmen have operated like stern father figures, pushing their workers like children reluctant to do well, but at the same time benevolently guaranteeing their jobs. Such bosses tend to be workaholics who are poor at delegating. Their authoritarianism can produce tremendous energy, but its limits become apparent as companies become more sophisticated, because it involves so much suppression of individuality. It may suit for as long as Korea is copying the development of others, but it directly hinders the development of the innovation and creativity that Korea's economy now needs.

Strong central leadership creates its own security. The Koreans do not see security in an organisation, and even less in a contract. Their loyalty is to the individuals who run organisations. Lifetime employment is guaranteed not by the duration of the company, but by the continuing relationship with the individual at the top. Although bosses have the authority to sack people on the spot, they rarely do. Firing someone is a last resort, something that is regarded as a severing of human relations. Confucian education requires a more benevolent approach. When the sons of founders take over, many people lose their jobs, but it happens very subtly. Often the new, young chairman knew the old guard when he was a boy. They probably called him by his given name, and he knew their weaknesses and perhaps felt how they manipulated or disappointed his father. His reluctance to rely on these people for advice when he becomes chairman becomes apparent. They quickly sense this and offer to resign. The resignation is quietly accepted, but they may keep their office and salary for as long as two or three years afterwards while they gradually ease themselves out.

Where the Korean system displays real weakness is in decision-making. Bosses guard the area of decision-making very jealously. The Daewoo chairman, Kim Woo-choong, for example, travels the world and frequently makes major corporate decisions on the spot after meeting government officials and businessmen in the country involved. Bosses characteristically do not permit credit to go to another, especially not to a subordinate. Usually, in a smaller corporation which is still run by its founder, there is only one decision-maker. For larger organisations, the process is more complex. Companies vary, but in general there is a consensus of sorts with consultation between varying levels of management. In government bureaucracies, there is more of a Japanese-type process with the ideas coming from the bottom up. The process is often slow and filled with paperwork.

Another characteristic of decision-making in business is the lack of long-term vision. There are various explanations, including the folksy one that Koreans have traditionally lived in clusters of houses, behind walls, in villages that are backed up against mountains (and hence can't see far into the distance). The scholar, Mark Setton, identifies the likely culprit as child-rearing habits: 'The focus is on immediate gratification of the child's demands, particularly the male child, not only during infancy but also during childhood when the sense of time and space is in a critical stage of development,' he says. Consequently, in adulthood, short-term sacrifice for a long-term payoff is not the popular way of doing things. So even if there is vision, the self-discipline needed to push it through comes in short supply. From this perspective, Korean companies might do better if they were managed by women.

'Young Korean women,' Setton says, 'are given much more rigorous training by their mothers under the principle that they are required to serve in the home, and this could be the reason why they appear to have twice as much self-discipline as the men. Unfortunately very few women as yet have policy-making roles, and Korean organisations are full of impatient males who want things done "yesterday" for results "tomorrow", irrespective of what may happen the day after.'

Setton also notes that Korean men generally are remarkably self-confident in their own opinions. It comes, he says, from an emotional impression of correctness rather than an awareness of objective facts, and again has its origins in the way they are treated as children. Parents do not boss their children around and criticise them as much as western parents. Rather there is much more positive reinforcement. When combined with the idea of face, in which admitting mistakes is taken as weakness, this confidence makes open discussion between superiors and inferiors extremely difficult.

'This discourages feedback, as inferiors become reluctant to speak their mind on matters of policy,' he says. 'Lack of feedback results in a lack of effective policy evaluation, which is the root cause of a characteristic common to many Korean organisations: development through trial and error, and more error.'

Officials in large Korean companies are often extremely hesitant about reporting upwards. In the case of the company which was developing the gear-less transmission, the inventors found with two Korean car companies that officials were unwilling to report their meetings to senior decision-makers.[197] Technicians were extremely enthusiastic about their project, but managers never heard of it.

'If a department head had recommended an untested idea and the company decided to do it and later it failed, he would be blamed. So why risk it?' said Lee Han-woo, a consultant for the inventors. 'If the project had succeeded, the credit would have gone to a higher official. The other risk is that these big companies are very proud. If someone goes and tells their boss there's a great idea outside, the boss might yell at them and say, "How come we didn't invent it?" Many new ideas and products end up this way.'

This nervousness that the hierarchical corporate structure creates can make for great comedy. One of the most popular TV shows in post-dictatorial Korea featured a buffoon of a boss whose aides all jumped to attention and cried 'Superb' every time he asked what they thought of his ideas. It had a Monty Python-like appeal for a while, and cheeky kids and students started doing it to their parents and to professors in class.

But this type of management environment can have serious, and tragic, consequences. Two air crashes in Korea in recent years are alleged to have occurred through a subordinate's unwillingness to correct a pilot. In July 1993, sixty-six people were killed when an Asiana 737–500 crashed into a mountain after the pilot made three 'reckless' attempts to land in bad weather. An official noted obscurely that the pilot 'appeared to have received no help from the co-pilot, Park Tae-hwan, who was inexperienced.'[198] In June 1991, the pilot of a Korea Air Boeing 727 landed at Taegu Airport without realising that his undercarriage wasn't down. The three members of the cockpit crew were jailed for several months for 'ignoring the manuals'. Somehow, all three misinterpreted warning noises. The point here is not that the co-pilots knew the plane would crash and kept quiet, but that the environment was such that one does not second-guess a pilot.

It is possible that this timidity by co-pilots may not feature when the pilot is a foreigner. A crash occurred at Cheju International Airport in August 1994, when a Korean co-pilot disagreed with his Canadian pilot and overreacted. The pilot was coming in too fast and was landing his Korean Air Airbus 300 too far along the runway. The crash happened when the Korean co-pilot tried to lift the plane up again. The plane skidded off the runway and burst into flames. Fortunately, all 160 on board were safely evacuated. The Cockpit Voice Recorder captured the final seconds (Time: 11.21 a.m.):[199]

- 21.22 Co-pilot: Go around
- 21.26 Pilot: Get your ha — Get off, get off. Tell me what it is.
- 21.33 Pilot: Get off
- 21.34 Co-pilot: Go around?
- 21.35 Pilot: No, no
- 21.43 Co-pilot: Reverse
- 21.46 Co-pilot: Brake
- 21.55 Pilot: What are you doing? Don't ... What man ... You're gonna kill us.
- 22.07 Pilot: Hold yoke
- 22.08 (Sound of crash)

For Koreans, decisions still seem to be negotiable long after agreement has been made. For westerners, this tendency can be infuriating. A foreign investment banker who had been involved in a complicated financing deal with a major conglomerate turned up at the final signing ceremony, with the heads of several affiliates in attendance, to find that the company's negotiator wanted to renegotiate a crucial term of the agreement. The banker refused to change his position and got aggressive, at some personal risk.

'Had they said the deal was off, it would have been very career-damaging for me,' he said. 'But I knew this was the only way to deal with the Koreans. The annoying thing was that this term had been in the deal from the beginning several weeks earlier.' He got his way after two hours and the ceremony went ahead.

This experience is a good example of a point that is often lost when we talk about the relationship-building and etiquette involved in doing business with Koreans. That is that you sometimes have to be stubborn and aggressive. Koreans see business less as a rational, legally based interaction than as a relationship. A westerner might take this to mean that one has to be more careful about getting on with people. This is true to a point. But in relationships, you sometimes have to be emotional, hard-headed, even bullying to get what you want. The Korean business environment can be very brutal and, contrary to the spirit of the cultural advice that business-men are given, it is my estimation that more western managers have lost out in business with Korea because of a failure to be aggressive than because of a failure to be polite.

The point is not so much that personal relations are important, but that there is a much weaker sense of law in Korean business relations than in international business. 'Western contracts may run to hundreds of pages in which everything is anticipated,' says Hong Suhn-kyong, an American-educated Korean lawyer. 'But a Korean transaction may be covered by just two or three pages. Koreans find it irksome that westerners insist on writing everything.'

For Koreans, a contract is part of the symbolism involved in beginning a relationship. The contract is only as binding as the personal relations. Furthermore, the contract may often be seen by the Korean side as only symbolising the relationship between those who signed it, not the two corporations. If relations are very close, then insisting on a contract can actually be taken as an insulting indication of mistrust. If contracts are broken, extra-legal channels are used to resolve a dispute. It goes to court only when all else has failed.

Koreans are familiar with the western approach to negotiations in which opposing demands are presented and followed by exchanges that aim to seek a mutually acceptable compromise. But they prefer to start with points of common ground and build on them, thereby avoiding the confrontation involved in expressing opposing views and finding compromise. But, as the investment banker's experience shows, when they feel it is necessary, they can be extremely bloody-minded in negotiations. They are experts at brinkmanship, wearing opponents down, hanging over the edge of the cliff by their fingertips before agreeing to compromise.

Despite what I have said about the need to be tough, politeness is also important. Koreans respond very well to courtesies. They are very intuitive when it comes to sensing what kind of person you are, and are prepared to overlook mistakes in manners. But it is useful to remember that with a foreigner, there are always some things you can forgive and some that are more difficult to overlook. Nose-blowing, especially if you do it noisily into a handkerchief and, for some gross purpose, save it in your pocket, is difficult to endure. Some western men, and not a few women, make a noise like a trumpet when they blow their nose. A quieter technique is recommended. Koreans are very good at accepting a gesture to good manners as being as good as the real thing. So, if a person must blow their nose at the table, they can do so without offending if they politely turn their head away.

Educational credentials are important for Koreans, so if you did not go to university or went to a really obscure one, it's best not to volunteer the fact along with your theory about what a waste of time college is. If you went to Oxford or Cambridge or an American Ivy League university, there is probably an association of Korean alumni. You might want to join it.

Koreans like westerners, and their forthrightness can make them very good company. They will ask questions such as where you come from, which college you went to and what your religion is, not to judge you but as part of their search for common points of reference. The religion question gets funny reactions from westerners, many of whom feel affronted as if they'd been asked their sexual orientation, but it's basically an attempt at friendship.

The name card is important for Koreans because it means they don't have to try to figure out your position. Of course, it will give them assumptions about your authority which may or may not be accurate. It's important when receiving someone's name card to treat it reverentially. One shouldn't feel, 'Oh, this'll be useful when I'm trying to remember your name,' and shove it in your shirt pocket. Koreans wince when pragmatic westerners do this. Another reason to be nice to name cards is that in Korea you need to relate to all levels. The irony about authoritarian structures is that everyone in the chain seems to want to assert themselves. Until they get the phone call from on high, lower officials may often just do their own thing. You need to see the top man to get things started, but after that you need to smooth the wheels at all levels. You also need to be able to assess where the decision-making power is, especially as the person you are meeting may be there only because he speaks English, and may have his own difficulties in conveying your needs to the decision-makers. Many small and medium Korean companies take the visits of foreign companies as an embarrassment. The sooner it's over and done with the better. The fact that they may be missing a business opportunity may not figure.

The Korean custom that western men take to most rapidly is the drinking ritual. Basically, when drinking alcohol with a Korean, you should endeavour to pour from the bottle into the other person's glass. If you don't notice his glass is empty and he starts pouring his own, just say sorry and it'll be OK. This habit goes down so well with westerners that it could go global, like *karaoke*. When you're really partying, the idea is to empty your glass and fill it for your friend to drink out of. The glass usually takes about a third of a pint. If there's a bottle of whisky, too, your host might pour a shot into a small glass and drop the whisky, still in the glass, into the full beer glass and invite you to knock it back in one. There are a lot of legless foreigners staggering around Korean streets at night. You also get used to sharing food from the same bowls, despite the high incidence of hepatitis. The hygiene factor is ignored for the sake of group solidarity. Given that an estimated 10 per cent of Koreans carry the virus, this is a level of risk that westerners are usually prepared to entertain only in sexual encounters.

Entertainment can be very expensive. When it comes to paying the bill, you don't see Koreans sneaking off to the toilet. It is a matter of honour to pay, so much so that wrestling matches often break out between men at the counters of bars and restaurants over who pays. These are pretend affairs, but given the Korean level of vigour, may strike the first-time visitor as serious altercations. Proposing to go Dutch is unbelievably mean. But what often happens is that one person pays and when you're outside, you can stuff a few notes into your friend's pocket. He'll resist. You'll insist. He'll resist. At this point I give up. One unwritten rule is that you pay if a person is travelling to your location. One should be sensitive about proposing a meeting at 11.30. As lunchtime in Korea is midday, there's an expectation that you'll have it together unless otherwise stated.

In general, a well-brought-up person can't go far wrong with Koreans. The most important point that can be made about the cultural-sensitivity advice is that Koreans do not expect foreigners to be Korean. They are much more familiar with western style than the West is with theirs. They understand that people are different. Given this, it is useful to remember that they expect you to live up to the highest standards of your own culture. In a way, they expect more logic and fairness from a western person. This level of expectation also applies to moral matters. Although many Korean business-men, especially of the older generation, consider it normal to be unfaithful to their wives with prostitutes and bar hostesses, they find it deplorable how some western men seem to engage in affairs that wreck marriages. The fact that many foreign businessmen feel laddishness is a necessary part of business has caused a lot of anguish to wives. But it is easy, if they wish, to signal that they don't like heavy drinking and that the idea of being entertained by prostitutes doing lewd things with eggs is unacceptable. There are other ways to develop relationships. Golf might be a better option.

Chapter Fourteen

WORKING AND CONSUMING

There are around 21 million workers in Korea, plus about 2 million students and housewives who work part-time. About 8 million of this number are industrial workers. Some 300,000 graduates enter the workforce each year.

The spectre of this workforce getting out of hand and becoming a political force had always haunted the managers of Korea Inc. This fear was also generated by the fact that unions had been used in south Korea, both by communists before 1948, and by the government since, to further political ends. Strong controls under the dictatorships of Park and Chun kept workers in line. The controls were also designed to keep wages low and exports competitive. Involvement of third parties in labour disputes was illegal, which virtually precluded efforts by labour specialists and political activists to advise workers and negotiate on their behalf. The government recognised only one union per company. These were centrally controlled through the Federation of Korean Trades Unions, an umbrella group with about 2,400 affiliated unions. Intelligence officials used to sit in on its meetings. Some companies refused to allow unions. In small companies, management could intimidate workers so that labour organisers could not find the minimum thirty employees necessary by law to agree to a union being formed. In companies which were unionised, the union leader's position was full-time and came with a salary paid by the company and privileges. In all, only 12 per cent of the 17-million-strong workforce in 1987 belonged to unions.[200] Strikes were suppressed by riot police, often violently.

Thus during the period of rapid industrialisation, the Korean worker saw no significant improvement in pay and conditions. Korea was reckoned by the International Labour Organisation in the 1980s to have the longest average working week in the world (fifty-three hours). Safety standards have also been appalling. Consider the following statistics: in 1994, for every 10,000 workers, 118 were involved in accidents. This compared with eighty for Taiwan and thirty-nine for Japan. The losses were estimated at $6.3 billion. Over 52 million working days were lost through accidents, which was thirty-three times more than days lost through strikes. Between 1964 and 1994, 39,000 workers were killed and 2.9 million injured in accidents at work.[201]

After pro-democracy protests in June 1987, workers were able to organise themselves. The first wave of strikes that followed were mainly to press for recognition of new unions created illegally by workers in opposition to the existing 'pro-management' unions. In the few weeks after the lifting of political restrictions, there were over three thousand strikes, paralysing car plants, coal mines, shipyards, electronics and textile factories. Employees struck at over two-thirds of Korea's big plants, which employed more than 1000 workers.[202] In Ulsan, 20,000 striking workers from seven Hyundai plants took to the streets to demand the resignation of the chairman Chung Ju-yung himself. Chung had refused to recognise a new union. In an incident typical of its kind, goons acting for the company had snatched documents which unionists planned to submit to register the union. In the end, the government ordered the documents to be returned and the registration was announced. Chung, humiliated by the change in government attitude, continued to oppose the union demands. Hyundai shipyard workers marched through Ulsan behind forklifts and cherry pickers, dressed in protective clothing and welding masks. Several hundred went on a rampage, setting fire to cars and wrecking the city hall. Hundreds of riot police took up positions by the Hyundai-owned Diamond Hotel and drenched the rioters in tear-gas. Eight thousand workers took over the Hyundai shipyard. Similar scenes were played out at the Daewoo car factory at Pupyong outside Seoul. In two massive pre-dawn blitzes, thousands of riot police invaded the two sites and arrested the strikers. The police were in full riot gear and carried fire extinguishers in case desperate strikers set themselves on fire. They placed mattresses around buildings to prevent protesters from making suicide leaps. Several tried to immolate themselves but were overpowered and at least two strikers were injured jumping out of a window.

These few weeks of turmoil created widespread fear that President Chun would use the military to re-establish order. But despite the drama of the Hyundai and Daewoo strikes, the government kept a hands-off policy.

Interestingly, there was some economic logic at work in this approach. Government economists had figured that the slowdown in exports would reduce a trade surplus with the United States and allay the real threat to the economy – protectionist retaliation from Washington. When it did intervene, it was mostly to pressure management to accept workers' demands.

After the summer of 1987, the genie was out of the bottle and in every sector workers began pressing for more say in management, improved conditions and better wages. It seemed that everyone with an issue demonstrated. I remember watching with some amazement a march of chanting publishers protesting Korea's signing of an international copyright agreement, and demanding the right to pirate foreign books. In another incident, street hawkers rallied outside the city hall in Seoul after police began removing their carts in a pre-Olympic clean-up of the city.

For several years, labour strife was an almost daily occurrence, particularly in the spring, the traditional time for wage negotiations. Samsung, with its more sophisticated management, managed to avoid a lot of the violence. But Hyundai's Chung Ju-yung, still the tough guy of Korean business, could not shake the view that workers had no right to make demands in his company. In one of the most dramatic cases, in 1989, a protracted strike at the Hyundai shipyard, which cost the company £70 million and forced about twenty suppliers to near-bankruptcy, was ended with a land-and-sea assault by 9000 riot troops.

White-collar workers have also been very active, with some major union activity in the 1990s in the banking sector and in schools. However, no political party has succeeded in gaining union support. The main political parties are financed by big business and try to appear to be all things to all people.

Although images of violent protest dominated foreign TV coverage of Korea for many years, the Koreans also have a well-earned international reputation for being hard workers. On construction sites in the Middle East and south-east Asia, they have impressed governments with their round-the-clock operations and their ability to beat deadlines. In this regard they are different from their brothers and sisters in north Korea, who lack the incentive for hard work.

One feature of workers in south Korea is a spirit of 'Can Do'. It is one of those countries where you can get a lot of things done immediately. The first time we got in a decorator to wallpaper our flat, the man slapped the strips on so quickly, I should have entered him for the *Guinness Book of Records*. The first time I moved house, I didn't have many possessions and I was able to flag down one of the hundreds of small trucks that cruise around Seoul, whose driver did an instant removal job. Another time when we moved, we arrived at a house, this time with a proper removal vanload of furniture, to find that the previous tenants had taken the linoleum and left us with bare concrete floors. While the removal men were having lunch and I was at the estate agent handing over the £25,000 rental deposit in cash, a friend who was helping out went to the nearest carpet shop and got all the floors fitted with linoleum in about an hour.

Car breaks down? No problem. Once I was on the motorway with my family when the accelerator cable snapped. We were spotted by a pickup vehicle that patrolled the roads looking for victims. In no time the driver and his mate had hoisted the car off its front wheels and were tugging us along the road. We were still in the car of course. Going along a road at about fifty m.p.h. on your back wheels with no view except the back end of a truck may be exciting for children but is unnerving for adults. We were pulled to a small village where they had a workshop. A lad was dispatched to the nearby town to get the part and we were shown the village restaurant. After some noodles and kimchi, the car was done and we were back on the road.

The downside of speed is poor quality. This is a particular problem for the Koreans, whose 'Can Do' approach is matched by a real 'That'll Do' mentality. There is a lot of peeling wallpaper in Korea. This is not simply a consequence of doing things too quickly. It is a feature of the 'Can Do' spirit that any amateur can do anything.

At work, Koreans refer to one another by their position. In an office, you won't hear, 'Hi, John, how's it going?' It'll be 'Honourable office manager, did section chief Lee call you this morning?' Promotion does not only mean a bigger salary and sense of career advancement. It also provides a title, which a person may use generally in society. Therefore, being promoted from section chief to department head is as important as rising from corporal to sergeant in the military. Many Koreans have been surprised when I told them of my experience in British factories of people on the shop floor who had turned down promotions because they did not want the increased responsibility.

In a social environment in which people are called by their job titles, the symbols of power become extremely important. Something like, say, arranging the telephone extension numbers in an office becomes important because numbers denote hierarchy. Similarly, getting the right office is not so much a matter of having the nice view out of the window as avoiding the locations deemed lower in the hierarchy. In one place where I worked, we tried to get around this visual hierarchy by arranging desks in an H-shape. But the Korean staff felt that the person who got to sit with his back to the door, in the horizontal line of the H, would be seen as the most junior and so subtly argued to avoid that place.

You will find when you walk into a Korean office that you can always immediately tell who is in charge. If there is ambiguity it may indicate some ambiguity in the office politics. In some joint-venture operations, for example, you may find that two people seem to have similar offices and similar-size furniture. This could be a case in which the boss from the operational viewpoint is a foreigner, assigned by head office, while the titular boss may be a Korean. This can be useful because it allows the Korean to relate to government officials as a company president and to the presidents of other companies as an equal. As his role is the social one, his office is usually uncluttered with paper.

For many years, the big western news agencies in Seoul were run by Korean reporters. As Korea became a bigger story, foreign correspondents were sent to run the offices. The relationship of these foreigners with the senior Korean reporter was often quite complex. The senior Korean usually remained as the official bureau chief while the foreigner was recognised by the government as the real power they had to deal with because he wrote the news. The staff played a dual game of deferring to the foreigner as the boss for news-gathering purposes and to the elder Korean as the wise paternal elder who, of course, would outlive all the foreigners.

Koreans are accustomed to such complex arrangements. Woe betide a foreigner who tries to play politics, though. In one news bureau, a foreign correspondent was asked by head office to recommend salaries and was provided with a budget for an office move. He saw this as an opportunity for a bit of western rationality and, being an experienced Asia hand, tried to signal to the Korean 'bureau manager' who never did any work that he, the 'correspondent' (lower title), was the real boss. To do this, he ordered a slightly larger chair and desk for himself for the new office. The bureau manager stopped coming to work. After a week, the correspondent went to the man's house and told him he was adjusting the furniture. Problem solved, and everyone went back to work as if nothing had happened.

In 1965, 37.6 per cent of the GNP was produced on the farm. In two decades that proportion had dropped to 11 per cent. As industry developed, people moved from the country to town and city in huge numbers. Three-quarters of the population lived in small villages when the Park Chung-hee revolution started. Now three-quarters live in urban spreads.[203]

The patterns of life on the farm typified the approach to work as industrialisation began. Farm life was characterised by periods of hard work followed by periods of waiting for crops to ripen. During this time, there would be work to do such as repairing thatched roofs and out-houses. All the relatives would turn up and muck in. While the women were in the kitchen keeping the supply of food and drink going, cackling and cursing, men would yell and bark out contradictory orders. Each time something had to be done, like lifting a beam, ten pairs of hands would go for something that required only two.[204] At work in modern environ-ments, Koreans also seek this kind of warm camaraderie with their peers. When the *Segye Ilbo* newspaper launched in 1989, journalists and editors built up their files and prepared dummy editions for several months before the actual daily newspaper was started. Timothy Elder, an Ameri-can hired for the international news desk, found an unusual routine dur-ing the months prior to publication.

'There wasn't actually so much work to do,' he said. 'So from our desk, everyone except the editor used to go out drinking together at night. They would end up getting home at four or five in the morning. They'd be at work at nine, and somehow manage to drag themselves through the morning. At twelve, they'd go off for lunch and then spend the afternoon together in the sauna. They'd come in later in time to clock off and then they were all out for dinner and more drinking. This routine went on day in, day out for months. The editor didn't join in because his peer group was the other editors. And I didn't need to go out with them because I'm a foreigner. I couldn't figure why the company would pay people whose pattern of work was like this. And why people would endure such an arduous lifestyle. Then it occurred to me that this was their way of bond-ing. Later, when the paper began, of course, there was no time to do this. In fact, people worked very hard. But they were able to do so because they felt part of a group that had bonded.'

Company training sessions for new recruits also serve a bonding pur-pose. The big companies have employee training programmes which strike the outsider as terrifyingly militaristic. Initial training may be a kind of three-month boot camp which is intended to develop attitudes and company spirit. One part of the Samsung training is to drop trainees off in a remote place with some company products, which they must sell in order to buy food and a ticket back to the training centre.

Interestingly, though, this process does not create loyalty to the company as an organisation. In the scale between individualism and group conform-ity, the Koreans are somewhere in the middle. The Koreans observe the form of the Japanese standard of company loyalty. But the reality of their behaviour is different. They tend to seek loyalty to a sub-group within a large organisation. This may be the department or section they work in. But in a big company, the sub-group is more likely to consist of equals, such as the new entrants in a particular year.

Wining and dining is a huge part of work in Korea. As a journalist, I used to organise my days in breakfast, lunch and dinner meetings, simply because it is so difficult to get information on the telephone. For business executives, the cost of dining out gets astronomical. The important thing to understand about this is that it involves more than just networking. There's a measure of loyalty that goes with it. They say that if you have coffee with someone, you will be acquaintances; if you have lunch you can be friends; but if you get drunk together you can be very close. I was close with two male journalists in the mid-1980s who told me that when they were younger they used to go out drinking and often 'share the same girl at the same time'. Both men later became government ministers. Middle-class Korean men have literally hundreds of acquaintances in different loyalty groups that they keep up with. In times of trouble, the strategy of exhaustive socialising pays off. Tax officials find when they raid the house of someone who has been designated by the Blue House for attack and start bundling up anything that could be of use in the investigation, the victim never calls his lawyer. He starts calling his contacts in the bureaucracy, usually people he's known since high school, to see if they can use their influence to get the audit cancelled.

I did some research into entertainment. It began one night in Itaewon, an entertainment district in Seoul near the American military base where shop and bar owners spoke English. I was with an economist, who was visiting Korea for the first time. He was an expert on the Philippines and was boundlessly enthusiastic about being in a country that was so much more dynamic and advanced. He saw everything in terms of economics.

A group of heavily made-up girls in long boots and micro-skirts were clustered around a lamp-post at the foot of a steep, narrow street known as Hookers' Hill.

'Hello,' they called at us. 'You-come-my-house?'

'Ask them how much,' my indefatigable friend urged.

'How much?' I asked one of the girls in Korean.

'Oh, you speak Korean. It's thirty thousand Won.'

'OK. Thanks,' I said and started to walk away. She looked quite hurt. 'It's not much. Why did you ask me?'

'*Kur-nyang*,' I said, using a Korean expression that means the equivalent of a shrug of the shoulders, as if to say 'I was just asking.' She muttered at my back.

'My God! That's cheap!' my mentor exclaimed too loudly. 'But it makes 'sense. They'll make up for the low price with volume.' I declined his request to go back and ask how many customers she had on an average night.

This encounter did pique my curiosity, though, about the whole issue of prostitution. In the 1980s, women's-rights campaigners were making astounding claims of the numbers involved in the sex industry. Eunice Kim, president of the Korea chapter of Asia Women United, a Protestant group, claimed there were one million prostitutes in south Korea. When taken as a proportion of the total population this figure represented around 10 per cent of adult women. In fact, the numbers included masseuses, employees of saunas, waitresses and coffee shop attendants, professions where many women could serve as prostitutes. As such, it was a hopelessly inaccurate measure, but even the more conservative put the numbers at the peak in the mid-1980s at around 600,000, which was about the same size as the country's army. But there is no doubting the client base. In the male-dominated society, where couples were traditionally pushed into arranged marriages by their parents and where all young men serve in the army, marital infidelity with bar girls and prostitutes is the norm.

Registered prostitutes are required to have regular health checks. They operate from garish shopfronts in specific areas of big cities and around American military bases. Most work in small inns with a madam and two to five other girls. Old women act as pimps and bring in the customers. One of these old ladies once guided me to a private house in Seoul, owned by a doctor, where three young women served customers. One, called Kyung-a, invited me to her room where I slightly nervously asked if I could interview her. It was my first time. Obviously accustomed to both nerves and strange requests, she sat warmly beside me and snaked an expert thigh around my leg. I whipped out my notebook.

'No. I'm serious. I'd like to interview you.'

'Sure,' she said, playing the game. 'Ask me a question.'

'No. I'm a reporter. I would like to interview you. I'll pay.' The 'reporter' word convinced her. It was my label.

'OK, then,' she said.

She took the money and gave brief answers to questions. I made a memo to myself not to interview prostitutes on the job. I should have taken her for a coffee. She corrected me on my friend's economic theories. The low price was because only Japanese would pay any more. It was not to encourage a higher turnover of clients – 'I only have one body,' she said.

She dreamed of getting rich. But it would only happen if she could one day meet a wealthy Japanese man who would take her under his wing.

Yoon Chong-a was a prostitute who converted to Catholicism and worked with an American nun in an outreach programme for prostitutes. 'I was from a very strict Confucian family and ran away to avoid an arranged marriage. If there had been someone beside me I could have got out earlier,' she said, referring to her role as a big sister to prostitutes. A significant number are unmarried mothers whose sense of shame leads them into prostitution. Some are abducted by gangsters, raped and forced into prostitution. Police broke five 'white slavery' rings and made forty arrests in one month during a crackdown in 1989. Prosecutors said that a gang in Seoul cruised the streets in four cars and had abducted twenty girls over an eighteen-month period. Around a hundred more were lured by advertisements for waitressing jobs and sold to brothels for up to £1200. Once in, their sense of shame and a system by which they become financially indebted to the madams, prevents them from leaving.

In the sex industry, there is a distinct class consciousness. Masseuses who work in barber shops in major hotels, and buildings owned by the government or the biggest conglomerates, consider themselves superior to their sisters in other barber shops, who provide what the local newspapers in periodic crackdowns refer to as 'lewd services', along with a shave and a trim. Similarly, women who work in Turkish baths would be shocked to be considered as prostitutes, even though they provide pretty much the same service. Among prostitutes around American military bases, there may be a distinction between those who exclusively service white or black men.

Some in the sex industry tell their parents they work at the telephone exchange (and so can't be called at work) or for trading companies that operate long hours. They often send their money home to help put siblings through school. Others have day jobs and work at night as bar hostesses and waitresses in establishments called 'room salons' where groups of men are served in intimate private rooms. As they get older, prostitutes find jobs in barber shops. Others become madams and pimps. Others may save enough to open shops or buy property. Many, of course, leave while they are still young and conceal their background in order to make respectable marriages.

The alternative for many young working-class women for many years was tedious and low-paid factory work.

There is no sentimental attachment in Korea to being a member of the industrial working class. There is sentimentality towards the farm, but no desire to return to it. In opinion polls on the subject, a huge majority of Koreans refer to themselves as middle-class.

As a middle-class consumer, the Korean is like the western consumer. She does not have strong religious or philosophical problems when it comes to buying certain types of food or fashion items. The main difference is that she has not been used to the quality and choice of products for as long as her western counterpart.

Despite their new democratic freedoms, Koreans still find it hard to resist government calls for austerity, which have come thick and fast as bureaucrats, alarmed by the worsening balance of payments, seek to defend the nation against invasions of foreign products. Consumers are not helped by the consumer activists, however, who see a lofty nobility in their cause and would be aghast at the suggestion that their real job is to help the selfish material interests of the consumer. They are looking out for the Korean economy itself and see their job as both the teacher and the union representatives of the housewife. As teacher, they educate and guide consumers into sensible buying habits; as unionist, they act on behalf of the consumer.

When Korea's economy began to take off in the late 1960s, consumer issues were one of a range of responsibilities that fell to women's groups. These associations conducted education programmes to help housewives adjust to modern urban life. For example, women were taught about modern plumbing, such as running water and how they shouldn't leave taps running, and how to use appliances such as electric washing machines and rice cookers.

Because consumer protection groups do not see government and business as their adversaries, they have been overdependent on government for funding and for laboratory services. (Big business also contributes to the groups, but for their non-consumer protection activities. In 1992, for example, the Daewoo Group reportedly donated 100 million Won to the YMCA.) Not surprisingly, then, various considerations tend to cloud consumer protection judgements. Specifically, when dealing with imported products and services, the groups behave in a united front with government and Korean business to favour the local over the foreign.

The Citizens Alliance for the Consumer Protection of Korea sees itself as one of the more modern and responsible groups. It specialises in food safety and includes many scholars in its ranks. However, far from adding a depth and sobriety to consumer activism, the scholars are often more emotionally nationalistic and less in touch with consumers than the conservative women who run the other organisations.

Sometimes, the government's own product testers come across as being a bit amateurish. In May 1992, the government's Consumer Protection Board reported finding methanol in a medicine called Gingkomin and in some bottled drinks available at pharmacies. The test was conducted on behalf of the Citizens Alliance. Shortly afterwards the government's National Institute of Health conducted a similar test and came up with no methanol. By the end of the month the Consumer Protection Board and the National Institute of Health tested the product once again with the Citizens Alliance and the Ministry of Health and Social Affairs looking on as official observers. The methanol was rediscovered.

In a product comparison test, the Industrial Advancement Administration gave A's to Philips Softone light bulbs in all categories except brightness. As its name suggests, the Softone is designed to soften the light, but the IAA did not have the international test standards for such coated bulbs. A TV report, which came out at the time of a Philips promotion, declared that the foreign bulbs were dim.

During an anti-foreign consumption campaign in 1996, the O'Kim's Irish Pub in the Chosun Hotel in Seoul was unable to import any Guinness beer. As the only place in Seoul where draft Guinness was available, this created some anxiety among certain foreigners as it occurred just before St Patrick's Day. The problem was that Guinness samples had failed a freshness test which measured carbonisation and patriotic officials were refusing to allow it to pass through customs. Explanations that, as Guinness is not a highly carbonised drink, it would always fail such tests, fell on deaf ears. This standoff went on for three months. Officials finally lifted the embargo after their overzealousness to protect the consumer was exposed in the *Financial Times*.[205]

PART FOUR

Politics

Chapter Fifteen

BREAKING THE LAW

I was driving along a road in Seoul one day, in heavy traffic, when a taxi cut in front of me. Drivers in Korea are so lawless, selfish and rude that you find yourself repressing road rage every few minutes. But this time, as I was forced to slow down to let him in, I did something stupid. I deliberately steered a few inches outwards so that he scraped my bumper. Thinking it was his fault, he made to stop, but I waved him on. My heart was racing.

About a week later, I did the same thing to a young woman driver who tried to jump a place as two lanes merged into a one-lane tunnel. This time we stopped and her male passenger was quite agitated because he knew I had refused to concede. I apologised and we drove off. My mouth was a bit dry and I felt weary, and not quite in control of myself.

Not long after, I was at a junction waiting for a gap to merge into the flow of traffic when a driver overtook the cars behind me and pulled alongside. I knew this one. Overtaking when merging on to a main road is a common trick. The queue-jumper is in the wrong, but you have to concede to avoid an accident. But instead of letting this fellow in, I pretended to look the other way and kept going so that as he turned, he dented his bonnet on my headlight. This time there was a bit of damage. He got out to remonstrate with me. I was justified because he was technically at fault, but in my heart I knew I was completely wrong. I had intentionally caused the collision. As I argued my case that it was foolish for him to overtake when merging on to a main road, I made broad arm gestures indicating two cars coming out and one – his – suddenly turning and crashing into the other. Other drivers stopped and, seeing the meaning in the arm movements, wound down their windows and expressed support for me. We parted to pay our own damages. After this incident, I began to wonder what was wrong with me.

I began a process of self-analysis – well, basically, staring out of the office window wondering what was up. I discovered in myself a buried anger whose cause still strikes me as odd.

This was in 1988 and I had been in Korea by this time for six years. I had been very caught up in the inspirational theme of Korean democratisation. Although westerners generally favoured the parliamentary opposition, led by Kim Young-sam and Kim Dae-jung, over the authoritarian government and its more radical opponents, these leaders were sufficiently flawed for me not to have too many illusions about them. What impressed me was the Koreans in general. What I saw happening was the creaking dinosaur of the country's political culture shedding a very ancient and scaly skin. Economic growth meant people could now make all kinds of detailed choices in their lives that they had been unable to make before. If you looked at the political facts, it seemed impossible to imagine democracy would ever arrive. But if you looked at the changing culture, it seemed inevitable. It had come in 1987 with a huge display of people power, which led to a democratic presidential election. These developments had all the feel of a miracle. It was the people, rather than individual leaders, who had brought it about. The following year, Korea hosted the Olympics. I was really looking forward to seeing the miracle-makers host the Olympic Games. I didn't expect my Koreans to rain on my parade. But rain they did.

As soon as the Olympic flame was lit, the Koreans began behaving abominably. It started with a column in the *Chosun Ilbo* newspaper, criticising the American athletes in the opening ceremony for waving and holding up signs like 'Hi Mom!' instead of goose-stepping in solemn ranks. This individualistic behaviour by the Americans was received by Koreans as contemptuous disrespect by the imperialist which had been controlling them for forty years. They were reminded of their dependency. NBC, the American TV network with the main rights to broadcast the Games to the world, had been running small features about Korea showing sweatshops and student demos. This was seen as an attempt to wreck Korea's finest hour. Korean spectators began booing American athletes, and cheering the Russians, because they were seen as America's enemies. When NBC zoomed in on a Korean boxer who did a forty-minute sit-down strike in the ring after losing a fight, the Korean media savaged the Americans for insulting their nation by not covering up this demo. A shop owner reported that some NBC staff had ordered some T-shirts from him with a picture of the boxing scene with the caption 'We're fighting. We're bad.' (Bad being

American slang for good.) Then a drunken American swimmer stole a moulding from the toilet of a hotel bar and was treated by the local media as if he were a nation-trasher. Some American and south Korean guards at the border truce village of Panmunjom even had a fist fight over the whole thing.

What became horribly apparent to me was that my fantasy of the Koreans nobly hosting a celebration of international harmony was a projection. In my mind, it had become a grand xenophobic show-off, a strutting on the stage by an immature people who had been hoisted high enough off the ground for the miserable north Koreans across the border to see the tongue they were poking out at them.[206] I regretted that I had trusted them with my idealism. A child of the sixties should have known better than to trust a generation who wear suits and ties even when they're off work. This betrayal shattered my view that people were basically good. At the time I was not really conscious of the profundity of this disappointment. But once I saw it for what it was, the road rage disappeared.

The lesson here was that all this could have been avoided if I had read into my subject before I had arrived and learned a bit more about the political culture of the Koreans, instead of projecting my own post-industrial idealism on to them. But it's never too late. I started reading up. I began to develop a fuller knowledge of the events of Korea's history, and of the political culture that underpinned them. I came up with my own metaphor for understanding Korea's political culture, and one which I propose as a short cut for anyone who lacks the time or inclination for study. Traffic. If you think traffic is an obsession of mine, you're right. It is. But bear with me as I desperately try to draw some meaning from the fact that during my thirties I wasted an accumulated total of around two hundred and fifty valuable, irreplaceable days commuting in Korean traffic.

The theory I'm working on, as yet untested in other countries, is that an astute observer can summarise the main features of a country's political culture after spending a little time on the roads. Politics is about the use of power and how people relate to each other in society. In our modern age, adults are at their most powerful when they are behind the wheel of a car. Furthermore, they are amid strangers. How they behave demonstrates their attitudes to power and other people's rights. Traffic behaviour illustrates how society regulates itself. An hour per country should be enough for a student trained in the highway code of political culture.

The first thing you may notice in Korea is that the main roads are ver good, in many parts much better than in Britain. Even minor suburbs may have six- or eight-lane roads. You'll also find that there are an awful lot of vehicles on these roads. Almost all are Korean-made, new and well looked after. Drivers carry a large waxed hand-mop in their car boots which they use to wipe the daily dust off their paintwork. A lot of cars have dents but these are panel-beaten pretty quickly. There isn't a big second-hand car market and no one drives old bangers.

What does this tell us about the political culture? This is a country with good political infrastructure. But it is very new. The institutions of democracy are there – a Constitution, a Supreme Court, a National Assembly, a Cabinet, a President, a system of local government. The newness of it and the opportunity for advancement mean that the individual citizen is pretty ambitious. There isn't an underbelly culture that romanticises itself or tries to justify its angry hopelessness. When they're down they tend to try to climb up. Part of this involves acting 'as if': i.e. you present yourself as if you are better than you are in order to become better. They wear suits and polish their cars all the time.

So far, so good. You could figure this out in ten minutes. But by then you will have come across your first accident. Korea is a very crowded country and people deal with this by ignoring each other. Strangers in the street are non-people and it doesn't matter if you bump into them or jostle them. The same mentality rules on the road. Other drivers are non-people. You see a gap and you go for it. Some do it skilfully and others uncertainly. You will notice that some drivers cross several lanes hoping that the nice people in other cars won't hit them. They look round or in their mirrors but in their uncertainty they do not see.

The reason such driving is common is that it is too easy to get a licence. The driving test is decided on a person's ability to manoeuvre a car around an obstacle course of beacons in first gear without bumping into them. Five minutes at the Testing Centre in southern Seoul, where you can watch people doing this, provides deep insight into the educational system in which Koreans, and their political leaders, have been raised. An examination is not devised as an objective arbiter of knowledge and competence. It is a gesture. Over 1.3 million people passed the test in 1996 and 1.08 million new cars hit the roads. 'Hit' is the operative word. These are among the most dangerous roads in the world. Measured in terms of traffic deaths per 10,000 vehicles, Korea was the world's third worst country in 1992 (after Botswana and Morocco).[207] With concerted campaigns, it managed to improve in three years to ninth place, but it is still scary. Thirty-five people die a day on the roads, seventeen are permanently disabled, and over 950 are treated for injuries.[208]

Similar to the unsure drivers are the unsure pedestrians. The next five minutes should be spent observing them. As a modern country, Korea has traffic lights and pedestrian crossings as we do. But many backstreets have neither pedestrian crossings nor pavements. Old women, especially, often seem to cross roads without looking, just hoping that they won't be knocked down. The problem is that they are thinking about the driver, not the dangerous weapon in his hands. If you step out into the road, you expect that people will move out of the way. The thing is that the elderly people, who are not drivers themselves, don't have a feel for how difficult this is to do at speed. Without stretching the correlation too much, we should note that this attitude reflects a very important feature of Korean political culture. That is, that people look not to the office, the constitution or the flag, but to the person in power. They embrace or reject not the principles or symbols of state, but the actual person who represents it. Thus falling foul of the law is not a problem as long as one hasn't fallen foul of the people who enforce it.

If we look from the point of view of the driver, we see another interesting parallel. Koreans tend to swerve out of the way of obstacles, rather than brake. There is always a way round things if you have connections, money, courage and imagination.

The road-wandering mindset is, of course, rural. And a keen observer would guess after a few minutes that Korea was not long ago an agricultural country, most of whose people lived a long way from paved roads. There is a distinctly rural feel to the city backstreets. The lack of pavements, the ambiguous road markings, shopkeepers and stallholders spilling illegally on to the streets, people spitting. The worst feature is the apparent unconcern for the safety of children. Korean homes are not big and they lack gardens, so children often play on the side of the street. By western standards, parents are incredibly blasé about the dangers, and a lot of children are killed on roads every year. A little boy was run over down our street. His parents had a small mirror- and picture-framing shop. The shop took up the equivalent of the lounge and they lived in the back room. The boy used to play on his tricycle just outside.

The second half-hour of research should be spent following professional drivers. These men, mostly, are not careless. The overriding problem is that they are lawless. It is worth looking at this more closely because it is the fundamental issue facing Koreans, in politics as well as on the roads.

Although truck, bus and taxi drivers and chauffeurs are low on the social totem pole, they are, of course, the professionals on the roads and they set the tone. Their counterparts in the political world are the professional politicians themselves. It is important to note that they are the worst offenders: bullying, selfish, and a law unto themselves.

Why do they ignore laws? Koreans are still governed by an ethos that is predominantly Confucian. In the classic Confucian tradition, the ruler was supposed to lead by moral example. A legal tradition developed for the benefit of assisting the ruler in this endeavour. In the first half of the twentieth century, the Japanese used modern law to invalidate Korean practice, destroy Korean culture, and cheat locals out of their land. Under Park Chung-hee, the government directed modernisation through laws. These laws are written in a vague way that allows government bureaucrats great leeway in interpretation. Thus, Koreans have always seen law as something given from above. The concept that law is created after debate by people who are elected, and that in theory they, the ordinary people, have a say in the development of the laws of the land, does not yet figure in the common perception.

The elected lawmakers in the National Assembly have done nothing to dispel this attitude, having occupied themselves with political struggle rather than debate over laws and issues. After weeks of drama and posturing in the National Assembly, whole lists of laws drafted by the presidential Blue House or by bureaucrats are approved without the assemblymen even really knowing what they are about.

In a western country, such apparent disregard would be taken as a serious flaw, because law is so important. The basic rules for conduct are contained in law. Social issues, such as fox-hunting and abortion for example, eventually become judicial questions. Once a new law is passed either allowing or banning something, an issue often disappears from the social agenda. In Korea this is not the case. Politics is not about issues or laws. It is essentially about social relations and who has power. For this reason, it has always been logical for the opposition simply to oppose and hinder government in whatever way it can, without bothering to develop rational argument. For example, opposition leaders protested diplomatic relations with Japan and the construction of the Seoul–Pusan expressway in the 1960s simply because they were government projects. No one holds this against them, but at the same time, Korean politics would have benefited from more reasonable behaviour. The failure to take rational positions on issues undermines popular sentiment towards politicians and has retarded the growth of rational, democratic thinking. But it can be understood in the context of traditional attitudes. One reason the Chosun period lasted for so long was that the rulers' emphasis on family as the prime object of a loyalty prevented the masses from forming into bodies that could oppose them.

When the dynasty collapsed, the society became atomised. In other words, prime loyalty of Koreans was not to their nation. As a consequence, activities which strike us as treasonable are severely punished only if they offend political power-holders.

By way of illustration, a highly credible accusation surfaced after the bidding for the 2002 World Cup that Korea had been the favourite but that FIFA decided on co-hosting between Japan and Korea after lobbying by a senior Korean official against his own country. The purpose of this lobbying was to prevent Korea's international football representative, Chung Mong-joon, a FIFA vice-president, from becoming a national star.

It is not surprising, then, that in an environment in which everything is situational, Koreans take a cavalier attitude to law. As laws do not govern human relations, they are considered a last resort. Resorting to law represents a loss of face because it means that superiors have lost control and inferiors have lost their deferential attitude. Disputes are solved by rearranging social relationships, not through laws.

Given the weak role of law, people naturally rely on their families and networks of alumni and hometown friends to get on in life. Networking is vital. The fall of a powerful political figure or the collapse of a network can close off access to opportunities for a wide number of people. When a powerful figure falls, his close associates fall too. Those who had connections to these associates hear a loud banging of doors being shut. They scramble to open alternative doors to power. The four presidents who ruled from 1961 until 1998 came from the south-east Kyongsang provinces. Kim Dae-jung, who is from the south-west Cholla region, has run in elections against all of them. He would win over 90 per cent of the vote from his home province, but be lucky to scrape 10 per cent from Kyongsang. It was assumed that most of that 10 per cent was from Cholla people living in the other province. As Kyongsang had double the population of Cholla, Kim Dae-jung was always at a disadvantage. The bias against Cholla spread to other provinces. The prospect of a Kim Dae-jung victory was very disturbing for a lot of people from Kyongsang and other parts of Korea because it threatened their networks. An invasion of resentful Cholla people into the corridors of power would mean that networks would fall and careers be wrecked. These fears explain how non-Cholla Koreans could accept the government's false accusations that Kim was a 'pro-communist' with north Korean connections without too much hesitation.

Koreans retained the old Confucian values through the system of education, not because their rulers embodied the Confucian values. In fact, Koreans are very mistrustful of political leadership. Kings were invariably considered as usurpers. Authority seemed to exist in order to steal people's money and make them suffer. Japanese rule was even worse. 'During that time, authority was considered evil,' says Roh Jae-won, a retired ambassador. 'Fathers told their sons, "Don't follow authority unless it's a matter of personal safety. Obey, but internally defy."' Thus, we might say that Koreans also defy law out of filial piety. It was law in the hands of bad rulers that made their parents and grandparents suffer.

This dislike of authority does not mean, though, that they considered their leaders to be illegitimate. Authoritarian rulers were mindful that their subjects did not like them. At the same time they knew that people were open to the suggestion that 'heaven' had put them in power, that even though they were repressive, somehow they were the right ruler. Chun Doo-hwan is a good example of a leader who was never seen as having the mandate of heaven. The permanent protests against his rule by students was a constant reminder of this fact. Heaven itself even seemed to conspire against him. One of Chun's projects was the creation of the Independence Hall, a museum to Korean suffering under Japan. But on the eve of its much-lauded opening in August 1986, a fire broke out and the roof was destroyed. Heaven was angry. So was Chun. Six electricians were hauled in by police and two of them imprisoned.

Given the absence of exemplary leadership, and of law, it should not surprise us that the Koreans are so fractious. There is a joke among political scientists that if you put two Koreans on a desert island, they would form three political parties: one each and a coalition. The names of parties change so quickly that it is difficult to keep track of them. With the exception of leftist parties, banned in south Korea, political parties represent neither a social class nor a particular philosophy. They are, in a sense, a gesture to democracy in an authoritarian political culture. Parties are built around powerful factional leaders. It takes a strong and ruthless figure, like Kim Il-sung and Park Chung-hee, to hold them together. Power acts as a glue, but, when out of power, parties come unstuck.

What counts is the faction. The key to holding a faction together is money. Kim Yong-sam and Kim Dae-jung, who were opposition faction leaders for decades, had this ability. One of Kim Dae-jung's aides told me after Kim had lost an election – and probably should have been replaced as leader – that the party's monthly costs were 300 million Won, and that Kim Dae-jung would remain in charge because he was the only person who could secure that amount from corporate donors with a single phone call.

The roots of the mistrust of leaders still remain. Democracy for Koreans at this stage means they can elect their leader and hold him accountable. But they still do not see their political leaders as their representatives. There is still a view that leaders are wrong, corrupt and working against the interests of the people.

If the spreading of democratic attitudes leads to trust and respect for law, we will see fewer punch-ups on the side of the road between drivers after an accident. Conflict need not be solved by force, or by a few banknotes, when there is rather a fair and objective system. An exchange of insurance details would be enough.

Chapter Sixteen

DICTATORS

Democracy has been the aspiration of the Koreans since their separation into two states in 1948. The leaders of both Koreas intuitively knew that their state had to be accepted as the true and legitimate 'democracy' of the people. The South's authoritarian rulers modelled their republic on the American system and always referred to it as a liberal democracy. The north Koreans also claimed it in their name – the Democratic People's Republic of Korea.

However, these rulers had very different ideas of what democracy was and none were seen by westerners as democrats. Even fifty years later, north Korea is still a communist dictatorship. It claims to act in the interest of the people, but does not permit free elections to test the claim, thus ruling it out as a democracy in the western definition. It is seen, in fact, as antidemocratic. North Korea's problem has been an ideological adherence to its view of history as a kind of permanent warfare that creates its own enemies and justifies force in suppressing them. It is more of a vast military base than a civilian community.

But it's not as easy to argue against those who believe in it as one might think. I once had great difficulty trying to explain to a tourist guide in Pyongyang why I thought that the north Korean elections he was telling me about were not democratic.

'What do you mean? They were elections and people could vote,' he said.

'But all the candidates were from the same party,' I said.

'That's what elections are,' he said.

'In some cases there was only one candidate,' I said. 'Also, everyone by law has to vote. No wonder they got a hundred per cent.'

'Well, we have elections laws, like you have election laws in your country. They are our laws.'

'But there are no opposition candidates.'

'Why should there be opposition? We're not opposed to each other.'

'Well, I mean, a different viewpoint. Candidates from a different party.'

'Why do you need different parties when the Workers' Party represents the people? Anyway, you can have different views in the same party.'

'Yes, but—'

'Anyway, these were candidates all chosen by the Great Leader.'

'Well, there's your problem.'

'What?'

'They couldn't take a different position from him. The Great Leader would have them shot.'

'Only traitors are executed. You don't allow traitors in your country, do you?' At this point another guide intervened and explained to the young man in Korean that my lack of understanding was because in Britain we are not united like north Koreans and that's why we have rival political parties.

South Korea's claim of being a democracy has also posed problems for the western commentator. Apart from a brief interlude in 1960, south Korea did not become recognisably democratic by western standards until 1987, and yet its spokesmen always insisted it was a liberal democracy. President Chun Doo-hwan had a spokesman who had been jailed as a student protester under the previous regime. This man invited a small group of western correspondents to lunch one day during a period of anti-government demonstrations in order to give us the government's views. We were sitting at a circular table in a private room of a restaurant. We started talking about the current crisis, which had started when the opposition party had walked out of talks on constitutional reform in the parliament and called for street protests. The opposition knew it was futile to negotiate democratic reform with a dictator who controlled the parliament. However, this move had created some moral confusion among western diplomats because the regime's allegedly democratic opponents were abandoning the democratic process for the streets, where there would be violence.

'The opposition have taken this undemocratic decision,' the presidential spokesman said reasonably. 'But we hope they will return to the table.' He went on to explain at length about the government's commitment to democracy and respect for human rights. After a few minutes of this, I became aware of motion in my peripheral vision. The journalist seated on my left, and directly opposite our host, had held out his hands as if gripping a rather large imaginary pole and began sliding them up and down in an extremely vulgar gesture which everyone pretended was not happening, but which effectively ended our host's pretence. He stopped what he was saying, and someone asked another question. I'd not seen a government spokesman silenced in this way before.

When countries are criticised for their lack of democracy, it is often pointed out in their defence that democracy takes a long time to develop. This is certainly true, and it is quite an acceptable response, unless it's coming from the people with the power to help it develop. Democracy is a political system that involves governance by popular consent, whose introduction involves a humbling of political authority which seems almost unnatural when we consider how human society has been ordered for most of history. It seems almost too much to expect the powerful to permit other people to be free. It is more natural for them to feel they are special, or even indispensable, because by some miracle of heaven they have been put in charge. More basically, when you have power, it is a horrible feeling to lose it. It is unreasonable to expect a leader to voluntarily relinquish power any more than a middle-aged man would voluntarily give up his job in mid-career to give a younger person a chance. If there's a threat that your successors might arrest or kill you, it amounts to foolishness to subordinate this personal risk to a national benefit that can only be imagined and which may be dubious. Democracy is, of course, a system in which these leaders have no choice. The system is greater than the leaders. The problem is that it is leaders who introduce the system. It therefore tends to develop very slowly, and needs to be forced along sometimes. But like economic development, once the model is established somewhere in the world, it is possible for others to imitate it and catch up. What we have seen with south Korea, then, is a 'catch-up' process. Or, if you like, a process of importing a foreign concept.

This catching up has not been easy. The Korean political culture was not conducive to democracy. The security threat from north Korea and the ideological anti-communism also hindered democratic development. Many foreign observers, especially those opposed to communism, could justify authoritarianism in south Korea. However, it is important to note that, for south Koreans themselves, culture and security may have been explanations for the absence of democracy, but they were never ultimately accepted as excuses.

Democratisation in south Korea has involved a process of imitation of America's institutions, and a changing of the political culture to make them work. It has been less clearly pursued as a programme, in the way that economic development was pursued. But if we view the events of the last five decades, we can see the process unfolding. The catch-up began with imitation and evolved into substance.

The Korean story is very complex, but we can identify some very simple issues which dominated politics over the decades. The first was the question of succession. Korean presidents have assumed the power of a monarch. Once in power, they quickly seem to have become gripped by the idea that the nation would be doomed without them. They responded by manipulating constitutions, parliaments and elections to make sure that they remained in power. It was not until 1987 that the country achieved its first peaceful, democratic transfer of power.

The first president was Syngman Rhee. He had an impressive background. 'Few heads in international politics have been battered longer or harder than his,' his biographer, Robert Oliver, wrote in 1951.[209] 'During a political career that began in 1894, Dr Rhee has spent seven years in prison, seven months under daily torture, and forty-one years in exile with a price on his head. He has directed a revolution, served as president of the world's longest-lived government-in-exile, has knocked vainly at the portals of international conferences, and finally shepherded his cause to success – only to see his nation torn asunder by a communist invasion.'

Rhee was born in 1875, and educated at a school run by American missionaries. He converted to Christianity. He founded the first daily newspaper in Korea and organised protests against corruption and against Japanese and Russian designs on Korea. He was jailed in 1897. For seven months, his head was locked in a wooden weight, his feet were in stocks and his hands cuffed. He was beaten with rods and had oiled paper wrapped around his arms and set on fire. 'His fingers were so horribly mashed that even today, in times of stress, he blows upon them,' Oliver wrote.[210]

After his release and the Japanese takeover of Korea, Rhee went into exile in the United States. He earned his doctorate at Princeton, where he studied under the future US president, Woodrow Wilson. He was one of the main leaders in exile and lobbied for decades for Korean independence. He married an Austrian woman, and by the time he returned to Korea after four decades, he struck people as being more of a foreigner than a Korean. He saw himself as the leader of a country that was half held by communist rebels. The rebels attacked in 1950 and Rhee's republic was rescued from destruction by the intervention of foreign power. Rhee was preoccupied with the big picture of national division, but was not able to reunify Korea during his twelve-year rule. He was incensed that the United States had not repelled the Chinese during the Korean War and he refused to sign the 1953 Armistice. He threatened to 'March North' and, although this was never backed up with military movements, it was years before people stopped taking it seriously.

Rhee's south Korea was a poor, agricultural country. Most Koreans were preoccupied with where their next meal was coming from. Rhee had no economic vision and the country lived off American handouts. During Rhee's 1948–60 rule, labour unions were used as a political arm of government. Teachers were pressured into joining his Liberal Party and required to investigate the political leanings of their students' parents. High school and college students had to join the Korean Student Corps for National Defence and receive military training and anti-communist indoctrination. The press was relatively free, although one leading newspaper, the *Dong-A Ilbo*, was closed down for a while because the Chinese character for 'puppet' was once used instead of 'president' in reference to Rhee, apparently by mistake.

Rhee considered himself above the fray of politics, but when he saw that he was not going to be re-elected in 1952, he descended into it.[211] At the time, the president was elected by the National Assembly. Rhee threatened to dissolve it if it did not approve a constitutional change to allow for presidential election by popular vote. He treated opponents as if they were enemies of the state. When assemblymen voted to have martial law lifted in Pusan, Rhee had half of them arrested. After a staged assassination attempt, police began to investigate alleged links to the opposition. Police claimed that an assemblyman called Chang Myon was working with assassins paid by north Korea to depose Rhee. Under this type of pressure, the Assembly voted 160 to zero for Rhee's constitutional amendments.

Rhee's vice-presidential running mate, Lee Pom-sok, who as home minister controlled the police, was behind much of the manoeuvring against the Assembly. Lee was a nationalist who had graduated from the Chinese Military Academy and fought the Japanese in China. He had held a general's rank and served on the staff of the nationalist Chinese leader, Chiang Kai-shek. In 1946, he had formed the Korea National Youth Association, which had the support of the US Department of Defense, and which he saw as the foundation of a future Korean army. This group soon claimed 1.3 million members. Pro-western and anti-communist, its members supplemented police units and fought against leftists. On the day before the election, Rhee, who was feeling threatened by his running mate and his large youth group, suddenly ordered his supporters to vote for a different vice-presidential candidate, who won.

Another constitutional amendment allowed Rhee to run for a third term in 1956. He won again. One opposition candidate died of a heart attack just before the election, but still received about 20 per cent of the vote. Another, Cho Bong-am, won 22 per cent. Cho was a former communist who had split with his former associates before the war over their subservience to the Soviet Union, and had later served as Rhee's agriculture minister. He argued that the way to defeat communism was to strengthen democracy and that it would be eventually possible to win peacefully in an all-Korea election. Leaders of his Progressive Party were arrested in 1958 for allegedly contacting north Korea. Cho was charged with spying and was sentenced to five years for contacting a north Korean agent. An appellate court sentenced him to death. He was executed in 1959.

Now in his eighties, Rhee became more isolated and his administration more inefficient. In 1960, he ran a fourth time and won 88.7 per cent of the vote. Twenty people were killed in election violence and many injured in protests against the widespread vote-rigging. These protests erupted into full-scale demonstrations. After several protesting students were shot and killed in the streets of Seoul, Rhee resigned in disgrace. He lived the rest of his life in exile in Hawaii.

Can we say that Rhee contributed to democracy? His republic had elections. It survived. That was about it. Despite the war and the poverty, Rhee could have done so much more. He had vast experience in democratic countries. He also had a mandate for vigorous action, particularly as he had had to deal with leftist guerrilla subversion, left-right violence and a civil war. However, he failed to institute the basic traditions of democracy – reasonably fair elections and a tradition of peaceful democratic succession. Had he lost to Cho Bong-am in 1952 or 1956 and stepped down in a dignified manner, or retired and let another candidate run, he may be remembered today with more affection.

Rhee's presidential system was replaced by a parliamentary democracy under premier Chang Myon. This government did not last long. In the freer environment, campus activists formed a Student League for National Unification, which advocated reconciliation with north Korea and the withdrawal of foreign powers, a position that was a radical change from the post-war years. They called for a conference between north and south Korean students. Rightist groups protested in nationwide rallies, raising fears of a return to the left-right violence of the late 1940s. Hundreds of teachers went on hunger strike when the government declared a new union illegal. Students demonstrated in sympathy after some teachers collapsed in class. Union leaders expressed their support for students who were trying to hold a North-South students conference, a move which was thought to reveal a political agenda, and further inflamed the right. Students decided to stage a march to Panmunjom, the truce village in the DMZ. When they heard that the military was rumbling about taking over to end the chaos, they began to tone down their activities, but it was too late. The leftist agitation had provided what one scholar has called 'useful justification' for a military coup.[212]

Park Chung-hee drove his tanks into Seoul at 5 a.m. on 16 May 1961, and seized power unopposed. Citizens adjusted to the new reality, but not without nervousness. The uncertainty was perhaps best characterised by a joke that circulated at the time. It tells of a soldier on guard duty on the Han River bridge on the day of the coup. He was – typically – asleep in his hut in the early hours of the morning, when General Park's convoy rumbled on to the bridge. Awakened rudely by mutineers who burst into his hut, the guard paused and made an instant assessment of his predicament. '*Inmin-guk Mansei!* [Long live the (north) Korean People's Army!]', he shouted, thrusting his arms into the air in welcome.

It is possible that Park had interrupted a real opportunity at this stage in Korea's history for economic development under parliamentary democracy. Others have their doubts that the civilian politicians would have been capable of it. The impression from many people is that Park was doing the country a favour by putting them under control. He had little respect for civilian politicians and brought many military officers to run government and state corporations.[213] Conservatives welcomed the change because they feared destabilisation by pro-North Korean forces. Bureaucrats also welcomed it because they had fewer politicians to worry about.[214]

Park claimed to have democratic goals. However, he had arguments for postponing them. Korea, he said, was in the 'top-knot and horsehair hat stage of old' and couldn't be changed overnight by the institution of democracy. It would take an industrial revolution. As western European democracy was unworkable at that stage, what he proposed was 'Administrative Democracy'. He said, 'The goal of the revolution is to weed out corruption, strengthen the autonomous ability of the people, and establish social justice. Therefore democracy should be established by administrative means, not by political means, during the transition period.'[215]

The transition period he was referring to was that between his 1961 coup and elections, which came in 1963. Park of course ran in those elections and continued to do so, changing the constitution and fiddling the results when it was necessary. The 'transition period' of his rule lasted for eighteen years.

Park earned a lot of respect during his first two terms of office, up till 1971. Had he stepped down at this point, as the constitution required, he would have done democracy the favour of having established a precedent for a peaceful transfer of power. However, events conspired to convince him that he was indispensable. Fear of north Korea had been mounting. In 1968, north Korean commandos reached the Blue House in Seoul before being stopped. Park wanted to drop south Korean forces in Pyongyang, but the Americans refused to permit retaliation.[216] Two days later, an American spy ship, the USS *Pueblo*, was captured fifteen miles off the north Korean coast. Its eighty-two crew members were taken prisoner. Again, as the United States was already at war in Vietnam, it was not prepared to retaliate and risk a second war in Korea. A few months later, north Korea landed over a hundred commandos on the south Korean coast. In another incident, a US navy reconnaissance plane was shot down by north Korea and thirty-one crew members killed. After US President Richard Nixon decided in 1970 to cut the strength of US forces in Korea by a third down to 43,000, Park became increasingly doubtful about the reliability of the United States as an ally. This lack of US resolve also reflected on Park himself. South Koreans felt secure in the American embrace and confident that north Korea would not launch a full-scale attack for as long as it feared it was going to war against America. Park's argument as to why he was indispensable was that he was the man who could maintain this 'special relationship' with the United States. When Park learned that it was Congress who called the shots, his aides began a programme of corrupt lobbying and gift-giving that ended in the 'Koreagate' hearings in 1978 which took the bilateral relations to an all-time low.[217]

As his second term came to an end, Park forced through a constitutional change to allow him to run again in 1971. Park almost lost this election. His opponent was Kim Dae-jung, a surprise compromise candidate between opposition factions. There was cheating on both sides, but with enormous funding and all the resources of the state at his disposal, Park had a huge advantage.[218] Even so, Kim Dae-jung managed to win 45 per cent of the vote.

In the following year, talks began with north Korea, and the two rival sides signed a historic agreement pledging to end their hostility. This process was treated internationally as if there had been a breakthrough. In fact, it was nothing of the kind because, as both sides knew well, there had been no significant power shift towards one side. The 'reconciliation' was a temporary lull. Ironically, their exposure to the north Koreans made Park nervous of his own opposition. Kim Il-sung had built up a communist personality cult and ruthlessly suppressed dissent. The result was, to his south Korean opponents' way of thinking, enviable. Such unity gave the impression of total strength. Dissent in the South gave an impression of weakness to north Korea and to Park and his followers. Park's response was to suspend the constitution and declare martial law. He introduced a new

'Yushin' (revitalising) constitution and had himself re-elected for a six-year term. His rule degenerated into repression. He even made it illegal to criticise the new constitution.

Park Chung-hee's chief lieutenants were younger officers who had played key roles in his coup. One was Park Chong-kyu, who was known as 'pistol Park' in 1974 after he shot at a gunman who tried to assassinate the president in a crowded theatre. The gunman, a north Korean agent, killed the First Lady. Cha Ji-chul was the chief presidential bodyguard. These two men increasingly controlled access to the president. On one occasion, when Park Chung-hee visited a province, the local governor went to light the president's cigarette with his lighter unintentionally set at high. The flame leapt out and startled Park. After the meeting was over, Cha is said to have stayed behind and beaten up the governor. A third aide was Kim Jong-pil, who was Park's nephew-in-law. Kim was the founder of the Korean CIA and tried to build up Park's Democratic Republican Party along the lines of the all-powerful Kuomintang in Taiwan, as a vehicle of perpetual rule. He saw himself as Park's successor. Kim is one of the great survivors of Korean politics and has the distinction of having been prime minister under two governments – under Park in the 1970s and under Kim Dae-jung in 1998.

The KCIA had sweeping powers and, under various directors, expanded and intruded into every sector. In theory, the agency was supposed to guard against north Korean subversion. Indeed, this capability grew more sophisticated in the 1970s, after North–South talks began. Despite an unsophisticated public face, the agency quietly developed detailed data about north Korea. At North–South meetings, for example, agents took samples of north Korean cigarette packets, glasses, bottles, tableware and anything else they could lay their hands on and used it to analyse north Korean manufacturing processes. Its domestic departments, however, investigated government opponents, devised plots to undermine them, controlled the media, spied in colleges and churches, and coordinated policy between government ministries. Agents kidnapped Kim Dae-jung from a Tokyo hotel in 1973 in what appears to have been a murder plot designed to look as if it was committed by north Koreans. The American CIA, alerted by Kim's supporters and by a former KCIA director, Kim Hyong-wook, intervened to save him.[219] Kim Dae-jung was dumped outside his home, shaken but unharmed, and barred from political activity for the rest of Park's term. Kim, the former KCIA director, testified against Park Chung-hee at the Koreagate hearings and later disappeared in Paris. It is assumed he was murdered by KCIA agents.

In October 1979, opposition leader Kim Young-sam was expelled from the

National Assembly and protests erupted in the cities of Pusan and Masan, his political home-base. At a dinner, Park Chung-hee scolded the KCIA director, Kim Jae-kyu, for failing to control the demonstrations. Kim said to do that they would have to kill 3000 protesters. Park apparently said that the Shah of Iran, who had recently been ousted, had failed because he was not prepared to kill enough of his own people. If necessary he, Park, would kill thirty thousand. Park's bodyguard, Cha Ji-chul, joined in the criticism of the KCIA chief. Kim had been frustrated for some time over his difficulties managing the politics of his job as KCIA chief, and over Park's criticism of his performance and Cha's interference. He left the room and returned with a pistol, shot Cha and then shot Park. Two women with them were unharmed.

Sensible assessment of Park is hindered by political labels. He seemed to progress through different phases. He was, in turn, a Korean nationalist in a Japanese uniform, a communist officer in the rightist south Korean army, and an anti-communist nation-builder. The labels get so confusing that they start to peel off. Park was a pragmatist, not an ideologue. By nature, he was said to have been austere and righteous. Ironically, if he had not been so closely allied with the United States and if he had played up the revolutionary, interventionist and collectivist features of his rule, Park may have received a better hearing in the court of the international left. He employed dictatorship in order to transform the economic base of society. But he did not see class warfare within society. He saw that among the classes of nations, Korea was a proletarian. In order to become strong, its workers had to work and its producers be favoured in order that they produce. From the point of view of democracy, though, while Park contributed greatly to the creation of a middle class, he obstructed political development in practice. Two decades after Rhee's departure, visible democracy had regressed. Park's state was more repressive than Rhee's had been during the Korean War. From this perspective, his gift to democracy was his sudden departure from the scene.

Two million people turned out in the streets of Seoul to watch the journey of his coffin to the national cemetery, and wonder about the future. The leader was still not elected fairly and there was still no peaceful method of power transition. Park did not even have a successor.

Chapter Seventeen

STRUGGLE FOR DEMOCRACY

The man who took over as acting president was the Prime Minister, Choi Kyu-hah. But in the Korean system, the Prime Minister's position was an 'acting' role anyway. Occasionally, the post would be filled by one of the power group who would add some weight to the office. But Choi was a bureaucrat, a political lightweight who lacked the character and the political power base to grasp the historical moment for democracy. He was elected president on 6 December 1979 by an electoral college. But he was unable to fill the power vacuum left by Park's surprise exit.

The next day, he abolished one of Park's Emergency Decrees, which had banned political assembly by students, demand for constitutional reform and circulation of rumours. The following day, he released Kim Dae-jung from house arrest and newspapers were allowed to mention Kim's name again for the first time in years.[220]

The real power in the country, though, was Chung Seung-hwa, the martial-law commander. Another army general, Chun Doo-hwan, who headed the Defence Security Command, the military intelligence agency which was investigating Park's assassination, thought that there were unanswered questions about Chung's own involvement in the assassination. Chun also had other problems with Chung.

Chun was the leader of the officers of the Korean Military Academy 11th class. This was the first group of professional army officers who had done a full four-year course. Older officers were either Japanese-trained or had graduated from the Academy after only brief training. The 11th class members, who graduated in 1955, were seen as the 'older brothers' of subsequent graduating classes and commanded intense loyalty. This group felt it had been deliberately denied promotion and held back by the generation which Chung Seung-hwa represented. When they heard that Chung planned to remove the 11th class leader from his powerful post and reassign him to a field command, they mutinied. On the night of 12 December 1979, Chun arrested the martial-law commander. Loyal troops came to Chung's assistance and a gun battle broke out in the streets of Seoul. Several soldiers were killed. One of Chun's group, Roh Tae-woo, ordered troops under his command down from the DMZ to Seoul, leaving a gap in the defences against north Korea. After this act of mutiny, there was no turning back. Fortunately for Chun and Roh, younger officers stood by them and they were able to take control of the military.

Like Park Chung-hee, Chun Doo-hwan was a poor boy. His story contains the familiar ingredients behind the Korean revolutionary achiever: devoted mother, pro-independence father, poverty and the helping hand of heaven. Chun was the seventh of ten children.[221] He came with portents. Two brothers had died before he was born and his mother was desperate for another son. Three years before his birth, she had a dream in which three majestic men and a woman walked down a rainbow to her house. In the dream the second man had a crown on his head. She went on to have three boys and two girls. One of the girls later died. The second son was Doo-hwan. When a wandering monk said she had the face of the mother of a great man except for her protruding teeth, she smashed them out against a log pillar. Chun's father once hurled a Japanese policeman who had insulted him down an embankment and nearly killed him. After this, the family thought it prudent to flee to Manchuria. While they were hiding on one occasion from bandits, Chun's baby brother, Kyung-hwan, started to cry. Neighbours whispered that they would have to strangle him otherwise they would all be discovered and killed. One was about to do it when the baby suddenly stopped.[222]

After this experience, the family returned to Korea and lived in Taegu. Chun was a good athlete and a natural leader. He joined the Korean Military Academy in 1951, where he captained the football team. In the army he was nicknamed Lieutenant Principle for his alleged uprightness. Two soldiers once offered him cigarettes as a bribe and he thrashed them with a pole. He married Lee Soon-ja, who was the daughter of the chief of staff at the military academy. In 1959 Chun went to the United States and studied psychological warfare and went through ranger training with three other Korean officers, one of whom was Cha Ji-chul, later to be Park Chung-hee's bodyguard.

On the day after Park's coup in 1961, Captain Chun allegedly demanded to see Park to confirm that he was not just another corrupt general.

According to the account in a later hagiography, Park agreed to explain himself to the young Chun. Park said he was opposed to the corruption and incompetence of the government and told Chun he planned to develop a 'nationalistic democracy'. Satisfied, Chun persuaded the military academy faculty and students to support the coup and led a march of eight hundred cadets into central Seoul where they were greeted by Park.

From 1970 to 1971, Chun commanded a regiment of the 9th (White Horse) Division. During combat duty in the Vietnam War he is said to have ordered his men to always wear clean underwear, saying, 'Do you want your enemy to see your dead body, should you die, in dirty underwear?'[223] Chun thought that, in Vietnam, internal strife was the source of the South's vulnerability to the North. He wrote in a letter to Park that south Korea needed a 'Koreanised democracy' to avoid the same fate.[224] Chun became a general and commanded the First Airborne Special Force. He was later the assistant to the presidential security chief. In 1978, he was appointed the commander of the First Division, a key division which includes the traditional invasion corridor north of Seoul. Chun apparently introduced the personal touch and managed to shake hands with each of the ten thousand men under his command. He oversaw the construction of a strategic defence wall near the DMZ and the discovery of a third north Korean invasion tunnel under the DMZ. In March 1979 he was assigned to command the Defence Security Command, the intelligence agency that polices the military.

The day after the '12.12' incident, as the struggle between the generals became known, it was business as usual as far as the rest of the country was concerned. President Choi was still in charge and Koreans still enjoyed their new freedom. In February, the civil rights of Kim Dae-jung and almost seven hundred other dissidents banned by Park were restored. When the new academic year began in March, students formed associations and took to the streets. Workers staged strikes to press their demands. The period came to be known as the 'Seoul Spring'. But all was not well. In parliament, politicians argued and held up the rewriting of the constitution. The economy was reeling under the effects of a global recession. The President did not really appear to be in charge. In April, Chun appointed himself head of the KCIA. In May 1980 the student protests against martial law gathered momentum and tens of thousands of students engaged in furious warfare with police. The scale of these events exceeded the 'chaos' that preceded Park's coup two decades earlier. On 16 May the ruling party leader, Kim Jong-pil, joined in the call for an end to martial law. But it was too late. On 17 May 1980, Chun informed the cabinet he was taking over and imposed his own martial law. Political activity was banned, leading politicians were arrested, media censored and universities closed. Troops arrested activists and went on to campuses to prevent students from gathering. Highly trained special-forces units were assigned to Seoul National University, and Chonnam and Chosun universities in the city of Kwangju, which was the capital of South Cholla province. This was not the first time the special forces had been used for police work. The elite troops had been used to put down the riots in Pusan and Masan the previous October. On that occasion, they had clubbed and beaten demonstrators, but not too much more than a protester who was grabbed would expect, not in daylight anyway. They saved their real beatings for night-time.

In Kwangju, it was to be different. The special forces behaved in broad daylight with such shocking brutality that the entire citizenry erupted in rebellion. Soldiers beat and bayoneted demonstrators and then went rampaging through the city. They barged into coffee shops and stormed on to buses, savagely beating young people of student age. Troops used flamethrowers on protesters. The hospitals began filling up with dead and injured.

Amid a general news blackout, the country was unaware of what was happening. In Kwangju itself, rumours flew that those directing the brutality were from Taegu, the capital of the rival North Kyongsang province. It was easy to believe they were being made an example of out of regional prejudice. Kyongsang people found various reasons to dislike Cholla. The region's politicians had been the reactionary landowners who opposed Syngman Rhee. Leftist guerrillas fought from mountain bases in the province even after the Korean War. The people were friendly, artistic, but couldn't be trusted; you get your money from them up-front. Under Park, this prejudice had become more exaggerated. As a result, Cholla was far behind the rest of the country. Its people's resentment was feared.

Tens of thousands of protesters piled on to the streets and fought back. A strategic manoeuvre by Kwangju taxi drivers forced the elite troops to retreat from the city. Rebels assaulted the prison where leftists and guerrillas from the conflict of the 1940s and '50s were still being held. Shim Jae-hoon, a Korean correspondent for *The New York Times*, recounted his thoughts as he approached the city. 'My first reaction was that I had survived Vietnam, but I maybe won't survive this. It seemed like full-scale warfare was taking place. There was smoke rising from several places in the city. There were long lines of refugees with bundles on their heads, escaping the city. Rebels had machine guns on trucks and were using walkie-talkies. They had been in the army so they knew what they were doing. There were armed citizens guarding places and snipers on the roofs wearing helmets. They had taken over a factory which made jeeps and trucks. It was civil war. I knew they'd get slaughtered.'

The mayor and a committee made up mostly of bureaucrats appealed for calm and persuaded citizens to return their weapons. But passions were still running high. Militants pretended to co-operate, and joined the committee. Once they had gained a majority, they took over.[225] The radicals called on young people to take up arms, and held military drills. A young man called Yun Sang-won emerged as the militants' chief strategist and another, Park Nam-son, led the armed rebels. Yun was an organiser in Kwangju for an anti-government group called the National Democratic Workers League. His plan was to resist for as long as possible to force Chun's regime to either surrender or to kill them and thereby demonstrate its barbaric nature. He wanted the United States to intervene and protect them from Chun's troops, but was not hopeful. In the end about a hundred and fifty armed rebels remained. They knew they would die

'We think the United States as an ally can exercise its influence on the Korean government. Since it hasn't done so, we suspect the US might be supporting General Chun Doo-hwan,' Yun Sang-won told foreign reporters.[226] The Americans were not exactly supporting Chun, but neither did they use their leverage to restrain him. The rebellion was quelled and the city retaken after an assault by paratroopers. Yun's body was among those found at the City Hall building, which the militants had made their headquarters. The final death toll for the nine-day event was over two hundred dead.

Government propaganda, media censorship, and popular prejudice against Cholla created confusion for years about what had actually happened in Kwangju. The fear of north Korea was played up. There were charges that the rebellion was directed by communist agents. Yun's associates, however, say that there was no such evidence and that Yun himself was very critical of north Korea.[227] During the uprising, rebel citizens were still reporting suspected north Korean agents to the local office of the KCIA.

The military claimed that they had American support for their actions in Kwangju. The Americans were not able to credibly defend themselves against this charge for reasons of miscommunication. Both the special-forces units who caused the uprising and the paratroopers who quashed it were outside of the Combined Forces Command. Chun did not need US approval to move them. For the Americans, this legal point limited their responsibility. To the Korean mind, however, such arguments about law are technical sophistry. Power politics is what counts. The Americans could have stopped Chun and didn't.

Where the Americans did act, though, was to save Kim Dae-jung. With baffling judicial logic, Chun's junta found Kim guilty of having master-minded the Kwangju uprising, despite the fact he was behind bars at the time, and sentenced him to death. In the face of criticism from the Carter administration, the junta waited until the November 1980 US presidential election. When Ronald Reagan was elected, they felt he would be more sympathetic to an anti-communist ally. They planned to execute Kim before Reagan's inauguration.[228] Carter officials met with Reagan's incoming national security adviser, Richard Allen, and conspired to save Kim's life. Allen met with Chung Ho-yong, one of Chun's junta and the commander of special forces, and offered Chun a state visit in exchange for commuting the death sentence. Chun, who had by now had himself elected as president, accepted the deal and became the first head of state to visit the newly inaugurated American president. This deal was never made public. As a result, news pictures of Chun and Reagan together convinced dissidents that the Americans had been backing Chun all along. This perception prompted anti-American protests which lasted a decade.

I first heard of this deal during a dinner with three dissidents in 1983, hosted by a close aide to Kim Dae-jung. One of the guests, a prominent anti-government lawyer, assumed I was an American and was distinctly frosty towards me. He shook hands coldly and responded to my English in laconic Korean. I didn't understand the origins of anti-Americanism in those days and perceived it as a kind of racism. I had a policy of not pointing out that I was British simply to squirm out of the line of fire. What's more, I was writing for an American newspaper. The host recounted at length this story of how the White House saved Kim Dae-jung. In his telling, there was another condition that Chun was forced to agree to. He was also made to promise that he would step down after his seven-year term of office was over, as the constitution required. The host described, with actions, how just before entering the room to meet Reagan, Chun was handed a piece of paper with these conditions written on in Korean. He nodded and was ushered in, the host said, giving a little nod and imitating Chun waddling in with his arm outstretched in greeting.

'How do you do?' the host said in exaggerated bad English. 'So, you see, Reagan saved D.J.'s life. Chun will step down in 1988,' he added confidently.

As this tale unfolded, a cloud of resentment lifted visibly from behind the eyes of the lawyer. He leaned over the table and, with a warm smile on his face, held out his hand to me.

'I am very, very sorry,' he said in flawless English. 'I had no idea about this.'

'Oh, don't worry,' I said.

'He's British anyway,' the host said.

I began to understand that anti-Americanism emerged as a necessary part of the Koreans' raging against their past. They were throwing off their own historical habit of dependency, rather than making valid comments about any particular American offences. As an essentially emotional issue, it lent itself, as politics so often does, to great ironies. One for me was that during the height of anti-American protests by students, the American military commander in Korea was the antithesis of what you would expect the chief representative of an 'imperialist oppressor' to be.

William Livesey was the commanding general of US forces from 1984 to 1987, and was also the commander of the Combined Forces Command, the arrangement under which the bulk of the Korean military fell under American command. At the time, Chun Doo-hwan ran a dictatorship which could only have survived with American support. Livesey, then, was one of the most powerful men in Korea for reasons of national defence and political symbolism. If you imagine the roles reversed, with a Korean commanding such a position in America, he would have the biggest car in Washington and swan into the White House as if he owned it. But Livesey was like a farmer-general. 'Farmer' is being polite. By British standards, where you expect your generals to be posh, he was a peasant who at times appeared like a buffoon. He was a very friendly, spontaneous and informal man. At press meetings, we always tried to get him to admit the political importance of his role, but he never would. His public-affairs officer would mutter a prayer for divine intervention to prevent the general from saying something that would end up on the front pages and cause riots. But, he'd just smile mystically and say in his broad Georgia accent, 'Ah'm a simple soldier. Ah don't understand these things but ah know what you guys are tryin' to git me to say, an' ah won't say it. Every morning, I jus' wake up and look myself in the mirror and say, "Livesey, look north."' I must say we correspondents really loved our sessions with this man. He loved his soldiers and could get tears in his eyes talking about them in interviews. He used to appear in advertisements on the American Forces Korea Network, which was a TV channel widely watched by the Korean public, advising the men and women in his command on safety and fitness. In one, he bounced into a car like a ham actor, snapped on his seat belt, turned to the camera and said, 'Buckle up! Ah do!' In an advert encouraging fitness, he began with the memorable line, 'If you ain't fit, these hills in Kor-riya'll kick your butt!'

Throughout Chun's rule, students protested continually. But this generation of campus activists was different from its seniors. The appearance of a new dictator, and the apparent ease with which democratic America backed him, influenced students away from American political values. During the 1970s, young intellectuals had sought freedom, democracy and human rights. In the 1980s, they turned to socialist revolution. The smell of tear gas hung almost permanently over the major campuses. Notice boards were plastered with revolutionary slogans and the thrill of a cause energised thousands of young men and women. Riot police, most of them young men on military service, became a permanent feature outside certain key university campuses. When there were demonstrations, they would don their padded uniforms and protective masks and fire canisters of tear gas into the university grounds to prevent protesters from getting off campus. Uniformed 'grabbers' in anoraks and gym shoes and helmets would try to grab student leaders. When protests were planned in the streets, the police gained advanced intelligence and posted men at subway stations and in the city centre. They would stop young people and check their IDs, and go through their bags to see if any were carrying leaflets. People became so accustomed to the sight of riot police that they forgot what a militaristic and often frightening impression they gave to foreign visitors. Platoons of riot police used to regularly drill in a park next to Dong-guk University in Seoul, right across the road from the deluxe Shilla Hotel, where visiting dignitaries and businessmen used to stay.

The protesting was relentless. The police became probably the best riot-control force in the world, able to clear a plaza full of protesters in a matter of seconds, by driving in from two sides pumping tear gas and making sure to give the students an escape route. The tear gas was especially strong. Even a day after a protest, it would hang in the air like an invisible sheet of pepper. Citizens learned not to rub their eyes and noses but to let their tears and mucus wash it out. Students seemed to develop a cockroach-like immunity and made it a point of honour not to wear gas masks (which were illegal). They would put toothpaste in their nostrils and under their eyes to cut the gas.

These students were remarkable for their selfless innocence. They had gained entry to university with the sacrifice of their families behind them. Before they did their military service, most of them were virgins. They drank and smoked but they did not take drugs. Most could not afford to go to discos and buy fashionable clothes. They did not have nihilistic or self-absorbed views of life. They had emerged from a childhood of swotting for exams into an environment which expected them to take responsibility for their country. One I got to know well was Lee Yong-ho, who was one of the top-scoring students of his year. The son of a construction worker, in 1983 he entered the economics department of Seoul National University, the leading college in the country. He eventually became an underground radical and dropped out to work as an industrial labourer.

'At the time I was too young to know about Korean society. I saw police on the campus, fighting with students and beating them. I was very shocked. I looked for seniors to explain about society. I felt I knew nothing. A high school friend introduced me to a senior and I joined his group studying about social science, Korean history and economics.'

Lee had joined an illegal 'circle'. In the second year, they studied books about economics, some of which explained Marxist and neo-Marxist theories.

'In Korea these kinds of theories were not even studied in universities. Some of the books were blacklisted and if you were caught with them you'd be charged with spying. I'd heard a story about a drunk who had shouted "Long Live Kim Il-sung" as a joke and been arrested for spying, so I was careful. We didn't really have any set programme or even know how to approach these books, so we just read them and passed them round.

'I was not a radical being inspired by radical texts, but an intellectual trying to understand things. I'm not sure about my friends, but it was the lack of freedom that radicalised me. Some people were more intellectual and others more political. If someone had read a book that no one else had, it gave them a kind of power over others. So group leaders would read books strategically and not hand them around. It's ironic because we studied about freedom of philosophy and thought, but the way some people used it was contrary to this freedom. Most of these circle members were the intellectual leaders of the student movement.'

Lee worked for three months in a factory, concealing his identity as a student, and then went to do his twenty-seven months' military service before returning to university. After graduating in 1990, he moved to Inchon, where he worked as a welder and factory worker.

'I was in a circle of old friends. Some were from my underground student circle, some from other circles, and some were labourers. We passed around books and talked of our philosophy and strategy for the labour movement. We didn't have a political strategy. There were other underground workers but we had no contact with them. In those days the government could catch nationwide organisations easily, so we didn't make one.

At that time, I read about Kim Il-sung's *Juche* theory. One Seoul National University law college student had written it down from north Korean radio broadcasts and distributed it to friends. One of my friends was a key member of his group. My impression was that real north Korean spies would have no way of finding out about these groups and contacting them. At that time, Korean nationalism was very popular among students and *Juche* emphasised strong nationalism. But all the time I was studying it I was haunted by the feeling that it was not logical. I couldn't understand the logic of the emphasis on the leadership. I struggled with my friend about that point. He insisted, 'Just believe and follow.' I felt it was comical for him to say this, but I couldn't say what I felt because others were taking it so seriously.

'I stopped the factory work after eighteen months. I felt I tried to be a labourer but couldn't be successful, so decided to quit. I was an educated intellectual, very different from workers. I can do more for society and myself as an ordinary educated man, not an underground man. I found I didn't like workers. This was not a class feeling. It's just that the culture of labourers was not mine. I didn't like the hard physical work because, when you're doing it, you cannot think of anything except work. Normally my mind was always thinking of things, but I couldn't think when I worked. Also, I felt isolated among workers. Our group didn't really try to make unions, we just gave them ideology. I felt I was useless, I couldn't do anything for them.'

Lee is now a chartered accountant doing the accounts of foreign and Korean companies. He keeps in touch with his old friends. 'Some are lawyers, one is in the opposition party, one is a businessman. We've all changed, but we've not talked about it. The value of it all was that we had freedom of speech and thinking within our own group. We couldn't change society by ourselves. You cannot take away people's freedom and no one should take the freedom from others. That's my basic thought. It's the conclusion of my ten-year activism. The thing we have in common is that we still share a feeling that we want to work for society. We still talk about the need to live a righteous and meaningful life and help society.

Some protests by students in the 1980s escalated into massive events. On several occasions students occupied campus buildings. Once at Sung-kyun-kwan University, students declared some student buildings a 'liberated zone'. Eventually riot police retook them. At Konkuk University in Seoul, fourteen hundred students were detained and thirty-four of them jailed under national security laws, after a siege. Tens of thousands of students were arrested throughout the 1980s. In 1985, radical students took over the American cultural centre library in Seoul for three days. American diplomats would not permit riot police to remove the students by force, and international TV cameras set up across the street. The boldness of this event released a pent-up resentment, which most of us covering it at the time were unaware existed. Many of the Koreans walking by seemed more impressed than shocked. This was just the first of numerous assaults on American targets through the decade.

Despite all this activity, the students were also remarkably ineffective. Demonstrations seemed to be ritualistic, rather than strategically designed to make a point. Citizens did not criticise the students, despite the constant tear gas and blocked streets. But neither did they support them. Student leaders seemed to be pursuing their own fantasy revolution, unaware that with their radical slogans and violence, they had little backing from the populace.

But one issue would not go away. That was Kwangju. Every year in May, memorial rallies were staged in the city and on campuses around the country. The ghosts of murdered protestors haunted Chun Doo-hwan throughout his rule.

In 1980, Chun had conducted massive communist-style purges. Over eight thousand officials were removed for corruption or other offences, or simply because the people drawing up the lists put their names there. Almost sixty thousand people were picked up in a drive to 'eliminate social evils'. Two-thirds of them were sent to 'purification' camps, where at least fifty died. News media were forced to close or merge, and several hundred journalists lost their jobs. Under new rules, newspapers were not permitted to have reporters in other cities and had to rely heavily on the state-controlled news agency.

In 1982, Kim Dae-jung was released and allowed to go to exile in the United States. Seoul had won its bid for the '88 Summer Olympics, which gave it a focus for political development. The country had to be ready for this crowning glory. The economy had picked up again. In 1985, Chun released many politicians from a ban. While Kim Dae-jung was in America, his faction, and that of Kim Young-sam, combined to form an opposition party. Within a few weeks of its formation, their New Korea Democratic Party won an impressive number of seats in the National Assembly. It began to press for a constitutional change to replace the electoral college system for electing the president, which the government could manipulate, to a direct popular election.

However, the National Assembly itself was a pretence. A proportional system was in place whereby additional seats were allotted to each party according to how many seats it won in the election. The way these were allocated allowed the ruling Democratic Justice Party to enjoy a clear majority, although it won only a third of the vote. The ruling party agreed to the opposition's demand for talks on constitutional change to allow for more democracy, but, with its majority, was not required to concede on anything. To create the necessary power shift to force a democratic change, the opposition politicians had to use other means. They took to the streets.

It would be a mistake to portray the struggle for democracy as a battle being waged by noble civilian democrats against a corrupt and brutal military regime. Opposition and government were part of the same authoritarian political culture. It was really this culture that was being rejected, and no single figure or party clearly represented the democratic alternative.

Chun was personally unpopular. Even those who could justify his usurpation of power found his dour public face, and the financial scandals associated with his family members, reasons to dislike him. I used to marvel at receptions where Chun would make a grand entry into a hotel ballroom flanked by security. He would stand at the front holding his drink and addressing people in general. A few people would go to the front and listen, but the rest of the room would carry on their own conversations, completely ignoring him. Nevertheless, this dislike did not translate into support for opposition. The government in general had significant support. It was seen as capable of managing the economy and the defence against north Korea.

In January 1987, a twenty-one-year-old linguistics student from Seoul National University died in police custody. Police had been dunking his head repeatedly in a bathtub and, in their zeal, smashed his windpipe against the side of the bath. Police tried to cover up the incident, but details leaked and inflamed the populace against the regime. Protests and memorial services were held throughout the country. Something had changed. After years of indifference to student demonstrations and opposition-party antics, this incident touched ordinary Koreans deeply. Chun had a new and fearful enemy – the mothers of Korean students. In a few months their voice would be heard.

In April, Chun announced that the talks the opposition were boycotting on constitutional change were off permanently. He said that any further discussion would threaten the peaceful transfer of power at the end of his term in 1988, and the Olympic Games later in the same year.

Around this time, in the foreign media, we began to have problems with the police. Korean and Japanese photographers had often run into trouble with police when they were covering demonstrations and anti-government events. We complained officially after one or two of our members were beaten. The authorities obliged by issuing armbands for specific events which identified us as foreign journalists, and police were told to allow us to do our job. Then the photographers and TV crews, who were almost all Korean nationals, began to notice strangers with 'foreign-press' armbands. We realised that the government was also issuing foreign-press armbands to police cameramen, who could get up close and get pictures of individual demonstrators. Students realised it too and there was a case of a photographer being mistaken for a police agent and manhandled by students. At this point we decided to distribute our own armbands, with each person's Seoul Foreign Correspondents' Club membership number and strict rules about not lending them to other people. The authorities did not appreciate this initiative. In a yelling match, an assistant minister of culture and information accused a small delegation, who had gone to explain the decision to him, of violating Korean national sovereignty. The foreign press nevertheless wore their own armbands for a ruling-party event the following day at which Roh Tae-woo was officially to be nominated as the party's candidate in the December 1987 presidential election. It was a timely moment, for it was that night that the fiercest and most sustained period of rioting began.

With the electoral college system, in which people voted for about five thousand people who elected the president, Roh was to be a shoe-in. The opposition was in disarray at this point and students had lost popular support. People had accepted that Chun had overcome his predecessors' weakness for perpetual rule and would actually step down. But this was no longer the issue. The problem was that he was afraid to allow a free vote and was putting his best friend in his place. An organisation of religious leaders and dissidents called for protests. At 6 p.m. that night, 10 June 1987, drivers were asked to peep their horns.

Several journalists were sitting in the bar of the press club, talking about our armband victory. Someone walked in reeking of tear gas, saying there was a bit of a demo going on somewhere. At six, we opened the windows to see if the people driving home from work were peeping their horns. At first, there was just the sound of traffic. But after a minute, it seemed that the normal erratic sound of horns was taking some shape. A long line of cars in convoy came down the street to the city plaza, with their horns at full blast, and the rush-hour traffic started to pick up the theme. Meanwhile, on the other side of the plaza, a cloud of tear gas appeared between the buildings. It was the bit of a demo. Thousands of people were already in the streets.

I drove around the city centre with another western reporter. Seoul had been the scene of several large-scale protests before, but nothing quite on this scale. The debris of street warfare was everywhere. Ripped-up paving stones and rubble, powder scars where tear-gas canisters had landed. We rescued two young women who were choking on tear gas, and dropped them at a subway stop. At one point, a crowd of several thousands was making its way along a broad road between the Namdaemum Gate and the City Hall. The car was completely surrounded by people and only inching along. People slapped on the bonnet and shouted. These were not only students. One or two people in the crowd gave us baleful looks. North Korean agents, fanatical anti-Americans, nutters who get drawn to mobs? A large man in a suit knocked on my window. I lowered it wondering what he was planning.

'The horn,' he said in English. 'The horn.' Of course, the horn.

I peeped the horn and the crowd around us erupted in joyous applause. I took my *'waeshin kija'* (foreign reporter) armband out of the glove compartment and held it up to the windscreen. The people roared again and slapped the car in support.

The protests spread to cities all over the country and lasted for days and days. Some students occupied the Myongdong Roman Catholic Cathedral the city centre. Riot police were positioned around it and the siege became a focal point. After a few days, it became apparent that these were more than student demonstrations. I found a coffee shop on the second floor of a building which afforded a view up the street to the Cathedral, and where you were protected from tear gas. One lunchtime, I watched as a man, carrying a briefcase, was stopped by a line of riot police from going down a narrow street, probably back to the bank where he worked. He went berserk and in his outrage looked as if he would take on the entire south Korean police force single-handed. He was manhandled away. On another occasion, a salaryman who had obviously given the police a mouthful was bundled into a doorway by police and about to be taught a lesson when he was rescued by some middle-aged ladies who weighed into the police as if they were naughty schoolboys. This was a middle-class revolution.

After *The Washington Post* reported that the middle class were taking on the government, the minister of culture and information came to the cathedral to take a look for himself, and suffered the indignity of being chased down the street by angry demonstrators. Chun knew he had a problem that was not going to go away. He held separate meetings with opposition leaders. Kim Young-sam came out of his meeting and said that Chun was still not prepared to concede. The riots picked up again and the government debated whether to introduce martial law and bring in the tanks. But the ghosts of Yun Sang-won and the others killed during the Kwangju uprising in 1980 were also in the demonstrations. The ghost of the future also haunted Chun. The Olympics were only a year away and Chun envisaged their opening by Roh Tae-woo, who would then be president, with himself sitting by his side, as the elder statesman, as a tribute to his achievement of the first peaceful, democratic transfer of power in Korean history.

The only way to break the impasses was to concede. On 29 June, Roh Tae-woo made a dramatic announcement in which he called for a rewriting of the constitution to allow for presidential elections by direct popular vote. The country was jubilant. On 1 July Chun approved. The opposition was back in business. Kim Dae-jung was released from a political ban. Kim Jong-pil had returned and formed his own party. Most people you asked wanted Kim Dae-jung, Kim Young-sam or Kim Jong-pil to be the next president. But a scholar at the time warned me about assuming that a ruling party victory by Roh Tae-woo could happen only if the election was rigged.

'Democracy for us Koreans means the right to choose our own dictator,' he said. His point was that when it came down to the vote, people would want a person they thought was capable of ruling and had the backing of the military.

In the end, this is what happened in the December 1987 presidential election. The opposition did the government the big favour of splitting the anti-government vote. The alliance between Kim Young-sam and Kim Dae-jung broke and they ran against each other. The government pulled out all the tricks. It controlled media. Pretending to report equally, it always began each news item with a report on Roh's campaign because his candidacy number was '1'. There was gift-giving on a scale which the opposition couldn't match. There was also a convenient reminder by the government of north Korea. A north Korean terrorist who had planted a bomb on a Korean airliner was caught in Bahrain and brought to Seoul on the eve of the election.

The advantage of the opposition was that it had more committed activist support and could produce more people at its rallies. Election workers tried to convince media of their own crowd estimates. Kim Dae-jung had the biggest rally of the whole campaign, on the Yoido Plaza in Seoul. He asked me how many I thought were there and looked very disappointed when I gave my estimate of 'over a million'. I found out later his aides had told him the crowd was nearer three million.

Kim Young-sam also got large crowds. Roh Tae-woo's looked as big, but when you were in them you could swing a cat around and not hit anyone. A lot of these ralliers were reluctant. A friend from Samsung told me that he had been ordered by the company to go to a Roh rally. He took his headphones with him and, while Roh was giving his speech, he was listening to Jimi Hendrix.

In the absence of credible polling, I was going on intensity and size of crowds as the measure of support. I thought Kim Dae-jung would win. But in the week before the election, all those people who didn't bother with rallies and were noncommittal when you asked them who they were going to vote for, like my landlord and other neighbours down the street, decided for Roh. In the end, Roh gained only 37 per cent of the vote, but it was enough to win. Kim Young-sam came second, DJ third, and JP fourth. The opposition complained of vote rigging. Dissidents tried to prove there had been a sophisticated fiddling of the vote count using computers and claimed that the military dictatorship was continuing to rule. Indeed, there had been some questionable incidents. A ballot box was removed from a polling station. Voting on military bases was not secret and soldiers were pressured to vote for Roh. Candidates violated spending limits. But by the standard of previous elections, this one was an improvement. The claim that Roh had won through fraud fell flat in the face of the opposition split. In the end, it was the procedure, not the personalities, which was important. There had been for the first time a peaceful transfer of power through a reasonably democratic election. Until now, democracy had been imitated. Now, its form was in place. Over the next decade the focus would be on developing the substance in terms of fairer elections, individual rights, and a democratisation of the culture. Democracy had only just begun.

Chapter Eighteen

HUMAN RIGHTS

Dictatorship is not as easy to recognise as one might think. Freedom exists along a scale and one person's experience of where a country is on it may differ from the impression outsiders get from news reports. It is especially difficult to measure when there is no legitimate opposition voice, and local people do not complain openly about their situation. When there is fear, people do not freely come up to you and tell you they are afraid. But there are other reasons than fear to keep quiet. Koreans felt ashamed of their human-rights problems and even dissidents felt torn about feeding international criticism of the Korean government. In the mid-1980s, one close friend in the opposition party proudly told me one day that he had just met with two visiting officials from Amnesty International.

'I told them things weren't so bad,' he said.

'What?' He was always complaining to me about the military dictatorship.

'I don't want to bad-mouth my country. This is our problem,' he said.

Also, it was not as if Koreans were lamenting their life in the 1980s. There was plenty to be proud of. The economy was marvelled at by foreigners. Seoul had hosted the Asian Games in 1986 and was hosting the Olympics in 1988. Authoritarianism had always been a fact of life, something that most people dealt with rather than thought was wrong and fought against.

In 1982, when I arrived, people were afraid to say what they thought. I learned to read between the lines to find out what was happening. A small item on the back page of the English-language daily *Korea Herald* saying that two students had been arrested for 'scattering leaflets' usually meant there had been a big demonstration. People didn't talk on the telephone because they assumed the phones were bugged. The coffee shops were full of rumours about corruption involving Chun Doo-hwan's wife, Lee Soon-ja, and others. You often felt that people were trying to overhear your conversations.

Sanitising news does work on apolitical people to an extent. I remember hearing a young European woman give a very positive briefing to a group of foreign visitors about Korea. It had never invaded another country, it had picked itself up from the ashes of war, and there was almost no crime. I found this last point a bit perplexing, especially as my house had been burgled twice that year. I questioned her about it and she said it was her impression from the newspapers. You couldn't pick up a newspaper without some reference either to how amazingly Korea had grown or to the Korean War or both. It's always a telltale sign of dictatorship when the media are short on news but heavy on past suffering and present success.

As the opposition parties became stronger during the 1980s, ordinary people spoke more openly of their dislike of the government. After the students occupied the American cultural centre library in 1985, intellectuals who had previously defended the government to me in terms of the need for vigilance against north Korea would launch into diatribes against America. Fear was being lifted and people were speaking out. It is hard to recapture the atmosphere of this fear once it has gone. It is also hard to appreciate the courage it takes to be at the front line of this process. Students used to risk thrashings and arrest. They had a strong internal cohesion which gave them courage. Often the stone-throwers at the front were being watched by older students from behind whom they were eager to impress. Before a demonstration, students would go through rituals. Once at Korea University, I watched hundreds of students, after a memorial for some students who had died in mysterious circumstances on military service, form a long snake, five abreast, with their arms over one another's shoulders. They ran rhythmically, like Zulus, and chanted in unison deeply from their stomachs before they went to confront riot police. Close up, you could feel how, for many, the exhilaration of solidarity was overcoming a natural nervousness. Some were twitching with adrenaline. This was how they prepared to do battle with the mighty power of the state. They were able to do so because the state, although repressive, had to pull its punches to maintain its rule. But nevertheless, it took courage to attack the fear that hung over all.

Opposition leaders, for all their subterranean fundraising and factional meandering that so often seemed to undermine the democratic cause, also exhibited courage. Kim Young-sam went on a protest hunger strike that lasted twenty-three days. Many had experienced torture. Kim Sang-hyun, a leading figure in the Kim Dae-jung faction, told me how he had been hung up and had the soles of his feet beaten by investigators pressuring him to link Kim Dae-jung with the Kwangju uprising. He brushed off this experience and felt that it was important to develop links and friendships with the ruling side to demonstrate that opposition was not to be feared unnaturally. Kim Dae-jung himself is a man of immense courage. I once saw him give an election speech in Taegu when supporters of his opponents started throwing missiles at him. He completed his speech without flinching, as two bodyguards, who had anticipated trouble, stood on either side of him desperately intercepting stones with Plexi-glas shields. In prison under death sentence in 1980, Kim Dae-jung had told his family to pass on the message to his supporters that, after his execution, there should be no revenge. A devout Catholic, he understood the importance of breaking the cycle of fear. After his release from prison, he still maintained that Chun and his lieutenants should be pardoned. He did not want them to hold on to power out of fear of retribution.

The massive people-power protests of 1987 resulted not only in a change in the way that the president was elected, but also in other democratic rights. The censorship of the press through government guidelines was stopped. Government controls of media and associations through licensing were lifted. Labour unions began to organise and demand their rights. Dissidents began demanding other rights.

The main source of human-rights abuse in south Korea has been, and continues to be, the domination of the legislature and judiciary by the executive branch. Thousands of students and dissidents have been arrested, for exercising rights which were recognised in the constitution, because the executive ordered a 'crackdown'.

The executive branch has justified authoritarianism by manipulating the nation's fear of north Korea. This fear was articulated by an ideology of anti-communism. Unlike communism, which proposed revolutionary change, anti-communism was essentially a negative ideology. Unlike democrats, who were also opposed to communism, anti-communists saw democracy as a convenient back door for communist infiltration and thereby justified authoritarianism. It is not difficult to relate to the south Korean predicament a few decades ago. There had been a war in which civilians had suffered terribly. On the Asian map, south Korea looked like a small white blob stuck on the edge of the huge, red, communist massif. There was only a ceasefire, not a peace. It was reasonable to assume that there would be another war. Middle-aged Koreans remember being taught in primary school that north Koreans were red devils with horns on their heads and believing it literally. In National Ethics classes, this nationalistic anti-communism was combined with traditional Korean ethics with filial piety as its main feature. The classes were compulsory at university until 1989, by which time they had become a bit of a joke. They are still taught in schools, although the 'National' has been dropped.[229] In high school, there was two hours a week military-style training for boys, and nursing training for the girls, which added to the war mentality. There was a midnight to 4 a.m. curfew until 1981, and until a few years ago, there were monthly air-raid drills in which the whole country came to a standstill for twenty minutes.

The legal instruments for repression were the National Security Law and the Anti-Communist Law. The latter was introduced in 1961 and repealed in 1991. The former remains in place. Over the years, people have been found guilty of aiding and abetting the enemy for the oddest of reasons. In one case, someone was found guilty for having asked a waitress not to turn off a radio in a restaurant after realising that it was tuned by mistake to a north Korean station. This was in 1968, before the authorities were able to jam north Korean broadcasts. In 1978, some philatelists were found guilty because they obtained north Korean stamps from international collectors. A pro-communist was defined as anyone sharing a 'world view or ideology with radical, socialist, anarchist, or communist inclinations'.[230] Agreeing with anything that north Korea agreed with, meeting anyone who may have visited north Korea, could be seen as evidence of guilt.

We should not be surprised to find that political research and analysis were not encouraged. The south Korean state did not trust its own people enough to allow them to study Marxism in any of its forms

As the government has become more confident, it has naturally felt less threatened by ideas and activities associated with north Korea. Since 1988, when the government stopped penalising overseas Koreans for visiting north Korea, it found it extremely useful to get briefings from Korean-American and other visitors to north Korea instead of treating them like spies.

Public debate on the unification issue even now is limited. It was once the exclusive province of the Blue House and the intelligence agency. The current president, Kim Dae-jung, was for years portrayed as a pro-communist because he had proposals for gradual reunification which were different from the government's. Crackdowns on 'leftists' continued under presidents Roh Tae-woo and Kim Young-sam into the 1990s. In one such campaign, in August 1996, police raided Yonsei University after a siege and detained almost six thousand students.

People continue to be arrested on vague grounds. In 1996, a singer and a publisher were arrested for making a songbook that apparently 'praised' north Korea. A student was arrested for putting a 'dangerous' opinion on a computer bulletin board, challenging the government's version of an incident in which a north Korean submarine ran aground on a south Korean beach.

Torture remains a problem, despite some attempts to improve police behaviour. The main cause is that prosecutors rely heavily on confessions obtained during interrogations. In addition, there are big incentives for police and intelligence officials to get results. One former policeman told me that his arrest and interrogation of a north Korean spy had made his career. Also, suspects may be held for up to thirty days before being charged. For some national security offences, this is extended to fifty days. Torture of political suspects became an issue in the mid 1980s after some criminal suspects and a dissident, Kim Keun-tae, sued their torturers. But abuse of suspected north Korean agents and common criminals is widespread. Sleep deprivation, threats and beatings are routine. Sexual insults and even assault of female detainees is not uncommon. These and any other tricks that work are designed to break a suspect's will and force a confession. An intelligence agent once admitted to me that with suspected pro-north Koreans, there are no rules during interrogation. It is assumed that, over the years, many have died during questioning. In 1985, a student, Kim Song-man, arrested after meeting some north Korean students in Europe, was forced during interrogation to write a suicide note to his parents, presumably in case he died under torture. Despite lack of evidence, he was found guilty of spying. He remains in prison. In 1995, an elderly scholar broke down and confessed to spying charges during a sustained period of interrogation, after agents showed him the suicide note of one of his children. In this case, some charges were dropped on appeal. But one can only guess at the numbers of people charged with offences that in a fair system would not be considered criminal, and the numbers who are serving jail sentences for confessing to crimes they have not committed.

Failure to observe procedure, such as obtaining search and arrest warrants, reading of rights and allowing suspects access to lawyers, are not yet grounds for dismissing cases. As a result, such violations are routine. Park Chung-ryol, the deputy chairman of the dissident National Alliance for Democracy and Unification of Korea, was arrested at 2.30 one morning in November 1995 by Agency for National Security Planning agents.[231] They had a warrant but wouldn't let him read it. He was taken to a police station and made to sign in, and then taken to an ANSP interrogation centre. This ruse was to get around the fact that the ANSP was no longer permitted to investigate certain offences. Park was read his rights and then immediately softened up with a beating. He was not permitted to remain silent, nor to contact his family or lawyer. He was interrogated all day by a team of fifteen people trying to force him to agree that he was a north Korean spy. He was allowed less than an hour of sleep a day. He was beaten, and forced to stand in a cold shower for almost an hour each day. He was also made to stay in the same position for hours. One such position was to kneel and hold a chair above his head. He was also taken to places in the countryside and ordered to look for a radio transmitter his interrogators said he had buried. They threatened to kill him unless he confessed to being a member of the (north) Korea Workers' Party.

Law continues to be used not to protect people and guarantee their rights, but for political gesture. Dissidents are punished harshly for crimes that touch a political nerve. When a prime minister, Chung Won-shik, visited Hankuk University of Foreign Studies, and was pelted with eggs and flour in 1991, public outrage lead to two-year jail sentences for the radicals involved. On the other hand, students and workers rounded up after protests are often released, despite having committed violence for which they should normally be charged, regardless of the political excuse for it.

On major national holidays, prisoners are pardoned. In 1998, Kim Dae-jung's inauguration was marked by an amnesty that covered release of political prisoners and ordinary criminals, parole, reduction of sentences, restoration of civil rights, removal of past offences of corruption from bureaucrats' records, and waiving of drunk-driving and speeding tickets. It covered an amazing 5 million cases. As a political gesture, this was an example of the use of executive power to demonstrate leniency to 'victims' of the previous administration of Kim Young-sam. Much as such amnesties are welcomed, they too represent an overruling of the judiciary.

Five years earlier, in March 1993, with his inauguration, Kim Young-sam conducted a sweeping amnesty for almost forty-two thousand prisoners. At the time, it was the biggest in Korean history and was designed to underscore the arrival of real civilian democracy.[232] On that occasion, I travelled down to a prison near Taejon, a city in central Korea. My interest was six men in their seventies who were being quietly freed after decades in solitary confinement. They were among a group of prisoners of conscience virtually unknown to the general public. Known as the 'non-converted', these prisoners were jailed on charges of subversion or spying for north Korea.

It was a wet and chilly day. All morning, criminals, mostly young men, came out and were greeted by family members and associates. Outside there was a group of about thirty students from a local university who had come to meet some fellow activists who were being released. They watched as an elderly man in a crumpled blue suit and, incongruously, a pink chiffon scarf tied around his neck, walked out of the prison gate. He was tall and scholarly. Beside him was a short, stocky man almost eighty years old, who had dark patches around his eyes and looked in poor health. Someone explained to the students that they were long-term prisoners. The students applauded and asked them to say something.

'Thank you for coming to meet us,' the stocky man said. 'I'm only an old man. There are younger men who should be released because they still have their life to live. I feel guilty in front of them.' He bowed and they applauded again.

'Grandfather, how long were you in there?' a student shouted out to the man with the pink scarf.

'Thirty-seven years,' he said. The students gasped in disbelief.

The two men walked down the road with family members. When I asked who they were, one of the human-rights activists, who had himself been a prisoner, pointed at the man with the pink scarf. 'His name is Hong,' he said. 'Often in prison you find a person who seems to forget about himself and takes care of others. He was such a person. He was in the cell opposite mine. Once I was brought back to my cell after being beaten. I felt so wretched and in despair. We were not permitted to talk. He stood at the door and watched me for hours. I could feel that he was willing me to feel courage. This was how I began to recover my spirit.'[233]

Another prisoner, called Lee Jong-hwan, was being released after forty-two years. We found out that, as he had no relatives to greet him, he had been taken out of a back gate by prison guards and driven to an old people's home about fifty miles away. I joined forces with two human-rights activists, who got the address. We found Lee sitting a little bewildered in his new room. He had a lean, wiry body, colour in his cheeks and a lively sparkle in his eyes.

'It hasn't sunk in yet that I've been released,' he said. 'I saw in the papers that they were going to free people who were over seventy years old, but I wasn't sure if I would be included. Even this morning the guards didn't let me know. They only told me as they opened the gate. Then I was driven here. I'm not sure if this is still a prison. I've been told I can't go outside the grounds without permission.'

'Don't worry,' said one of the activists. 'That applies to the other people as well. It's because the management is responsible for your welfare.'

What does a man think of in those first moments?

'I felt gratitude to dissident and church groups lobbying for the political prisoners and regret that all the long-term offenders were not released,' he said.

Among those still in prison was Kim Sun-myung, who had been arrested in the same month as Lee, October 1951, during the Korean War. He would eventually be freed in August 1995 after almost forty-four years in prison.

Kim and Lee were both south Korean-born communists.[234] Kim was a private in a reconnaissance unit in the north Korean army when he triggered a booby trap and was captured by American soldiers. Lee was a political operative, picked up by US forces as he crossed the border into south Korea. Both were sentenced to fifteen years as 'collaborators' by a military tribunal. The following year, they were retried as 'spies' and sentenced to life. Ahn Hak-sop was another soldier in the north Korean army. In 1953, he was captured in a battle with south Korean troops. In prison, it was discovered he was actually a south Korea-born volunteer. He was badly beaten and charged with collaboration. Family members, meanwhile, were unable to get permission to visit him because they lived in a restricted area on Kanghwa Island, near the DMZ. A relative finally obtained the necessary pass, but it was too late to plead for leniency. A military court had, a week earlier, sentenced him to life imprisonment. The relative was told that had she arrived before the trial and paid 7000 Won (about at current rates), she could have obtained his release.

These men were jailed less than halfway through Syngman Rhee's term as president. They were kept, for the most part in solitary confinement, through the rule of Rhee, Park Chung-hee, Chun Doo-hwan, Roh Tae-woo and into the administration of Kim Young-sam.

'In the fifties the prisons were not fit for humans, just beasts,' said Kim Sun-myung. 'There'd be from fifty to a hundred people in a large cell. Many were near starvation. When an inmate died, we tried to put him in a sitting position so he looked alive and after roll-call we got his ration.' For ten years after the 1961 military coup, all visits and letters were banned. It was during this period that the prisoners disappeared from public knowledge.

Ideological offenders were given an opportunity to change sides. In a system which the Japanese had used to great effect against independence activists, and which was formally adopted by south Korean authorities in 1955, they were able to swear loyalty to south Korea and be pardoned. Kim, Lee and Ahn declined because they saw themselves as POWs. In 1972, when the Yushin constitution was announced, there was a new policy of persuading inmates to convert. They were required to sign two conversion documents, one a declaration regretting past activities and the other an oath of allegiance to south Korea. Compliance entitled a prisoner to basic privileges and made him eligible for parole and amnesty. By this time, the numbers of ideological prisoners had increased. Some were captured north Korean agents. Others were anti-government leftists accused of being pro-north Korean. They had various reasons to resist. The north Koreans knew that if they converted, their families still in the North risked loss of status or worse punishment. Li In-mo was a north Korean war correspondent, treated as a guerrilla because he had been captured in 1952 in the mountains with partisans left behind after the communist army retreated. In north Korea, his wife had privileges as the widow of a war hero. (It was only in 1991, three years after Lee's release from prison in the South, that she heard he was still alive.) Several were dissidents who had falsely confessed under torture to being north Korean spies. They wouldn't recant because to do so would require them first to admit they were guilty of the crimes for which they had been sentenced.

For some it was a simple matter of principle. 'I couldn't lie. I couldn't cheat my conscience,' said Kim Sun-myung.

Refusal required great courage. At first, prisoners were severely beaten. At least seven died under beatings, survivors say. Until this time, if prisoners had been in solitary confinement, it was because of the lack of facilities. But now it became policy to keep the unconverted from influencing others. Kim Sun-myung said he spent a total of thirty-five years in solitary cells. When these measures failed, more subtle means were used. Wardens brought political scientists to discuss the errors of communism and encourage prisoners to recant their beliefs. Family members were also brought in to pressure them to sign. There were also occasional 'educational' day trips to a textile plant near Taejon and for lunch at the Kum River resort run by the Hyundai Group to show how the country was changing.

Since 1985, the unconverted have been kept in Block 15 of Taejon prison, a three-storey building separate from the rest of the prison. Conditions are basic. In winter there is no heating. Each cell has a wooden floor and a solid steel door. Food is passed through a small hole in the door. The back of each cell has a small, barred window and a squat toilet, which attracts rats and, in the baking summer months, hordes of flies. The large container under each toilet is emptied every two or three months by a detail of ordinary criminals. The political prisoners are not allowed to talk to each other, or to other criminals in the prison, such as the toilet detail and the prison barber. At the end of each corridor there is a door where a guard sits. If a prisoner wants something, such as writing paper or a newspaper from the prison shop, he pushes a button in the cell which lights a red light by the guard's desk.

Visits were restricted to family members. Since his wife died in 1953, Lee Jong-hwan had received almost no visits. Once a relative came with some deeds of land that Lee owned, to ask him to sign it over. He refused. North Koreans and prisoners whose families had disowned them had no visitors.

Conditions began to improve after June 1987, when Korea began to democratise. After prisoners protested by kicking their cell doors, they were permitted to see special TV programmes. From 1988, recorded radio news has been broadcast once a day and since 1989, prisoners who received money from their families have been allowed to buy one newspaper a day. Books on Marxism are also permitted although political works on north Korean Communism are banned. Guards stopped beating those found secretly communicating with inmates in neighbouring cells.

When the story of these forgotten men was revealed in 1990 by two Korean-Japanese prisoners, Suh Sung and his brother Suh Joon-sik, who were freed after an international lobbying campaign, there were around seventy unconverted prisoners, and a similar number who had converted and were awaiting release. International human-rights groups have no access to the prisoners, and little is known about their cases except that they were tried during dictatorships under dubious circumstances. Amnesty International adopted them as prisoners of conscience after satisfying themselves that the prisoners were not terrorists and had not committed violence.

Four years before Kim Sun-myung's release, I managed, with the help of a Korean-American human-rights activist, to trace his brother. When we went to the house, the brother was not there but his son gave us a work address. Kim's brother managed an electronics shop in the Myongdong district of Seoul. The next day I went to see him. He seemed very embarrassed to see me and ushered me out quickly to a coffee shop. 'No one here knows I have a brother,' he said. 'Even my son didn't know. But I had to tell him last night after you visited our house.' The family came under such pressure that, in 1968, he decided to register him as having died. Their mother, who was in her nineties when he was finally released, did not know Sun-myung was still alive.

'I went to see him once about twenty years ago, but he was still a crazy Red,' he said. 'He brought so much grief to the family. All he had to do was sign the form and he could have been released.'

As this reaction indicates, it is very difficult for south Koreans to permit communists their human rights. Even now there is scant interest, let alone sympathy, from the generation which experienced the war, in this issue of long-term prisoners. But for many younger Koreans, their continued incarceration is a shocking measure of the need to improve the level of individual rights. In 1996, twenty long-term unconverted prisoners remained at Block 15. There were at least a hundred and fifty political prisoners including students and trades unionists in jail at the beginning of 1996, and over four hundred and fifty people were arrested under the National Security Law during the year.[235]

Chapter Nineteen

THE KOREAN DISEASE

The ground floor of the hospital teemed with people. Patients lined in unruly queues to pay fees and waited as young ladies packaged their medicine. Nurses bustled purposively. In-patients wandered around. You could tell them from the out-patients because they were the ones wearing pyjamas. A friend and I were visiting a colleague who was in recovery from a cancer operation. Eyes followed our western faces as we made our way through the lobby to the stairs. This was one of those moments, like coming out of a crowded cinema after seeing a movie in which all the heroes were western men, when you feel your foreign-ness in Asia. We could have been a pair of missionary doctors. We found Tae-won lying weakly on a bed in a private room.

'Hey, you shouldn't have come.'

'How are you feeling?'

'OK,' he said. 'The surgeon said everything is OK.'

Tae-won explained that when he was diagnosed with bowel cancer, he had managed to queue-jump the waiting list for operations thanks to a friend who knew the surgeon. The specialist had explained the options. If the cancer was small, it would be an easy matter to cut it out and reconnect the bowel. If it had spread, a more complicated procedure would have been necessary. If it had spread hopelessly, the surgeon would only be able to sew him up again and send him home.

'I paid him a million Won last night,' he said.[236]

'Is that how much it all cost?' I asked.

'No, that was extra. To make sure he did a good job.' He laughed. But he was serious. It was a bribe. He had paid the cost of the most expensive of the three options in case the surgeon was tempted to perform the pricier

233

operation when it was not absolutely necessary. As it happened, Tae-won had a small cancerous part removed and was as right as rain in no time.

I'd long had my doubts about the Korean medical profession, ever since an encounter with a leading specialist in fertility who had inserted a gloved finger into my rectum and shoved my prostate in front of two male assistants. What got to me later, though, was that after further embarrassment, this inquisitor declared that my sperm count was low. What a liar. He said that the 'best drugs' were not available through the hospital pharmacy but it just so happened that he had some and was able to provide them at a rather high price. This happened at one of Korea's best establishments. The doctor was a professor, the equivalent of a Harley Street specialist. My suspicion was that he was feathering his nest. But I wasn't taking any chances, so I paid up, and was declared fertile a few weeks later.

A doctor at another hospital later indirectly confirmed my suspicions when he told me that a head of department could earn as much as 20 million Won a month, ten times his salary, with backhanders from drug companies to push particular products.

A lot of money also passes hands in schools. It has long been customary for parents to pay under-the-table money to teachers. In fact, in some of the better schools, teachers more than double their salaries with these unofficial payments. 'I pay my daughter's teacher about a hundred thousand Won a month,' said a friend who lived in the posh Apkujong area of Seoul. 'I don't want to, but I'm afraid that if I don't she'll end up having a seat at the back of the class.'

The media are another area in which there has been significant corruption. A practice of accepting 'white envelopes' containing cash from news sources is believed to have begun in the 1960s when Park Chung-hee consolidated his power. Many people associate the corruption in modern times with the military, which had access to American military aid goods such as clothing, jeeps and blankets which were recycled on to the black market. When the generals took power there was a lot of dirty linen to hide, so to speak, and they bought off potential whistle-blowers, who were mainly journalists. The *chaebol* also had reasons to keep journalists on their side.

'I first noticed it creeping into the news room some time around 1965,' said one older journalist. This was at the time when agents of the Korean CIA started visiting editorial offices of the main newspaper to demand that certain stories be edited or spiked. The cash began to flow for reporters who worked on the economic and political desks of newspapers. The practice became so prevalent that on some papers in the 1970s, political and business reporters actually received no salaries. As salaries did improve, reporters and desk editors who did not interact with sources, were often compensated with an additional monthly allowance.[237] Reporters would argue that giving a photographer, say, 50,000 Won to submit the best of his pictures of you to his editor was the equivalent in Britain of giving him a cup of tea. They denied that it actually made any difference. The point is often made, that, in fact, the white envelope reflects more of a relationship-building goodwill gesture than a bribe. A ruling-party politician, who later became the chairman of the National Assembly's Culture and Information Committee, once complained to me that he would give money to journalists and they would still go ahead and write negative stories. Even if the money did not function as directly as a bribe regarding a specific story, the corrupting effect of this practice was much broader and more pernicious than those involved would admit. South Korea once had thriving and feisty media. Through the 1970s, however, they were silenced by a combination of suppression and self-censorship of which the white-enveloping was a part. The result was that in the 1980s, when Koreans were jockeying for democracy, all the calls for freedom of the press were coming, not from journalists, but from outside the media. Many honest reporters saw this clearly. One celebrated journalist used to return government-issued *chonji* (cash gifts) by registered mail, addressed to Park Chung-hee.

The white envelope issue exploded in 1990 when the media broke a taboo and reported negatively on themselves. The first case came after it was revealed that the group of journalists for the major media which covered Seoul City Hall allegedly shared 40 million Won from the Hanbo Housing Co. The revelations surfaced after Hanbo officials were arrested on charges of bribing government officials and politicians to permit construction in a green belt area. Shortly afterwards, there was a case which involved 90 million Won apparently split between twenty-one reporters on the Ministry of Health and Social Affairs beat. These corruption stories were broken by the *Hankyoreh Shinmun*, a low-budget, low-circulation paper which pioneered new ethical standards in Korean journalism. At its launch in 1989 it declared itself opposed to the white envelope and made it clear it would not be influenced by the power or money of government and big business. Its reporters, many of them political dissidents, earned half as much as their colleagues on other papers. The paper's leftist editorial stance gave it the image of the outsider, and its influence was therefore limited. However, once the story had broken, the establishment media could not ignore it. Two news organisations fired their reporters involved in the Health and Social Affairs Ministry case.

Choo Don-shik, a senior editor of the *Chosun Ilbo*, the country's leading paper, drew up some basic no-white-envelope guidelines. In a newsroom ceremony, the paper's 270 reporters and editors pledged not to accept cash or valuable gifts, nor to accept any invitations which implied a request for favourable reporting. The paper also started to pay for the space, telephone and fax facilities provided to its reporters in government ministries and cover reporters' and editors' expenses. The *Chosun Ilbo*, however, was one of the few papers which could afford to take this moral high ground. Nevertheless, this stand, taken in November 1991, put all media on notice that there was no argument in defence of the white envelope. It was wrong.

Corruption in business and in the civil service appears to have occurred on a massive scale. Since 1987, when the media began reporting more regularly on corruption, it has been almost impossible to open the daily paper without reading of a fresh case. Construction and defence are two notorious sectors. The most dramatic examples in recent years have been the collapse of the Songsu Bridge and of the Sampoong department store, both in Seoul, within a few months of each other. Both cases were the result of corruption.

The Songsu Bridge was one of the twenty or so bridges that span the Han River, which cuts through Seoul. I knew this bridge well, enough to even recall its bumps. The collapse happened shortly before 8 a.m. on a weekday in 1994 when the bridge was solid with rush-hour traffic. Within minutes, there were TV pictures, interrupting morning children's TV, presenting the unbelievable sight of the bridge with a forty-eight-metre section span missing. At least ten vehicles, including a packed bus, were on it when it dropped to the river. Thirty-two people died.

Addressing the old sense that the spiritual roots of disaster lie in the morality of the leadership, the president, Kim Young-sam, said, 'Meeting with reproach and criticism against the government, I feel from the bottom of my heart that I lack virtue as President.'[238]

The prime minister offered to resign and the outgoing mayor of Seoul was detained for questioning. The chairman of the Dong-Ah Group, whose construction subsidiary had built the bridge fifteen years earlier, was taken in for questioning. The premier's resignation was rejected by the president, and the mayor was let go. Although the Dong-Ah boss had been the chairman of the construction affiliate at the time, he claimed that it was a titular position and that his late father had been in charge. Experts eventually concluded that flawed welding, lack of routine maintenance, and failure to keep traffic within the weight limit of eighteen tons per span were to blame. Two Dong-Ah officials were sentenced to two years in prison for ignoring safety standards.[239]

The Sampoong department store was a posh, five-storey building in southern Seoul. Its collapse in June 1995 had come with signs. Fifteen days earlier, diners reported a crack in the ceiling in one of the restaurants on the top floor. On the morning of the collapse, the floor of another restaurant had cracked and water began dripping through the ceiling of adjacent restaurants. Management closed off the fifth floor. At 1 p.m. the air conditioning broke down and power went out mysteriously. Management had an emergency meeting at 3 p.m. and then left without notifying staff or shoppers of their concerns. Shortly before 6 p.m., a 100-metre-wide section of the top floor collapsed and the store caved in on hundreds of shoppers.

The rescue effort dominated the news for the next two weeks. This was a tragedy of mind-boggling proportions for Koreans. It came on the heels of the bridge collapse, and also a gas explosion during subway construction in Taegu in April of the same year, which had killed 101 people. Citizens began to worry as they drove to work, shopped and slept at night, about things they had hitherto taken for granted. The sight of the gigantic rubble on live TV screens for days was a reminder that their nation had overreached itself, that its leaders were incompetent and the populace was flawed. A self-revulsion surfaced. The amateurish rescue effort seemed to add to this feeling. Great heart was in evidence, of the sort in which twenty yelling people tried to carry a single stretcher. Journalists and TV cameras crawled over the rubble, hindering the rescue effort. So much water was used to damp the dust that it was feared survivors in the basement levels were being drowned by the rescuers. Family members of victims tried to march to the Blue House to demand that the president order the central government to take over the rescue work from Seoul City. On another day, a mob of the bereaved beat up a local government official at a memorial service for victims. For sophisticated Koreans, it was as if the third world was crawling over the ruins of their collapsed dream.

But there were moments of great exhilaration, such as the night when rescuers dug down to a basement and found twenty-four cleaners in their fifties and sixties who had been huddled in a basement thirty metres underground. They were pulled out through a narrow hole one by one, their heads wrapped in towels to protect their eyes from the camera lights. Then, incredibly, a young man was pulled out alive on day nine. Three days later a young sales assistant was rescued. Then another young woman was found alive on the sixteenth day. These three attractive young people became instant celebrities and accelerated the national healing.

Inspectors checked over the collapsed pillars and found they were 25 per cent smaller in diameter than the plans said they should have been. Sticking out of them were only half the number of reinforcing rods that there were supposed to be. Prosecutors said additional construction on the top floor, and the relocating of water tanks on the roof, had been done without any structural calculation. In a miserably familiar process, the Sampoong chairman, the architect and some government officials were arrested.

This series of accidents rattled the confidence of Koreans, many of whom saw it as the comeuppance of a nation that posed as developed but was still operating in a backward way. The anxiety lasted for some time. Shortly after the Sampoong collapse, news reports that a sand shortage during the building boom in 1989 had meant that hundreds of thousands of homes had been built with sub-standard cement created a broader scare that even their apartment blocks may collapse. Inspectors worked overtime until people's minds were put at rest.

Corruption is a fact of life in Asia. Each new administration in Korea has sought to curry popular support and legitimise its rule by exposing the corruption of its predecessor. But it has continued. The higher the position, the bigger the amounts. From the top, corruption has flowed downstream, like a lazy river of filth, leaving its scum lines everywhere.

But when Kim Young-sam came into office in 1993, and he backed up a pledge to cure what he termed 'the Korean disease' by declaring his own assets and announcing that his presidential Blue House would no longer collect political funds, the establishment took notice. Cabinet ministers and ruling Democratic Liberal Party leaders were ordered to make public declaration of their assets. As a result, several top lawmakers, including the speaker of the National Assembly, were forced to quit after revelations that they had amassed wealth or committed other 'irregularities'. When the new Cabinet held its first meeting, it pledged to take the initiative in 'rooting out corruption'. A few days later, with some media prompting, four ministers were themselves rooted out. First to go was Kim Sang-chul, the new mayor of Seoul, a ministerial-level post, for illegal use of greenbelt land. He was followed by Park Yang-il, the Health-Social Affairs minister, dismissed for alleged property speculation, and the Justice Minister, Park Hee-tae, under fire because his US-born daughter dropped her Korean citizenship in order to enter a prestigious Korean university under a quota reserved for foreigners. The Construction Minister, Huh Ja-young, was fired for alleged 'financial irregularities'.

Prosecutors formed special task forces as part of the war against corruption in officialdom. Soon the wave swept through all sectors. The top brass had been exempted from having to publicly declare their assets thanks to the Army Chief of Staff, Kim Dong-jin, who had successfully persuaded the Blue House that it would be bad for discipline, and would help north Korean intelligence develop profiles on south Korea's generals. But this line in the sand was soon crossed. In April 1993, government prosecutors filed bribery charges against two top military officers in the opening volley of a broad drive against corruption in the military. A retired Marine Corps commander, a former chief of naval operations and three other officers were arrested in a promotions-for-cash scandal.

A retired admiral was charged with taking the equivalent of about £300,000 from six naval and marine corps officers for promotions between 1989 and 1991, when he was chief of naval operations. One of these officers was charged with having raised his cash from junior officers whose promotion he arranged. This promotions scandal was just the tip of an iceberg. Just as professors frequently have to donate to colleges to buy tenure, and lawmakers have to donate to party coffers to secure positions, paying for promotions was a long-standing practice in the Korean military. The actual transactions were usually conducted by ambitious wives.

Universities were also targeted, and the widespread practice of private owned colleges accepting donations from wealthy parents to secure places for their children was exposed. In one celebrated case, Hong Jung-hee, an Ehwa Women's University professor and the godmother of the Korean classical ballet world, was jailed for taking the equivalent of tens of thousands of pounds at a time from parents. Again, this was the tip of the iceberg. In fact, the tips of two icebergs, the educational and the artistic. Paying professors was common, as was paying for roles in performances and bribing judges for places in competitions.

The ferocity of Kim Young-sam's anti-corruption drive silenced the critics who figured that he lacked the moral and intellectual courage, and freedom from political obligations, to effect significant reform.

But even those registering their approval did so with some reservations. By forcing through laws requiring seven thousand top public officials to declare their assets, and by outlawing the use of false names in financial transactions, the new president was clearly signalling an effort to put an end to corruption, rather than just root out opponents and swing others around to his agenda. Nevertheless, there were sufficient elements of this latter aspect of the classic anti-corruption drive to make people feel ambivalent. Although some of Kim Young-sam's allies suffered in his campaign, the main casualties appeared to be his political opponents. One was Park Chul-on, a former prosecutor who, as an in-law of former President Roh Tae-woo, rose to become one of the most powerful politicians in the late 1980s. Once heralded as the architect of Roh's *nordpolitik* outreach to the communist allies of rival north Korea, which led East bloc states to recognise south Korea between 1988 and 1992, Park was accused of receiving a £400,000 white envelope from the godfather of Korea's one-armed-bandit salons in exchange for getting tax officials to stop an investigation. Park denied the charges and said he was a victim of political revenge. 'I am helpless, like a fish on the chopping block,' he told the reporters, who were positioned outside the Prosecutor General's Office to catch the latest victims of the anti-corruption drive.

At first, people kept their heads down and waited for a return to business as usual, but as the campaign continued, it began to be taken more seriously and people began to get the message that the old ways of doing business were changing, perhaps for ever. Lawmakers looked for new, ethical ways to raise cash. Politicians formed support groups to raise funds, ending the traditional collusion between lawmaker and businessman. The military and judiciary set up internal procedures to get rid of corruption.

However, animosity began to develop towards Kim Young-sam himself. The opening move of his campaign – the declaration that now he was in the Blue House, he would not take a penny of under-the-table money – led to an obvious question. What about before? Obviously, he was giving himself an amnesty. He also rejected calls for investigation into the crimes of his predecessors, Chun Doo-hwan and Roh Tae-woo, on the grounds that it was important to respect the office of the presidency in the interests of political stability. The victims of his reform campaign were not given any such grace. The common practices of the past were now declared crimes for which they could be prosecuted. This unfairness highlighted the sense that, impressive though the campaign was, the president was imposing his idea of 'democracy' on the people, rather than allowing democratic institutions do their work on the basis of fair and justly applied law.

In my more cynical moments, the entire anti-corruption campaign struck me as sophisticated political manipulation by a president determined to keep his opponents and every other potential opponent guessing. This cynicism reached its zenith at the point at which the campaign seemed, to international society, to be most impressive – the arrests of the former presidents. In June 1995 the ruling party fared very badly in local government elections. There were rumblings that the remnants of supporters of Chun Doo-hwan and Roh Tae-woo were going to split from Kim's ruling camp and use the ex-presidents' slush funds to finance a new political party.

This event never happened. An opposition politician claimed in the National Assembly that the former President, Roh Tae-woo, had amassed a large fund for political use. Many analysts figured the information had been slipped to him from the goverment. Roh went on television and admitted he had a fund of the equivalent of US$650 million. Chun was later alleged to have an even larger fund. Everyone had known that presidents were given large amounts of money by *chaebol* chairmen for their political funds, but these figures were so staggering that Kim Young-sam could no longer protect his predecessors. Roh Tae-woo and Chun Doo-hwan were arrested. Laws were quickly amended to allow them to be prosecuted for their 1979 *coup d'état* and the massacre of protesters in Kwangju in 1980, even though a court had earlier ruled that the statute of limitations had run out on these crimes. The heads of the *chaebol* were interrogated and several were tried with the former presidents. Chun was sentenced to death and Roh to twenty-two-and-a-half years. These were commuted to life and seventeen years respectively on appeal. (Chun, Roh and seventeen co-defendants were amnestied in December 1997 by President Kim on the request of Kim Dae-jung, who had just won the presidential election.)

The trial was seen internationally as signifying the arrival of true democracy and justice in Korea. It certainly furthered the process, established under Roh's rule, that former presidents could be held to account for wrongdoings. (Several of Chun's family members and associates had been jailed on charges of corruption and abuse of power under Roh. Chun was not himself tried, but had returned his political funds (although not all, it turned out), and spent two years in internal exile in a Buddhist temple.)

However, the key test of the democratic progress, and the measure of success of the anti-corruption drive during Kim Young-sam's rule, was that his own son unexpectedly fell victim to it. When Hanbo, the country's second-largest steel company, collapsed in 1997, investigators found its chairman, Chung Tai-soo, had been giving enormous bribes to politicians, bureaucrats and bankers. Chung was sentenced to fifteen years for bribery, fraud and embezzlement, and four lawmakers, a former home affairs minister and the heads of three banks were given sentences ranging from three to seven years for bribery. The president's son, Kim Hyun-chol, was also investigated in connection with this case and eventually jailed on charges of bribery and tax evasion. Prosecutors said he had hidden his money in over a hundred bank accounts.

What this case demonstrated was that a president can no longer even protect his own family while he is in office. For Kim Young-sam, it was an unintended consequence of the campaign he had unleashed so dramatically at the start of his rule. But it indicated the extent of its success.

Chapter Twenty

TOWARDS THE THIRD
MIRACLE

In other parts of east Asia, such as China, Japan, Hong Kong and Taiwan, economic development seems to suit the character of the people. As people often note, the Chinese come across as natural entrepreneurs. They do not have to be organised into making money, just allowed to do it. The Japanese may not appear to be so individually entrepreneurial, but they work well together. The Koreans are different. In comparison with their neighbours, they seem emotionally complex, too dominated by other considerations. Their emotions often subvert pursuit of what would appear to be their best interest. For example, at this time of writing, the Koreans are being helped through a financial collapse by the International Monetary Fund. And yet, instead of taking the money, and attacking their, albeit difficult, problems, they become distracted by issues of pride. They continued to conceal the extent of their difficulties even to the IMF, which would help them. They seem to refer to events as if the IMF is the problem. They talk of 'overcoming the IMF' when in fact the IMF is helping them overcome themselves. I make this point not to suggest the Koreans are especially incompetent. Far from it. As we have seen, they have developed in a remarkable way. Economic crises are in some regards a natural part of change, and no country has escaped them. The point is that the Koreans often seem such unlikely candidates for economic success.

No one in 1945 could have imagined that Korea would become such an important international economy in such a relatively short time. Korea grew because it is a child of superpower division. Were it not for the Cold War rivalry, and its primary interest to protect Japan, America would not have found an interest in Korea. A futurist might have guessed that Korea by the end of the twentieth century would have been a communist state like China, or an authoritarian socialist state like Burma, of minimal relevance to the West.

The story of the two Koreas is not a tale of two bickering brothers in the family of nations. It is more like the Man in the Iron Mask. Each considers the other to be an impostor. Each has cast the other into a dungeon, refusing to recognise its right to exist. Each fears the other's murderous intent.

Unification is the stated goal of both sides. An innocent traveller may wonder, then, why has it not happened? When asked this, Koreans of north and south tend to blame others – foreign powers, political leaders. In fact, the answer lies in the meaning of the division. Two options were created and one choice is to be. Unification is a win-lose affair. It is important to note that the two Koreas have not unified because, for both, each unification goal has meant the removal of the other side. The goal of the communists was a communist Korea; the goal of the anti-communists was a Korea without communists. Until now, the Koreans would not permit two states to exist. Even the various proposals that would officially allow two sides to exist until they gradually merge are designed as hostile, slow-motion takeovers.

From the start, military force was the most obvious first path to unification. From 1945, there were numerous border skirmishes started by both sides. In 1950, after the United States withdrew from the South, the North got the approval from its allies for its plan to try to unify by force.[240] It launched a full-scale war, but failed. Close study of the period suggests that in the context of the left-right struggle of the time and given the fact that Kim Il-sung may have been misled into believing that his troops would be welcomed by south Koreans, the conflict was almost inevitable. It is possible, on the grounds that Kim's attack was an attempt to unify the nation, that moral condemnation will fade with the passing of the generations which suffered. This really depends on whether future generations of Koreans identify with south Korea of the 1950s, or whether they see a unified Korea as a wholly new and different state, born of reunification. If the former, it is possible that Kim Il-sung will go down as one of the greatest villains of Korean history. If the latter, then the division itself will be seen as the main culprit.

Kim Il-sung's case will not be helped by the fact that he continued, after the war, to pursue the forceful approach by other means.

The two Koreas needed outside mediation for their problem. In the 1970s, the American statesman, Henry Kissinger, suggested 'cross-recognition' of Seoul and Pyongyang by each other's main allies. One problem with this suggestion was that, for the Koreans, as we have seen, their deeper struggle has been with traditional dependency on outsiders. There's a fine line between support and domination when it comes to having superpower allies. Unification may not have been possible while the superpower allies were opposed to one another. Now that the Cold War is over, it is apparent that the key actors preventing reunification are the Koreans themselves. Reunification will not happen until the Koreans want to do it. The other issue has been that these allies naturally have their own considerations regarding diplomatic relations with their ally's enemy. In the end, Pyongyang's main allies opened embassies in Seoul when it suited them, and despite furious objections from north Korea. This happened between 1989 and 1992. So far, Seoul's allies have had no wish to unconditionally open relations with Pyongyang.

America is the key nation in the Korean question. It has had its own reasons to hate north Korea. Barring Iraq in the 1990s, north Korea may be the most demonised state in the American political imagination simply because it has had no defenders, interpreters or lobbyists in Washington ever since it was founded. Even the American left shunned north Korea, apart from one or two obscure associations, such as a visit to Pyongyang in the 1970s by the Black Panther leader, Eldridge Cleaver. It was on the official list of terrorist states. The images associated with north Korea were of fanatic violence and irrationality: brainwashing of Korean War POWs, the 1976 axe murder of two American officers in Panmunjom. North Korea was a weird and vicious cult as far as Americans were concerned. The little information that came out confirmed that the feeling was mutual. North Korea used to refer to Americans as 'wolves in human form', and withheld information from its citizens that might prove otherwise. Ordinary north Koreans are unaware that Americans have landed on the moon, and have never heard of Elvis Presley, Michael Jackson or Coca-Cola.

After the collapse of the Soviet Union, north Korea began to get nervous. It was accustomed to playing off China and the Soviet Union for aid. With the Soviets gone, in 1991, Kim Il-sung felt he needed relations with the United States, either because he felt vulnerable, or because he wanted to find a new superpower to play off against China, for aid. He invited the former president, Jimmy Carter, and the evangelist, Billy Graham, to visit. Carter declined several times on the instructions of the State Department. Kim skilfully used a nuclear development programme in the early 1990s as a lever to get Washington into bilateral talks. At this time, however, it was almost taboo in Washington to propose a policy of talks, let alone diplomatic relations, with Pyongyang. North Korea then created full-blown panic by withdrawing from the international Nuclear Non-Proliferation Treaty, and eventually forced America to change its position.

By some irony, analysts and officials in Washington responsible for north Korea policy held a significant policy meeting in April 1993, on the day after an FBI attack on a religious group near Waco, Texas, after a long siege, killed seventy-two people. Analysts drew a comparison between the Branch Davidian cult and its leader, David Koresh, and Kim Il-sung's north Korea, and made the point that north Korea should not be painted into a corner.[241] From this point, the consensus grew that Washington and Pyongyang should talk, simply because the alternative was escalating tension. The talks were not easy, and many policy-makers came to believe that it may even make more sense to make a pre-emptive military strike against north Korea before it developed nuclear weapons. Tensions between these policy-makers peaked in the late spring of 1994, and were defused by a visit by Jimmy Carter to north Korea. Kim Il-sung died in July 1994, but as a result of his agreement with Carter, talks were revived and eventually an agreement was signed. However, as of this writing, there are still no diplomatic relations in place. The Korean War armistice has not been negotiated into a peace.

With America now at least willing to talk to north Korea, the main obstacle to reconciliation is the Pyongyang government's fear for its own survival. How can it deal with the obvious fact of its failure? As it began to face this dilemma, its problems mounted after disastrous harvests throughout the 1990s, and floods in 1995 and 1996, which devastated farmland. The regime has tried to portray itself as struggling with natural disasters. However, it is becoming increasingly apparent to its own citizens, whom it can no longer feed, that it is struggling with its own failure. After Kim Il-sung's death in 1994, his son, Kim Jong-il, officially mourned for three years before taking over. Although for north Koreans this mourning was in keeping with Confucian practice, it created a bizarre sense of a nation in limbo. During this period of limbo, the country laboured under worsening food shortages. International aid agencies reported that some areas of the country were suffering famine.

Pyongyang knows that the worst thing that can happen is for it to cease to be a military threat and become a 'humanitarian problem'. It is not confident that, given the choice, south Korea and America will permit it to survive. Therefore, it continues to be difficult and talk belligerently. It seeks ties with and aid from America and Japan. Beyond that, it wants to be left alone. The irony is that the authors of the *Juche* ideology of self-reliance, that speaks so deeply to the Korean soul, are coming round to a kind of welfare dependency on foreign power, while the south Korean 'puppets' they have been insulting for decades have created an independent economy in the global system.[242]

Time may be running out for the north Koreans. The regime has lost the affection of the people as a result of the famine. It may be just a matter of time before it loses control.

At present, north Korea's main strength is that it remains capable of waging war. It has been developing weapons of mass destruction. Despite an agreement with the United States not to use its nuclear-energy programme to make weapons-grade material, there is actually no means of verifying compliance. It also has biological and chemical weapons. While its conventional capability is affected by economic decay, the mass-destruction weapons are relatively cheap to produce and are thus immune to the wider collapse. It is possible that the Kim Jong-il government may become more desperate.

Since Park Chung-hee, the south Korean strategy for reunification has been to build national power. This has given us the economic and political 'Miracles on the Han River'.

Unification was not envisaged as a practical possibility by the south Koreans until the collapse of western communism and the unification of Germany. Seoul sent analysts to its embassy in Germany to study the details of the process and began to look very realistically at how it might work. They came to a startling conclusion. If the North were to collapse, the economic and social burden of reunification might ruin the South. Various calculations were made about the cost of reunification. The figures were rather meaningless because they were based on some wild assumptions about the north Korean economy, but the results were sufficiently alarming to pose an unusual problem for the south Korean government. It realised it had to oppose unification. I first became aware of this when a senior foreign ministry official in 1991 told me in an off-the-record chat in very forceful and clear terms, 'We do not want unification.' Until then, in all my time in Korea I had only ever heard one person say that and she was a barmaid, saying that she didn't like the idea of serving drinks to poor north Koreans. I thought the diplomat was joking. But he was dead serious and expressing it clearly so that I would understand. When I asked him for an on-the-record version he said, 'We Koreans want the peaceful and democratic unification of our country. This should happen in a step-by-step way.' Then he added, off-the-record again, 'Maybe in about thirty or forty years' time.' In fact, this has become the consensus in south Korea. What the south Koreans want now is reconciliation, not reunification. This does not mean they oppose unification entirely, but simply that they prefer postponement.

The north Koreans do not yet believe this is the south Korean position. They see over the DMZ a reflection of their own motivation – that, if there is an opportunity to unify, the South will go for it.

Although there is deep mistrust on both sides, there is a common and ironic moving away from reunification as a policy goal. A sensible solution would appear to be for north Korea to formally give up its goal of communising south Korea and negotiate a reconciliation in order that it may develop its economy and enter into an arrangement with south Korea for step-by-step reunification. The dilemma for the regime is that the rationale for its existence and the intense militarisation of its society is based on the perceived threat of south Korea and the need to 'liberate' it. To change this stance and accept the legitimacy of south Korea and live beside it as the poorer brother may be impossible for the son of Kim Il-sung.

However, it may be possible for his successor. A successor may be able to disclaim responsibility for the past and propose dependency on south Korea. Such an arrangement may be considered a miracle of sorts for it is really reconciliation, not the final political arrangement, that will mark the key moment of reunification.

This situation would suit the north Korean government, and the south Koreans. However, it might not suit the north Korean people. If their government has to continue to repress them brutally to make them comply with a postponement of unification, they may take to the streets in the manner of south Korea in 1987, or worse, in the manner of Kwangju in 1980. At that point, people power may force unification. Perhaps then, the Koreans of both sides and their political leaders would simply have to do it.

Whichever scenario unfolds, gradual or rapid reunification, we await the deciding moment of the reunification of the divided country. What would make it a miracle would be a peaceful process by which the north Koreans are generously treated and embraced in a single state which is democratic and based on the free market. This state would either be an expanded south Korea or a new state based on the systems that south Korea has been developing. From then, it would simply be called Korea.

Chapter 21

NEXT GENERATION

It has been five years since this book was written and, given the pace of Korean development, five years represents a generation.

For the new generation, the big picture remains the same. The two Koreas are still divided. In south Korea, democracy gains ever greater expression – indeed, for young people, dictatorship is pre-history. They've heard of it, but are not so aware of the details of how it interfered in people's lives. Despite the continuing protest culture, tear gas was not used once during the five-year term of President Kim Dae-jung (1998–2003). The economy continues to grow. In north Korea, the people still labor under the rule of Kim Jong-il. They are recovering from the famine of the mid-90s, but malnutrition remains a problem and the country relies on international aid.

The south Korean government undertook a major change of approach to the North and introduced a 'Sunshine Policy' of engagement, ending decades of Cold War containment. But despite some high points – most notably a historic summit in June 2000 in Pyongyang between Kim Dae-jung and Kim Jong-il – and an increase of exchanges between the two sides, this led to nothing that we could characterize as a breakthrough. In fact, the increased exposure to the North has underscored for south Koreans the differences between the two peoples, differences which seem to grow with every year that they remain apart.

A foreigner can walk the streets of Seoul now and be ignored. Even kindergarten kids, emerging from a subway station with their teachers for a downtown excursion, will ignore Caucasians. Back in pre-history kids in groups might take up the cry, 'Hello! Hello!' but not any more. My theory is that the change is due to the fad for coloring hair. There was a time

249

when foreigners joked about the fact that Koreans all had black hair – can you point Mr. Kim out? Yes, he's the guy in the crowd over there with the black hair, ho ho – but now women of all ages color their hair and quite a few young men do, too. With all those blond and redheaded Koreans around, kids have to look closely to realize you're a foreigner. Then, if they do notice, they might surprise you with a proper English sentence, 'Hello. My name is Kim Young-hee. How are yoooo?' So intense is the parental drive for them to get on in life that kids are being taught English in kindergarten.

The most notable feature of the new Koreans is how Internet-connected they are. As we have noted, there is a tendency of Koreans to hurl themselves with unrestrained vigor into whatever they do. In the last few years, they have been hurling themselves into cyberspace. As a result, south Korea is without a doubt the most wired-up nation in the galaxy. By mid-2003, 70 per cent of the country's 46 million people had broadband Internet connections at home. Watch the people flow down any city street and count how many are using their cell phones, most of them high-speed third-generation models. Companies are working on a plan to build base stations everywhere that will allow people to make wireless connections to the Internet wherever they are. The Korean company NCSoft is the world's biggest online gaming network. Seventy per cent of equities trading is online. Around 10 million Koreans chat online, 1 million use video chatting, 3.6 million have avatars – little thingies that represent you in chat rooms and email. There's an association of psychologists specializing in Internet addiction. Its head, Kim Hyun-soo, was quoted in *Forbes* saying that 40 per cent of teenagers and 10 per cent of the general population are addicted to the Internet.[243] Sex figures pretty highly in all this, with the Internet accounting for a massive surge in teen prostitution and marital infidelity.

The Internet boom, which was unexpected, was ironically helped along by the 1997 Asian financial crisis – now known simply to Koreans as 'The IMF,' after the bailout by the International Monetary Fund. Many bright young people laid off from the big conglomerates went on to create the Internet companies that provided the software, so to speak, to the hardware of the broadband network, which had already been laid.

These new Koreans are going to places like Croatia for their summer holidays and to New Zealand for their honeymoons. They're different from their parents in that they're comfortable eating foreign food and drinking wine. When they travel overseas, they don't need an emergency kit containing instant noodles and kimchi.

We got a good look at the new Koreans in the summer of 2002 during the soccer World Cup. When Korea and Japan bid for the event, the governing soccer body FIFA stunned both by deciding that they should cohost. Given that this is the most widely watched event across the globe, cohosting was a risky proposition for the Koreans, who feared they would be upstaged by superior Japanese organization. But, in the end, the Korean effort was stupendous. The centerpiece of the preparations was the high-tech World Cup stadium in Seoul. In a nice piece of symbolism, the modern facility was part of a development that included a park atop two very large flat hills, which were once the city's garbage dump. In fact, the site is believed to be the world's largest landfill. Once a flat island in the Han River, the daily refuse thrown out by the citizens of Seoul grew over three decades into two massive mounds. These were the source of the stink that wafted over the city when the wind was blowing east. Now, drained and greened, they are a place for relaxation. The methane from the refuse is used to power the park's lights.

In early 2002, in the lead-up to the May 31 kick-off, the issue of dog-eating came up, just as it had prior to the 1988 Seoul Olympics. FIFA was being lobbied by activists in Europe and asked Chung Mong-joon, the cochairman of the Korean organizing committee and himself a FIFA vice-president, to do something. Chung decided he couldn't. In a TV interview, animal rights crusader Brigitte Bardot aggressively attacked the practice and riled the Korean press. Unlike in 1988, when dog soup restaurants were closed down or renamed so that foreigners wouldn't know what they were, this time the Korean response was 'up yours'. It's enough that laws are now in place regarding methods of slaughter (although enforcement remains questionable), the Koreans thought. The new self-assertion, taken nervously, I should add, had an interesting effect on foreign reporters. Instead of the usual snide stories about Rover being served up for Sunday lunch, reporters began going out and sampling it for themselves.

Before the World Cup, officials in Seoul were concerned that the media and public would behave badly if the Korean team didn't do well. Or worse, got beaten by the US. Earlier in the year, during the Winter Olympics in Salt Lake City, we'd had a taste of that bad behavior when an Australian judge ruled that a Korean speed skater had blocked another in a gold medal race and disqualified him. When the gold went to the second skater, an American, the entire Korean nation, it seemed, went apoplectic. McDonald's and other US brands were boycotted. Commentators foamed that the Olympics were being rigged in favor of the US to soothe the wounds of September 11. (Americans in Korea, meanwhile, were asking, 'What is speed skating?')

As it happened, though, the Korean team played superbly. With each game more and more red-shirted supporters turned out in the streets to watch the matches on giant screens. For foreign visitors, joining these crowds was the experience of a lifetime. The young people who made up the crowds were not soccer fans – in fact, they didn't always seem to understand the action well. They were fans of Korea. They roared as each player's face came up on the screen before kick-off and, amazingly for a people noted for xenophobia, they saved the biggest roar for a foreigner – Guus Hiddink, their team's Dutch coach. At the end of the match, the hundreds of thousands in the street picked up the newspaper they had been sitting on in the road and swept their rubbish into heaps to make the cleanup easier for the garbage men.

And when their team scored, 46 million Koreans erupted. Watching the Korea-Portugal game on screens set up in the Italian restaurant in the basement of the Seoul Finance Center, I remember bouncing up and down on the sofa seats with a bottle of Heineken frothing in my hand and hugging complete strangers. Such is the power of the 'beautiful game', as Pele has called it, that in those moments Korea was a nation gone nuts. In the stadiums, the Korean matches were electrifying as the Red Devils supporters – who were real soccer fans – led the crowds. One of my friends, a British sportswriter, said he thought Korea-Italy was the best football match he had attended in his life, both for the quality of the play and the atmosphere in the stadium. Korea won, cheered along by the Red Devils slogan of 'Again, 1966', a reference to the upset during the World Cup in England in 1966 when north Korea beat Italy to get through to the quarterfinals. (At that time, the dictatorship in south Korea did not allow the news to be reported. Koreans remember learning that seven teams had made the quarterfinals, and thinking it was odd that one was missing.)

The Koreans beat Poland, drew – fortunately – with the US, and beat Portugal, Italy and Spain to get to the semifinals, where they were beaten by Germany. For that last match, my wife and I were in the section of the stadium where, at the start of each half, a massive flag rolled out over our heads and thousands of us swayed under it. The Germans scored one goal. At the final whistle, the Korean crowds savored the end of their dream and then the Red Devils struck up a chant of 'Kenchanna' (It's OK), and as the players left the field the whole stadium picked up the hauntingly uplifting melody of the Korean folk song *Arirang*. Hiddink became the most-loved foreigner since General Douglas MacArthur. His trademark enthusiastic uppercut every time his boys scored inspired a nation and was repeated ad nauseam on TV. Corporations began analyzing his management techniques to see if there were lessons for business. There were. Some were strategic – Hiddink focused on fitness to the extent that his team was the fittest of the tournament. Others cut through cultural nonsense. For example, Hiddink ended the practice of younger players having to wait until the older players had their food before they got theirs, and generally bowing and scraping around them. He also selected his players solely by ability, rather than by seniority. Basically, the kind of stuff foreign business people had been trying to tell Korean managers for years. Kim Dae-jung made Hiddink the first honorary citizen of the Republic of Korea, ever.

In a tragic accident in June 2002, during the World Cup, two little girls were crushed by a US military vehicle on maneuvers on a public highway. Some weeks later, this accident was stoked up by activists into another full-blown and prolonged spasm of anti-Americanism. When a US court martial in Korea found the driver and the commander of the vehicle, both US soldiers, not guilty of negligent homicide, the nation went ballistic. Many Koreans, fed by Internet disinformation, thought the killing was deliberate and even those who knew it wasn't thought the two men should be sacrificed to assuage public anger. Protestors started holding candlelight vigils in downtown Seoul near the US embassy. In a small park nearby, activists set up an exhibition of the 'crimes of American soldiers', showing some very unpleasant pictures of murdered prostitutes and other such victims. One diplomat told me he'd seen some nuns in the park innocently wearing 'Fucking USA' badges, after the title of a current song.

In some ways, it seemed that Koreans were drawing deep into their modern history and expressing their complex frustrations at their dependency on the US. At another level, it seemed as if they were trying to rediscover the sense of community through street events that they had experienced during the World Cup. Faced with the image of hundreds of protestors shredding a giant Stars and Stripes, some US commentators wrote columns suggesting that perhaps the US should pull out its troops if they were not wanted. In response, Korean NGOs then accused the US of yet another crime – failure to understand their anti-Americanism. Only a minority want the troops out, they claimed. The majority just want the US to have a less condescending attitude toward Korea. At that point, I had a revelation: Americans are from Mars, Koreans are from Venus. After years of trying to figure Korea out, I realized that my approach had been wrong. These two countries need a therapist, not policy wonks.

One of the ironies of Korean frustration with the US is that it is perpetuated by a certain intellectual cowardice on the part of opinion leaders and politicians who fail to articulate the positive aspects of the alliance and fail to condemn acts of anti-Americanism out of fear of being branded traitors. This cowardice makes sense because Korean politicians recognize anti-Americanism for what it is – passing emotion. They do not take it literally and figure that the best thing to do is get on the right side of it.

The protests over the death of the two girls carried on into the presidential election campaign in late 2002. Lee Hoi-chang, the candidate for the normally very pro-American opposition Grand National Party, signed a petition calling for a revision of the Status of Forces Agreement, which allowed the US military custody of the two soldiers, and had a photo opportunity with the dead girls' parents.

Chung Mong-joon, the FIFA vice-president, was also running. For a long time, polls suggested he would be the most popular candidate. After Lee pulled ahead, Chung joined forces with Roh Moo-hyun, the ruling Millennium Democratic Party candidate. Roh, a straight-talking, self-educated lawyer – who declined to sign the anti-American petition, saying it was 'not appropriate' – had been selected through a primary system, which was being used for the first time in Korean politics. His party's leaders were so convinced that this had all been a mistake that they hardly bothered to campaign for him.

On election day in December, something unusual happened. By around noon, exit polls indicated that Roh, who was popular with young people and who, despite his refusal to sign the SOFA petition, was benefiting most from the anti-US sentiment, was losing. His supporters, who had been making heavy use of the Internet, went on to chat rooms and sent out hundreds of thousands of e-mails and text messages to encourage people to get out and vote. After lunch, exit polls showed Roh had pulled ahead. That night, as the votes were counted, I had some friends round for an election party. My house was directly opposite the home of Lee Hoi-chang, and the police and TV crews parked outside added to the atmosphere. Very quickly into the count, however, it became apparent that Roh was going to win. Lee left his home to make a concession speech and by the time he returned, the TV cameras had all left. When we called out to him from the balcony, he looked up, waved, and stepped into his house. It was a moment that seemed to mark the end of an era. Had he won, Lee would have represented a continuation of the same generation of political leaders that had ruled for the last forty years.

The outgoing president, Kim Dae-jung, retired as the grand old man of Asian democracy, ending a remarkable political career that began in the 1950s. Although no single figure led the Korean democratic struggle, Kim more than any came to represent the dogged determination of the Koreans to shake free from their ancient culture of authoritarianism. Kim chalked up some remarkable achievements. He introduced some vigorous reforms in the financial sector and attracted record-high amounts of foreign investment to stabilize the economy after the financial crisis. He personally encouraged Internet use. Women's rights improved markedly under his watch. Civic groups became increasingly active. Kim Dae-jung's finest moment came when he was awarded the 2000 Nobel Peace Prize for his contribution to democracy and for the summit with Kim Jong-il.

Despite all this, a sense of failure infects perceptions of his rule. Like his democratically elected predecessors, Roh Tae-woo (1988–93) and Kim Young-sam (1993–98), Kim Dae-jung enjoyed approval ratings in the 80s and 90s at the start of his term. By the end, it seemed as if, apart from family members, no one could find anything good to say about him. Even in his birthplace of Hawi-do, a remote island off the south coast, people were grumbling when I visited in 2001. The reasons are difficult to fathom. If you asked people why they disapproved of Kim Dae-jung, they couldn't tell you, and if you reminded them of his achievements, they would become irrational. There were the usual corruption scandals, even involving his own sons, two of whom were jailed. There were failed policies, most notably in health insurance. But these alone did not explain the gut disapproval. It was in part driven by the unrelenting negativity of the major media to Kim Dae-jung, a position which was itself puzzling.

The simple explanation for this phenomenon is that, however hard they try, Korea's democratic presidents have failed to meet a level of expectation that was set by a very undemocratic president. Koreans are haunted by the ghost of Park Chung-hee. The father of modern Korea shuffles and whispers in their minds, telling them that presidents have to match up to his nation-building standard. And so far not one has asked how this is possible when he's limited to a single five-year term, when you have to persuade rather than issue orders, and when, anyway, the nation is built? In other words, no president has articulated the limitations of the democratic presidency. Instead, with each election, the triumphant winner implies with grand egoistic vision – restructuring politics, ending corruption, unifying with north Korea, saving the planet, greening the galaxy – that he has unlimited power. In short, presidents raise expectations and then fail to follow through. When he took over in February 1998 during the financial crisis, Kim Dae-jung had a perfect opportunity to keep expectations low and make a Churchillian declaration that he had nothing to offer but blood, sweat, toil, and tears. Instead, he promised that the crisis would be solved in three years. His administration did a stellar job of stabilizing and restructuring the economy, but he wasn't getting sufficient approval points for it because he had promised more.

At a deeper level, the democratic presidents have disappointed because their mindset and style of governance has remained authoritarian. For all his democratic beliefs, Kim Dae-jung had been a factional boss who had operated in an authoritarian culture all his life. Despite the democrats at the helm, the tendency has remained for officials to operate in a top-down manner. Policy is often developed and implemented with a minimum of debate.

One case in point was how the new system for rendering Korean words into the Latin alphabet was foisted on the world in the summer of 2000. The original idea behind the new system was to get rid of the diacritic marks that distinguish different vowel sounds because English computer keyboards didn't have them. This was sound in principle, but there appears to have been no real debate between the committee of experts tasked by government with devising the changes and the people most likely to be impacted. As a result, there was no consideration of making exceptions for proper names. Thus, the city of Pusan overnight became 'Busan'. The metropolitan government of Inchon considered resisting when it was ordered to reinvent itself as 'Incheon', but quickly caved. All over the country soft consonants became hard – Kwangju became Gwangju, Taegu became Daegu – and certain 'o' sounds became 'eo'. According to the plan, company names and even personal names are scheduled to be changed in line with alphabetical correctness within the decade. In truth, though, it's hard to imagine all the Gims and Barks in Gorea going along with it.

Whether President Roh Moo-hyun can articulate the limited powers of the presidency and sufficiently reduce expectation to retire popular in 2008 remains to be seen. But he did get off to a good, humble start. In one of his victory speeches, he said that, as president, he'd like to pop out occasionally from the Blue House to a roadside tent to knock back a few glasses of liquor with the people. He also gave his first interview to an Internet-based publication.

Roh also demonstrated that he can risk unpopularity to do what is right. In January 2003, during the transition period, an official at the Ministry of Finance and Economy received a call from Moody's in New York advising him ahead of time that the ratings agency planned to downgrade Korea's sovereign rating.[244] The reasons cited were continuing anti-Americanism, the election of a new president whom *The New York Times* had referred to in one story as radically pro-labor, and the ongoing issue of north Korean nuclear weapons development. All of this was dampening investor confidence, Moody's said. The Korean official invited Moody's to send researchers to Seoul to meet the transition team before making its judgment. The offer was accepted. Within a few days, Roh had publicly called for a halt to anti-American protests, had met with the commander-in-chief of US Forces in Korea, addressed a joint meeting of the American and European chambers of commerce in Seoul, and given interviews to *The New York Times* and CNN. The wave of anti-American sentiment subsided and Moody's was duly impressed with the transition team. (Eventually, the rating was downgraded, but the reason given was the north Korean issue).

A central theme of Roh's presidency will be his vision of Korea as a hub of Asia. This is not new. The outgoing government had already been saying that Korea has to develop a niche as a northeast Asian logistics hub if it is to survive in the face of an economically developing China. The notion has been extended to include the idea of the country as a financial hub. At the time of writing, the hub idea is more of a slogan than anything else. Banners proclaim 'Dynamic Korea, Hub of Asia', although it is not quite clear who they are aimed at. An indication of the kind of effect of such sloganeering is that, among the 7,000 or so entries in an Internet-based competition to come up with a slogan for Seoul in 2002, several hundred entries suggested 'Hub of Asia'. In fact, there were even a dozen misspelled, 'Herb of Asia'. The winner was 'Hi! Seoul'. Personally, I still like an old one that proclaimed, 'My Seoul, Our Seoul' (you have to say it out loud). There is considerable cynicism in the foreign business community about Korea's ability to become a hub. In logistics, becoming a hub means increasing transshipment cargo to China. But why would Chinese ports sit back and let this happen? If it is to become a financial hub, Seoul would need to become international like Singapore. It's hard to imagine the Koreans discovering the pragmatic openness necessary for this. True, we have learned by now not to doubt the Koreans when they put their mind to something, but my money is on this national vision being quietly replaced by something else.

But, as with everything to do with Korea, any forecasting about national vision is clouded by the question of how to resolve the matter of north Korea. That question gained intensity in the post–September 11 world. While the two Koreas are playing out the last act of the Cold War, their allies now view the standoff through the lens of the War on Terror. north Korea's inclusion in the Axis of Evil, with Iraq and Iran, in US President George W. Bush's 2002 State of the Union address put the spotlight on Kim Jong-il. A few months later, while the case of war was being built against Iraq, US assistant secretary of state James Kelly went to Pyongyang for talks and surprised his hosts by producing some kind of proof – we're not sure what – that north Korea was working on a covert nuclear program. Instead of lying, the north Koreans decided to come clean. Yes, we are, they said. This bombshell confession made headlines around the world. Aside from the possibility that north Korea might use such weapons itself, the specter of it selling weapons and know-how to rogue states and to terror groups sent shudders through Moscow and Beijing, as well as Seoul, Tokyo, and Washington. The admission nullified the spirit of Pyongyang's 1994 agreement with the United States to close down its plutonium-based nuclear program, if not the letter – this new program is different in that it is based on enriched uranium. In response, the Korean Peninsula Energy Development Organization (KEDO), the consortium formed between the United States, south Korea, Japan, and the EU to supply new light water reactors and oil to north Korea as part of the 1994 deal, elected to suspend the oil shipments.

At this writing, Kim Jong-il seems willing to bargain the nukes away for security guarantees from the United States, which would ensure his regime's survival. In an ironic shift, south Koreans are in favor of providing such guarantees, while US policymakers are torn between 'regime-changers' who see no gain in dealing with a man – Kim Jong-il – who President Bush considers to be evil, and those who would be more pragmatic and negotiate the nukes away.

But, you have to ask, what kind of assurances could the US and its allies give that the paranoid regime in Pyongyang could trust enough not to want to develop some new 'insurance policy' of mass destruction? Probably none. A deal may be signed, but the regime of Kim Jong-il will continue to focus its binoculars on external enemies to justify the awful dictatorial controls that keep its people in misery.

The sad fact is that the standoff between the two Koreas may yet go on for a lifetime. Or it may end sooner. Either way, when it does happen, it will be thrilling and good, for Korea will once again be whole.

Notes

1 In 1234. Ref. Lee Ki-baik, *A New History of Korea*, translated by Edward W. Wagner (Cambridge, Mass: Harvard University Press, 1984), p. 170.

2 The tensions were defused after a visit to north Korea by the retired US President, Jimmy Carter, in June, 1994.

3 Kim Dae-jung, 'Is Culture Destiny? The Myth of Asia's Anti-Democratic Values' in *Foreign Affairs*, Nov./Dec. 1994, p. 194. This paper was a response to Lee Kuan Yew, the Singaporean leader, who is perhaps the most prominent advocate of an Asian form of democracy.

4 Simon Winchester, *Korea: A Walk Through the Land of Miracles* (London: Grafton Books, 1988).

5 Told to the author by Kim Zohng-chil, the tour organiser, and later vice-president of the Korea National Tourism Corporation.

6 After a visit to east Asia in 1911. Quoted in 'The Webbs and the Non-White: A Case of Socialist Racialism' by J.M. Winter in the *Journal of Contemporary History* vol. 9: 1, pp. 181–92.

7 James Kirkup, *Streets of Asia*, 1969, quoted in *The Travellers' Dictionary of Quotations*, ed. Peter Yapp (London: Routledge & Kegan Paul, 1983), p. 619.

8 Ibid.

9 James Cameron, *Point of Departure*, 1967, quoted in op. cit., *The Travellers' Dictionary*.

10 P.J. O'Rourke, 'Seoul Brothers', chapter in *Holidays in Hell* (Vintage Books, 1992). My attention was first brought to this article by two unhappy Korean soldiers in the library of the main American army base in Seoul, who asked, 'Do you think we have pizza faces?' They had been reading the piece, in which O'Rourke described Koreans as having 'pie plate faces' (meaning flat). He apologised for this slur after complaints by Asian-Americans.

11 Isabella Bird Bishop, *Korea and Her Neighbours* (first published 1898. Reprinted Seoul: Yonsei University Press, 1970), p. 27.

12 Ibid, preface.

13 Yonhap news agency, Seoul, in English, 9 June 1997.

14 I am grateful to Peter Bartholomew for this insight.

15 Sung-kyun-kwan is as old as Oxford and Cambridge. The oldest buildings date from the end of the fourteenth century. The wood is newer, from the middle of the seventeenth century.

16 *Korea Herald*, 10 July 1989. I am grateful to Ken Kaliher for providing this from his collection of news clippings.

17 *Korea Herald*, 27 May 1984. Also supplied by Ken Kaliher.

18 The word itself is not unique. The Korean character for *han* is shared by the Chinese, who pronounce it *hen*, and the Japanese, who pronounce it *urami*.

19 Personal email, 1 March 1998. Freda cited Chon I-du, *Han ui kujo yon'gu* (A study of the structure of han). (Seoul: Munhak kwa Pipyongsa, 1993.) I am also grateful to Moon Tahn Il, who participated in the newsgroup discussion on *han* from which Freda's quotation is derived.

20 John Gustaveson, my former business partner, first drew my attention to this unusual contradiction.

21 For a fuller analysis, see Hahm Pyong-choon, 'Shamanism and the Korean World-view', in *Shamanism: the Spirit World of Korea*, ed. Chai-shin Yu and Richard Guisso (Berkeley, California: Asian Humanities Press, 1988).

22 For this information I am grateful to Kim Won-pil, who met some of this group's members in north Korea in the 1940s. The group was the Pyongyang branch of the Holy Lord Church, a sect based in pre-war north Korea. The leader, Huh Ho-bin, and her members were arrested and jailed by communist authorities in 1946 and their fate thereafter is unknown.

23 This figure is from Lee Yo-han, a Unification Church minister who approached different groups in the 1950s and '60s in an effort to convert them. It is possible there were many more than Lee was aware of. He said that the messianic groups began to decline in the 1960s. Author's interview.

24 From a question-and-answer session with American followers during a US tour in March 1965, published by the Unified Family, Washington, DC, 1967. Ref. MS-1, p. 1.

25 Ref. Felix Moos, 'Leadership and Organisation in the Olive Tree Movement' in *Transactions, Royal Asiatic Society, Korea Branch, Vol XLIII* (Seoul: RAS, 1967).

26 Park's movement declined after his death.

27 Ref. Kang Dae-bong, *Ki: No Way?* (Seoul: Un-lip Publications, 1989).

28 See, for example, William Franklin Sands, *Undiplomatic Memories* (Seoul: Royal

Asiatic Society, 1975), p. 16. Sands was an American diplomat in Korea from 1896 to 1904.

29 Kim Jung-eun, personal email.

30 The market to foreign cigarettes was opened a few years after this incident. I am not sure whether MacArthur had a hand in it.

31 One ambitious former journalist told me in the 1980s that he had been advised by a fortune-teller to join the ruling party, although he was identified with the opposition. He took this advice and won an election.

32 Story told to me by the lawmaker Shin Kyong-shik, who accompanied the agent and had his own fortune read at the same time.

33 There are 275 surnames in Korea and 3349 clans. The more common names, such as Kim, Park and Lee, are grouped in numerous clans which are identified by the birthplace of the common ancestor. Hence the Kims from the town of Andong.

34 I am grateful to Mark Setton for some of these points. Personal email.

35 'Seoul man kills self over mom's remarriage', *Korea Herald*, 5 October 1985.

36 These points are taken from a talk on Korean culture Setton gave to a western business group in Seoul in 1994. Author's notes.

37 One study claimed that Korean soldiers conducted twelve massacres of a hundred or more civilians and dozens more of over twenty civilians as reprisals for attacks or mines, or simply as warnings. See Noam Chomsky and Edward S. Herman, *The Political Economy of Human Rights, Vol 1: The Washington Connection and Third World Fascism* (Boston: South End Press, 1979), pp. 321–2.

38 According to government figures, 183,142 Korean children were adopted between 1953 and 1993. Of these 72.1 per cent were by foreigners. These figures obviously do not include secret adoptions.

39 In the best of environments, a woman has roughly a 20 per cent chance of conceiving. With IVF, more than one egg is inserted to increase the chances of success. In Britain, the number is limited for medical reasons to three. On average, Korean clinics have a 25 per cent success rate.

40 Before the November 1997 currency crisis terms, this represented an annual income of £38,000 (but £20,000 by the end of the year).

41 *Korea Times*, 23 November 1997. Around 80 per cent of rape and molestation cases involved people known to the victim.

42 The *Daehak* was in Koguryo, the most northerly of the three states at the time on the peninsula. The *Kukhak* was in the Unified Shilla dynasty.

43 See Gregory Henderson, *Korea: The Politics of the Vortex* (Cambridge, Mass., Harvard University Press, 1968), p. 89.

44 Underwood's great-grandfather was the first Presbyterian missionary in Korea, and founded Yonsei University.

45 For example, all but one of the national daily newspapers use a combination of Korean script and Chinese characters. Many official government publications make predominant use of Chinese characters, which sends even educated Koreans to their dictionaries. North Korea uses only Korean script.

46 Typically, though, these controls are ignored and parents are willing to pay huge fees.

47 Chang Young-hee, essay 'A Mother's Dream' in *Crazy Quilt* (Seoul: Dongmoon Press, 1990), pp. 193–4. This book is a collection of her columns from the English-language daily *Korea Times*.

48 One American ambassador in Korea was fond of telling audiences that there were more Koreans with PhDs from American universities working in the Korean government than there were Americans in the vast American bureaucracy with similar degrees.

49 Ref. Lee Ki-baik, *A New History of Korea*.

50 I am grateful to Kim Ju-ho, editor of the *Ju-gan Jong-kyo Shinmun* (Weekly Religion) for this explanation.

51 Emperor Yao ruled in China.

52 Ref. *Sourcebook of Korean Civilization: Vol 1*, edited by Peter H. Lee (New York: Columbia University Press, 1993), pp. 6–7, which offers a translation of the myth from *Samguk yusa* (Memorabilia of the Three Kingdoms), I:33–34, written by the monk Iryon (1206–1289).

53 The *Kogi* (Old Record) and the *Wei shu*, by Pei Sung-chih (360–439). Dates uncertain. The Tan-gun legend is also depicted on the Wu family shrine built in 147 in Shantung, China, according to the *Sourcebook of Korean Civilization*, p. 5.

54 The more important dynastic ancestor at least for the ruling Yi clan at that time was Chi Tzu, a Chinese sage whom legend also credits with settling in Korea and calling the state 'Choson' in the twelfth century BC.

55 This began in 1909 with the founding of *Taejong-kyo*, a religion which worshipped Tan-gun, and was given shape by nationalist historians in the 1930s who also promoted the myth of Mount Paektu, on the Chinese-Korean border, as the birthplace of Tan-gun and all Koreans. I am grateful to Pai Hyung-il for these insights.

56 Even court documents were thus dated. I have a copy of a 1955 case in my files which is dated 'Tan-gun Era 4288'.

57 South Korean archaeologists believe this tomb, whomever it belongs to, dates to the later Koguryo period.

58 The full names and the official English version are: *Choson Minju-jui Inmin Gonghwa-guk* (Democratic People's Republic of Korea) for the North, and *Dae-*

han Min-guk (Republic of Korea) for the South. (The vowels in *Choson* are different. The second one is rendered in English as either versions of words as either 'o', 'eo' or 'u'.)

59 Koryo in the Chinese characters means 'high and beautiful' but is believed to be a short form of Koguryo, the name of an earlier dynasty. The English word Korea came from the Portuguese, Corea, the rendition of the Japanese pronunciation of Korai. Ref. James Scarth Gale, *History of the Korean People*, ed. Richard Rutt (Seoul: Royal Asiatic Society, Korea Branch, 1972), Rutt's notes p. 323.

60 I am grateful to Martina Deuchler for bringing this to my attention.

61 *Sourcebook of Korean Civilization*, p. 38.

62 *Haedong kosung chon* (Lives of Eminent Monks) by Kakhun, excerpt transl. in *Sourcebook of Korean Civilization*, pp. 75–8.

63 Ref. James Scarth Gale, *History of the Korean People*, pp. 158–9; *Sourcebook of Korean Civilization*, pp. 59–61, 109–13; and Richard Saccone, *Koreans to Remember* (Seoul: Hollym Corp., 1993), pp. 79–82.

64 Chong-wan became a Buddhist nun and Kim married his own niece.

65 *Sourcebook of Korea Civilization*, pp. 108–9.

66 Ref. Han Woo-keun, *The History of Korea* (Seoul: Eul-yoo Publishing Co. 1970), transl. Lee Kyung-shik, ed. Grafton K. Mintz, ch. 8.

67 Carter J. Eckert, Ki-baik Lee, et al., *Korea Old and New: A History* (Seoul: Ilchokak Publishers, 1990), p. 49.

68 The actual modern border of north Korea and China was established in the fifteenth century.

69 Carter J. Eckert, Ki-baik Lee, et al., *Korea Old and New*, p. 63.

70 *Koryo-sa*, 88:3a. Transl. in *Sourcebook of Korean Civilization*, p. 324.

71 King Sonjong (reigned 981–997). See *Sourcebook of Korean Civilization*, pp. 319–20.

72 The Koryo scriptures are one of twenty versions in East Asia.

73 Ha Tae-hung, *Behind the Scenes of Royal Palaces in Korea* (Seoul: Yonsei University Press, 1983), p. 10.

74 Mark Setton, *Chong Yagyong: Korea's Challenge to Orthodox Neo-Confucianism* (Albany: State University of New York Press, 1997), p. 19.

75 Ha Tae-hung, *Behind the Scenes of Royal Palaces in Korea*, p. 5.

76 The other options were Muak valley in the Shinchon area of modern Seoul and a site near Mt Kyeryong near the city of Taejon. Some construction began at the Mt Kyeryong location.

77 Neo-Confucianism was developed by the Chinese thinker Chu Hsi in the twelfth century.

78 This arrangement traces back to seventh-century China.

79 In the late nineteenth century, parents of children in Christian Sunday schools protested the teaching of western-style dancing because it reminded them of the butcher walk.

80 The children of *yangban* concubines were classed as *chung-in*.

81 For more on this, see 'Tigers in the Tree: Korean Family Lineage Records', a paper by Hildi Kang in *Transactions, Royal Asiatic Society, Korea Branch, Vol..66* (Seoul: RAS, 1991). Her Kang clan register was published in 1710 and updated in 1774, 1805, 1855, 1918 and 1979.

82 William Franklin Sands, *Undiplomatic Memories* (reprinted, Seoul: Royal Asiatic Society, 1975), p. 52–4.

83 Such an attitude in many ways lasted up until the 1960s. The conspicuous consumption of modern Koreans cannot simply be explained by economic factors. There has been a significant shift in thinking away from the ascetic Confucianism of the previous centuries.

84 *Book of Filial Piety (Hyo-kyong)* referred to in Wanne J. Joe, *Traditional Korea: A Cultural History* (Seoul: Chungang University Press, 1972), p. 305.

85 The monk, Moohak, also predicted the Yi family would rule for twenty-eight generations and 513 years, which was close. In all, twenty-seven kings ruled for 519 years.

86 The system was originally called *Chongum*, meaning 'correct sounds', and renamed *Hangul* ('great letters') in the twentieth century.

87 Ha Tae-hung, *Behind the Scenes of Royal Palaces in Korea*, p. 132.

88 Ibid., p. 145.

89 This was in 1762. This incident is recalled in great detail by the prince's widow in her memoirs, which provide a fascinating glimpse into the court in eighteenth-century Korea. See *The Memoirs of Lady Hyegyong*, transl. by JaHyun Kim Haboush (Berkeley: University of California Press, 1996).

90 Richard Saccone, *Koreans to Remember* (Seoul: Hollym Corp., 1993), pp. 92–5.

91 None of these vessels appears to have survived for any length of time. It has been suggested that possibly they weren't as seaworthy as the history books say.

92 For detail of this period, see *Hulbert's History of Korea Vol. II*, ed. Clarence Norwood Weems (New York: Hillary House Publishers Ltd, 1962). For the modern update, see *Korea Herald*, 18 November 1993.

93 This word is commonly written *gye* or *kye* in English. It rhymes with 'yeah'.

94 Wanne J. Joe, *Traditional Korea: A Cultural History*, p. 419.

95 This was how the upper classes saw foreigners. Ordinary folk were more likely to be awe-struck, then curious, and then friendly in encounters with foreigners.

96 William Franklin Sands meeting the governor of Hwanghae province some time between 1896 and 1904. Ref. *Undiplomatic Memories*, pp. 22–3.

97 The steamship was salvaged and copied. Two replicas were built but were unworkable.

98 Yi Kyu-tae, *Modern Transformation of Korea* (Seoul: Sejong Publishing Co., 1970), p. 258.

99 Carter J. Eckert, Ki-baik Lee, et al., *Korea Old and New*, p. 204.

100 Kabo was the name given to the year 1894.

101 Yi Kyu-tae, *Modern Transformation of Korea*, p. 28.

102 Ibid., p. 66.

103 Carter J. Eckert, Ki-baik Lee, et al., *Korea Old and New*, p. 240.

104 Ironically, an earlier rule forbade Koreans from taking Japanese names in a crackdown on conmen posing as influential Japanese.

105 Ref. Peter Bartholomew, 'Choson Dynasty Royal Compounds: Windows to a Lost Culture', in *Transactions: Royal Asiatic Society, Korea Branch Vol. 68* (Seoul: RAS, 1993).

106 This government building was finally demolished in the 1990s. The others remain to this day, although the Chosun Hotel has been modernised beyond recognition.

107 Arakawa Goto, a Diet member and newspaper editor. Quoted in Peter Duus, *The Abacus and the Sword: The Japanese Penetration of Korea 1895–1910* (Berkeley: University of California Press, 1995), pp. 397–8.

108 Ibid., p. 401. Quoting a writer named Okita Kinjo.

109 *Kyongsong Ilbo*, Sept. 20, 1916, quoted in Yi Kyu-tae, *Modern Transformation of Korea*, p. 131.

110 Carter J. Eckert, Ki-baik Lee, et al., *Korea Old and New*, p. 257, compares 1937 figures for bureaucrats in Korea (52,270 Japanese and 35,282 Koreans) with the similarly populated French colony of Vietnam (2920 French officials, 10,776 French troops, and 38,000 Vietnamese officials).

111 Yi Kyu-tae, *Modern Transformation of Korea*, p. 247.

112 These two were related by a man called Kwak No-pil, a Christian who the thought police suspected was a communist. He was released without charge after two months. His torturers were Korean policemen. Author's interview.

113 Told to me by Lee's grandson, Lee Dae-young. Lee Myong-nyong was one of the thirty-three signers of the 1919 declaration of Korean independence.

114 Yi Kyu-tae, *Modern Transformation of Korea*, p. 49.

115 Henry Appenzeller, the first Methodist missionary, in a letter 4 July 1890, quoted in Martha Huntley, *Caring, Growing, Changing: A History of the Protestant Mission in Korea* (New York: Friendship Press, 1984), p. 131.

116 This was the view of William Blair, a leading American Presbyterian missionary at the time. See *The Korean Pentecost* by William Blair and Bruce Hunt (Edinburgh: Banner of Truth Trust, year unknown), pp. 84–5.

117 This was one item in Wilson's famous fourteen-point declaration which outlined the American agenda for the Versailles Peace Conference.

118 Details taken from *The Korean Situation: Authentic Accounts of Recent Events by Eye Witnesses*, compiled in 1919 from mission reports by the Federal Council of the Churches of Christ in America.

119 Mrs Chun was still living in the village when I met her in 1985. She said her bitterness had evaporated a few years earlier after an emotional encounter with some young Japanese seminary students, who had visited her to apologise for the atrocity. The students later donated $12,000 to help build a new church in the village.

120 According to Korean figures. The Japanese government claimed 533 dead and 12,522 jailed.

121 Most 'white rice' went to Japan. Ordinary Koreans ate rice mixed with other grains.

122 America and Australia had anti-Japanese immigration policies.

123 'What the Japanese required after 1931 was active support and participation in their economic and military plans, not the indirect support of a portion of the elite and the grudging, sullen passivity of the Korean common man.' Carter J. Eckert, Ki-baik Lee, et al., *Korea Old and New*, p. 306.

124 See Bruce Cumings, *The Origins of the Korean War: Liberation and the Emergence of Separate Regimes 1945–47* (New Jersey: Princeton University Press, 1981), pp. 27–31.

125 This figure represented 16 per cent of the population.

126 This is the speculation in a 1994 report on the issue by the International Commission of Jurists, a United Nations group based in Geneva.

127 It took almost fifty years for this issue to come to light because of the reluctance of victims to come forward. In 1993, 121 former comfort women had registered in Korea for government benefits. In 1995, the Japanese government issued its first official apology. For detail, see *True Stories of the Korean Comfort Women*, ed. Keith Howard (London: Cassell Academic, 1996).

128 Richard E. Kim, *Lost Names: Scenes from a Korean Boyhood* (New York: Praeger, 1970), pp. 87–115.

129 For a very detailed analysis of this period between the end of the Second World War and the beginning of the Korean War, see Cumings, *The Origins of the Korean War*.

130 For example, in the 1980s, there was some flood aid from North to South, and, once, some separated family members and performing artists crossed both

ways during a brief thaw in relations. A little-known, but privileged, group of eight Czechoslovak, Polish, Swedish and Swiss officers from a permanent Neutral Nations body supervising the armistice were the only people permitted to go back and forth between Seoul and Pyongyang through Panmunjom.

131 A German ambassador to south Korea, talking to journalists in Seoul after Germany had reunified. Author's notes.

132 As an example of this fractiousness, with political freedom under the Americans in the South over fifty political parties were formed.

133 The following details are from: author's interview in 1988 with Moon Bong-jae, the youth group's president in 1948; other interviews on Cheju Island; and 'Internal Warfare in Korea, 1948–50: the Local Setting of the Korean War' by John Merrill in *Child of Conflict: the Korean-American Relationship 1943–1953*, ed. Bruce Cumings (Seattle: University of Washington Press, 1983) pp. 133–68.

134 As an indication of how paranoid people were, one refugee Protestant minister told me that his next-door neighbour almost reported him as a communist. The reason for suspicion was that the minister used to pray in church with his eyes open. The neighbour's wife managed to persuade the husband not to report him to the police. He learned this only after they became close friends.

135 See Cumings, *The Origins of the Korean War*, pp. 201–9.

136 Donald Stone Macdonald, *The Koreans: Contemporary Politics and Society* (Boulder, Colorado: Westview Press, 1996), p. 197.

137 Gen. Charles Helmick, cited in Mark L. Clifford, *Troubled Tiger: Businessmen, Bureaucrats and Generals in South Korea* (New York: M.E. Sharpe, 1994), p. 29.

138 A speech by then-Secretary of State Dean Acheson excluding south Korea from the US defence perimeter is believed to have been a factor in the North's decision to invade.

139 South Africa provided air units, and Denmark, India, Norway and Sweden provided medical units. Italy, not a UN member at the time, provided a hospital.

140 These details from Joseph C. Goulden, *Korea: the Untold Story of the War* (New York: Times Books, 1982), p. 231.

141 Gregory Henderson, *Korea: The Politics of the Vortex*, pp. 163–4.

142 Interviewed in south Korea, 1985.

143 Han had a copy of a US 8th army film which shows him at the site explaining in English to an American army chaplain what had happened. The film was discovered by a Korean TV researcher. Incredibly, one of the survivors had also survived the executions at sea the day before, after he'd concealed a razor in his mouth and cut the rope. He was Han's source for the information about the first effort to weigh bodies with rocks and dump them in the sea.

144 It is possible that some of these people went voluntarily, but their families may believe, or have found it wiser to assume, that they were unwilling.

145 Casualties from Macdonald, *The Koreans*, p. 52. Other figures from Lee Ki-baik, *A News History of Korea*, p. 380, and Andrew C. Nahm, *Korea: Tradition and Transformation* (Seoul: Hollym, 1988), pp. 481–2.

146 This was known as climbing the 'barley ridge'. The starvation came after the rice supplies ran out and before the winter barley crop ripened.

147 Macdonald puts the figure at $1.6 billion for three years after the war. Total US aid to Korea from 1953 to the mid-1970s, when it ended, was $6 billion. Military assistance was said to be valued at $7 billion. Ref. Macdonald, *The Koreans*, p. 198.

148 Macdonald, *The Koreans*, p. 199.

149 Song Byong-nak, *The Rise of the Korean Economy* (Hong Kong: Oxford University Press, 1990), p. 80.

150 A clause in the ruling Workers' Party constitution calls for the communisation by whatever means of south Korea. For this reason, south Korean governments have tended to reach for their guns when north Korea mentions the word 'peace'.

151 Four known assassination attempts: a commando raid on the Blue House in 1968; a bomb at the National Cemetery in 1970 detonated as it was being planted, the day before Park Chung-hee was due to visit; an assassin in 1974 missed Park, but killed his wife; a bomb in Rangoon in 1983 missed president Chun Doo-hwan, but killed seventeen others. An intelligence official said there was an earlier, unpublicised attempt against Chun, but the author was unable to confirm this claim. It is not known if south Korea made attempts on Kim Il-sung. When asked about the known incidents, a north Korean told me that the 1968 attack was revenge against the alleged murder by Park of a go-between sent by north Korea to propose talks, and that the 1983 attack was revenge for some undisclosed incident in north Korea which authorities blamed on the South.

152 The Japanese government has a list of ten people it believes were kidnapped by north Koreans.

153 This story told by the man's brother-in-law, a Korean-American who went to north Korea on a family reunion visit in 1991.

154 See Chapter 18.

155 This was in response to a question about whether north Korea would open its economy as China had done. Lunch meeting, April 1994. Author's notes.

156 This change was also generational. The post-Korean war generation in north Korea is less passionate about the 'Great Leader'. I am grateful to several Russian correspondents formerly based in Pyongyang for this observation.

157 Apocryphal, because, although it was a story that circulated at the time, I could not confirm the quotes.

158 Clifford, *Troubled Tiger*, p. 29.

159 These are Bank of Korea figures.

160 These details are from Michael Keon, *Korean Phoenix: A Nation from the Ashes* (New Jersey: Prentice Hall International, 1977).

161 These practices were not unusual for poor families, according to Cho Gab-je, author of *Nae mudum-e chimul baetora* (Spit on My Grave), a biography of Park serialised in the *Chosun Ilbo* newspaper 1997–8.

162 Manchukuo was the name of the state the Japanese militarists created in Manchuria. The figurehead emperor Pu Yi awarded Park a gold watch at the graduation.

163 Clifford, *Troubled Tiger*, pp. 35–7.

164 Alice H. Amsden, *Asia's Next Giant: South Korea and Late Industrialization* (Oxford University Press, 1989), p. 72.

165 The American CIA figured that the North was ahead of the South until the mid-1970s.

166 Lee was the foreign minister and one of seventeen people in Chun Doo-hwan's entourage killed in Rangoon, Burma, in 1983, when a bomb was set off by north Korean commandos.

167 Kim Jae-ik, who was also killed in the bomb blast in Rangoon in 1983, and Kim Ki-hwan, a former professor at the University of California at Berkeley.

168 Pyongyang blew up a south Korean airliner in 1987 on the eve of the meeting at which its allies were making this decision in what appears to have been an effort to create a pretext of poor security for an east bloc boycott.

169 Recalled in private email to me by Larry Moffitt, then executive director of the World Media Association, based in Washington, DC, which had organised the trip.

170 In Japan, the *zaibatsu* were broken up by the Americans immediately after the war. They regrouped in what are known as *keiretsu*, a looser association of companies with business relations.

171 These failures included the company owned by Lee Hak-su, a businessman who financed Park's coup.

172 Chung lost, and the winner, Kim Young-sam, removed similar ideas of grandeur from other businessmen by prosecuting the septuagenarian on charges of violating election funding rules. The Hyundai man was given a three-year sentence, suspended out of consideration for his age.

173 Francis Fukuyama, *Trust: the Social Virtues and the Creation of Prosperity* (London: Penguin Books, 1996).

174 Ibid., pp. 127–8.

175 Ref. *Business Groups in Korea: Characteristics and Government Policy*, by Lee Kyu-uck and Lee Jae-hyung, Korea Institute for Industrial Economics and Trade, November, 1996.

176 These examples are from Amsden, *Asia's Next Giant*, p. 73.

177 Actually, a bank will cash a promissory note early, at a discount.

178 For a detailed account of Chung's story, see Donald Kirk, *Korean Dynasty: Hyundai and Chung Ju Yung* (New York: M.E. Sharpe, 1994).

179 The British pronunciation of 'Hey-yoon-die' may draw blank stares in Korea, where it is 'hyondeh'. The word means 'modern'.

180 Clifford, *Troubled Tiger*, p. 116.

181 Ref. 'High Priest of Steel' chapter in Clifford, *Troubled Tiger*, pp. 67–75.

182 Kim Woo-choong, *Every Street Is Paved with Gold* (New York: William Morrow and Company, Inc., 1992), p. 62.

183 Ref. Clifford, *Troubled Tiger*, pp. 118–9.

184 A north Korean source revealed that in a 1993 visit, Kim had emptied his plate almost before the 'Great Leader' Kim Il-sung had started. Later in the meal, the Daewoo chairman got into an argument with Kim Il-sung's son, Jong-il, the source said.

185 According to a former Daewoo executive who accompanied Kim on the trip.

186 The details of this case were shared on condition that the companies in question not be identified.

187 A study of eight industries by the management consultancy McKinsey & Co. found Korean firms on average to be 51 per cent as productive as American companies. Cited in the *Far Eastern Economic Review*, 30 April 1998, p. 13.

188 Details from author's interview, and from James Harting, 'Selling Coca-Cola in Korea', a presentation given to the marketing committee of the American Chamber of Commerce in Seoul, December 1997.

189 'Web site', *The Economist*, 13 December 1997.

190 'Daily News Analysis March 2, 1998', SsangYong Investment & Securities (http://www.ssyisc.co.kr/english/research/980302/980302.htm).

191 The following explanation was given with a request that the company not be identified.

192 'Lessons Unlearnt', *The Economist*, 21 December 1996, pp. 105–6.

193 IMF figures as of 20 December 1997, quoted in *VIP Economic Report*, February, 1998, published by the Hyundai Research Institute.

194 In December 1997, 1226 small and medium companies went bankrupt.

195 'Daily News Analysis March 2, 1998', SsangYong Investment & Securities (http://www.ssyisc.co.kr/english/research/980302/980302.htm).

196 These details from author's interviews, and from William Rylance, 'Perspectives on Amway Korea's Soap Opera', *The Journal*, American Chamber of Commerce in Seoul, Nov./Dec., 1997, pp. 49–54.

197 See Chapter 11.

198 *Korea Herald*, 30 July 1993.

199 *Korea Herald*, 17 August 1994.

200 Government figures quoted in *Korea Herald*, 21 July 1995.

201 Ibid.

202 Government figures quoted in Clifford, *Troubled Tiger* p. 276.

203 The proportion of Koreans living in towns of over 50,000, from 1960 to 1987, changed from 28.5 per cent to 68.7 per cent, according to government figures quoted in Song, *The Rise of the Korean Economy*, p. 69.

204 For an in-depth description of this life, see Victor Brandt, *A Korean Village: Between Farm and Sea* (Cambridge, Mass.: Harvard University Press, 1971). Brandt lived for a year in his wife's home village as part of his research.

205 Author's interview with *FT* correspondent John Burton.

206 The South Koreans had proposed co-hosting with Pyongyang, but reluctantly. They had to be persuaded by US officials. North Korea rejected the idea when it was clear that Pyongyang would not get equal billing with Seoul.

207 This reckoning is based on Korean government statistics cited in *Korea Times*, 8 January 1996.

208 Calculated from National Police Administration statistics for 1996.

209 Robert T. Oliver, *The Truth about Korea* (London: Unwin Brothers Limited, 1951), p. 131. Oliver was an adviser to Rhee.

210 Oliver, *The Truth about Korea*, p. 133.

211 Ref. Richard C. Allen, *Korea's Syngman Rhee: An Unauthorised Portrait* (Rutland, Vermont: Charles E. Tuttle Co., 1960), p. 40 ff.

212 Sungjoo Han, *The Failure of Democracy in South Korea* (Berkeley: University of California Press, 1974), p. 178.

213 For example, through the 1960s, fifty-five of 125 ministerial posts went to people with a military background. Only five went to civilian politicians. These figures compare with eleven military and fifty-eight civilian politicians out of the 138 ministers under Rhee. Ref. Yang Sung-chul, *The North and South Korean Political Systems: A Comparative Analysis* (Boulder, Col: Westview Press, 1994).

214 One bureaucrat in the budget office at the time said that, under Chang Myon, his office spent most of its time coaching ministers and other officials how to deal with endless questioning by assemblymen.

215 Park Chung-hee, *Our Nation's Path* (Seoul: Hollym Corporation, 1970), p. 199.

216 These details from Robert Boettcher, *Gifts of Deceit* (New York: Holt, Rinehart and Winston, 1980) pp. 78–98.

217 For more on this episode, see Boettcher, *Gifts of Deceit.*

218 A senior figure in Kim Dae-jung's campaign team said that they countered ruling party gift-giving with crafty tricks. They went knocking on doors pretending to be from the ruling party and gave small gifts to voters. Later, others would come round officially from the Kim campaign and give more expensive gifts.

219 Ref. Kim Byong-kuk, *Kim Dae-jung* (Seoul: Ilweolseogak Publishing Co., 1992), pp. 89–97.

220 Kim Dae-jung was alluded to as a 'person out of office' in the media.

221 These details are from Cheon Kum-sang, *Chun Doo-hwan: Man of Destiny*, translated by W.Y. Joh (Los Angeles: North American Press, 1982).

222 'Baby Chun' was appointed head of the Saemaul Movement by Chun Doo-hwan. He later served several years in jail for corruption.

223 Cheon Kum-sang, *Chun Doo-hwan: Man of Destiny*, p. 77.

224 Ibid., p. 82. Apparently, this was a phrase that Park picked up from Chun.

225 The following details are from 'Yun Sang-won: the Knowledge in Those Eyes', a moving tribute to the militants' courage by American reporter Bradley Martin, in *Kwangju in the Eyes of the World*, a collection of reports written by foreign correspondents published by the Journalists' Association of Korea in 1997.

226 Ibid., pp. 70–1.

227 Ibid., pp. 92–3.

228 See Richard Holbrooke and Michael Armacost, 'A Future Leader's Moment of Truth', *The New York Times*, 24 December 1997. Holbrooke and Armacost were the US Department of State officials instrumental in saving Kim's life.

229 National Ethics classes are now optional at several universities where they have been turned into Peace Studies or Women's Issues.

230 Quoted from a government publication by Park Won-soon in *The National Security Law: Instrument of Political Repression in South Korea*, p. 33. This is a booklet published in Los Angeles, 1993, by Korea NGOs' Network for World Conference on Human Rights, et. al. The above examples of NSL arrests are also from this booklet.

231 These details from 'Republic of Korea: Summary of concerns on torture and ill-treatment', Amnesty International, October 1996, pp. 5–6.

232 Kim was capitalising on the feeling of many Koreans that Roh Tae-woo was not a democratic president, even though he had been democratically elected in 1987, because he had been one of the military coup makers in 1979.

233 The older man was Kwon Yang-sup, 78, a cab driver and former member of the communist South Korean Labour Party (SKLP). He had been in prison since 1972.

234 Details about long-term prisoners are from my interviews 1991–5 in south Korea with Lee Jong-hwan, Kim Sun-myung, Wang Yong-an, Suh Joon-sik, Li In-mo, Kwon Oh-hun, and human-rights officials. In north Korea, interviews with Li In-mo's wife, Kim Sun-im, and in 1994, after Li had been permitted to return to north Korea, with both together.

235 Ref. Chapter on Korea in *Amnesty International Report*, 1997.

236 About £900 at the time.

237 Called *nae-geun su-dang* (desk-job allowance). As one example, an assistant editor on one national daily in 1990 told me his allowance was 140,000 Won a month.

238 Ref. *Korea Herald*, 25 October 1994.

239 A rebuilt Songsu Bridge was opened in July 1997.

240 For more on this period, see Robert R. Simmons, *The Strained Alliance: Peking, Pyongyang, Moscow, and the Politics of the Korean War* (New York: Free Press, 1975).

241 These details are from one of the analysts at the meeting.

242 I am grateful to Aidan Foster-Carter for this point.

243 The details in this paragraph are from Benjamin Fulford, 'Korea's Weird Wired World,' *Forbes*, July 21, 2003.

244 Author interview.

Selected Bibliography

Adams, Edward B. *Korea Guide: A Glimpse of Korea's Cultural Legacy*. Seoul: Seoul International Publishing House, 1976, revised 1995.

Allen, Richard C. *Korea's Syngman Rhee: An Unauthorised Portrait*. Rutland, Vermont: Charles E. Tuttle Co., 1960.

Amnesty International. *Amnesty International Report, 1997*. London, 1997.

Amsden, Alice H. *Asia's Next Giant: South Korea and Late Industrialization*. New York and Oxford: Oxford University Press, 1989.

Bishop, Isabella Bird. *Korea and Her Neighbours*. First published 1898. Reprinted Seoul: Yonsei University Press, 1970.

Blair, William Newton. *Gold in Korea*. Topeka, Kansas: Ives & Sons, 1957. (Recollections of one of the first Protestant missionaries to Korea.)

Boettcher, Robert, with Freedman, Gordon L. *Gifts of Deceit*. New York: Holt, Rinehart and Winston, 1980.

Brady, James. *The Coldest War*. New York: Orion Books, 1990.

Brandt, Victor. *A Korean Village: Between Farm and Sea*. Cambridge, Mass.: Harvard University Press, 1971.

Chang, Young-hee. *Crazy Quilt*. Seoul: Dongmoon Press, 1990. (A collection of essays by a newspaper columnist.)

Cheon, Kum-sang, *Chun Doo-hwan: Man of Destiny*. Translated by Joh, W.Y. Los Angeles: North American Press, 1982.

Cho, Lee-jay and Kim, Yoon-Hyung (editors). *Economic Systems in South and North Korea*. Seoul: Korea Development Institute, 1995.

Cho, Lee-jay and Kim, Yoon-Hyung (editors). *Economic Development in the Republic of Korea: A Policy Perspective*. Honolulu: East-West Center, 1991.

Clark, Allen D. *A History of the Church in Korea*. Seoul: Christian Literature Society of Korea, 1971.

Clark, Donald N. (editor). *Korea Briefing, 1991*. Boulder, Colorado: Westview Press, 1992.

Clifford, Mark L. *Troubled Tiger: Businessmen, Bureaucrats and Generals in South Korea*. New York: M.E. Sharpe, 1994.

Covell, Jon Carter. *Korea's Cultural Roots*. Seoul: Hollym Corp., 1981.

Crane, Paul S. *Korean Patterns*. Seoul: Royal Asiatic Society, 1967.

Cumings, Bruce. *The Origins of the Korean War: Liberation and the Emergence of Separate Regimes, 1945–47*. New Jersey: Princeton University Press, 1981.

Cumings, Bruce (editor). *Child of Conflict: The Korean-American Relationship, 1943–1953*. Seattle: University of Washington Press, 1983.

Cumings, Bruce. *Korea's Place in the Sun: A Modern History*. New York: W.W. Norton & Co. Inc., 1997.

De Mente, Boyd. *Korean Etiquette & Ethics in Business*. London: Merehurst Press, 1988.

Deuchler, Martina. *The Confucian Transformation of Korea*. Cambridge, Mass.: Harvard University Press, 1992.

Duus, Peter. *The Abacus and the Sword: The Japanese Penetration of Korea 1895–1910*. Berkeley: University of California Press, 1995.

Eckert, Carter J. and Lee, Ki-baik, et. al. *Korea Old and New: A History*. Seoul: Ilchokak Publishers, 1990.

Fehrenbach, T. R. *This Kind of War: A Study in Unpreparedness*. New York: The Macmillan Company, 1963.

Gale, James Scarth. *History of the Korean People*. Edited by Richard Rutt, Seoul: Royal Asiatic Society, 1972.

Goulden, Joseph C. *Korea: The Untold Story of the War*. New York: Times Books, 1982.

Ha, Tae-hung. *Behind the Scenes of Royal Palaces in Korea*. Seoul: Yonsei University Press, 1983.

Halliday, Jon, and Cumings, Bruce. *Korea: The Unknown War*. New York: Pantheon, 1988.

Han, Sungjoo. *The Failure of Democracy in South Korea*. Berkeley: University of California Press, 1974.

Han, Woo-keun. *The History of Korea*. Seoul: Eul-yoo Publishing Co., 1970.

Hasting, Max. *The Korean War*. London: Simon & Schuster, Inc., 1987.

Henderson, Gregory. *Korea: The Politics of the Vortex*. Cambridge, Mass.: Harvard University Press, 1968.

Holles, Robert O. *Now Thrive the Armourers: A Story of Action with the Gloucesters in Korea, November 1950–April 1951*. London: George G. Harrap & Co. Ltd, 1952.

Howard, Keith (editor). *True Stories of the Korean Comfort Women*. London: Cassell Academic, 1996.

Huntley, Martha. *Caring, Growing, Changing: A History of the Protestant Mission in Korea*. New York: Friendship Press, 1984.

Hyegyong. *The Memoirs of Lady Hyegyong*. Translated by JaHyun Kim Haboush Berkeley: University of California Press, 1996.

Janelli, Roger L. with Yim, Dawnhee. *Making Capitalism: The Social and Cultural Construction of a South Korean Conglomerate*. Stanford: Stanford University Press, 1993.

Joe, Wanne J. *Traditional Korea: A Cultural History*. Seoul: Chungang University Press, 1972.

Journalists' Association of Korea, et. al. *Kwangju in the Eyes of the World*. Seoul, 1997. (A collection of reports written by foreign correspondents.)

Keon, Michael. *Korean Phoenix: A Nation from the Ashes*. New Jersey: Prentice Hall International, 1977.

Kim, Byong-kuk. *Kim Dae-jung*. Seoul: Ilweolseogak Publishing Co., 1992.

Kim, Chang-ha. *The Immortal Juche Idea*. Pyongyang: Foreign Languages Publishing House, 1984.

Kim, Dae-jung. *Mass Participatory Economy*. Lanham, Maryland: Center for International Affairs, Harvard University, 1985.

Kim, Dae-jung. *Prison Writings*. Berkeley: University of California Press, 1987.

Kim, Hyun-hee. *The Tears of My Soul*. New York: William Morrow and Company, Inc., 1993. (Written by a north Korean terrorist.)

Kim, Il-sung. *With the Century* (5 volumes). Foreign Languages Publishing House, 1992–4. (Autobiographical work in English.)

Kim, Joungwon Alexander. *Divided Korea: The Politics of Development, 1945–1972*. Cambridge, Mass.: East Asian Research Center, Harvard University, 1976.

Kim, Richard E. *Lost Names: Scenes from a Korean Boyhood*. New York: Praeger, 1970. (Also, Seoul: Sisayongosa, 1970. Reprinted, New York: Universe Books, 1988; Berkeley: University of California Press, 1998.)

Kim, Woo-choong. *Every Street Is Paved with Gold*. New York: William Morrow and Company, Inc., 1992.

Kirk, Donald. *Korean Dynasty: Hyundai and Chung Ju Yung*. New York: M.E. Sharpe, 1994.

Lee, Ki-baik. *A New History of Korea*. Translated by Edward W. Wagner, Cambridge, Mass: Harvard University Press, 1984.

Lee, Peter H. (editor). *Sourcebook of Korean Civilization* (2 volumes). New York: Columbia University Press, 1993–96.

Macdonald, Donald Stone. *The Koreans: Contemporary Politics and Society.*. Boulder, Colorado: Westview Press, 1988. Third edition, 1996.

Merrill, John. *Korea: The Peninsular Origins of the War*. London: Associated University Presses, 1989.

Nahm, Andrew C. *Korea: Tradition and Transformation*. Seoul: Hollym Corp., 1988.

Nam, Hong-chin. *A Life Story of President Kim Young-sam*. Translated by Lee Sung-kyu, Seoul: Bansok, 1993.

276

Noble, Harold Joyce. *Embassy at War*. Seattle: University of Washington Press, 1975.

Oberdorfer, Don. *The Two Koreas: A Contemporary History*. Reading, Mass.: Addison-Wesley, 1997.

Ogle, George E. *South Korea: Dissent Within the Economic Miracle*. London: Zed Books, 1990.

Oliver, Robert T. *The Truth about Korea*. London: Unwin Brothers, 1951.

Paik, George L. *The History of Protestant Missions in Korea, 1832–1910*. Seoul: Yonsei University Press, 1971.

Paik, Sun-yup. *From Pusan to Panmunjom*. Washington, DC: Brassey's (US) Inc., 1992.

Palais, James B. *Politics and Policy in Traditional Korea*. Cambridge, Mass.: Harvard University Press, 1975.

Palmer, Spencer J. *Confucian Rituals in Korea*. Berkeley: Asian Humanities Press, year of publication unknown.

Pang, Hwan-ju. *Korean Review*. Pyongyang: Foreign Languages Publishing House, 1987. (Handbook on north Korea.)

Park, Chung-hee. *The Country, the Revolution and I*. Seoul: Hollym Corp., 1963.

Park, Chung-hee. *Our Nation's Path*. Seoul: Hollym Corp., 1970.

Park, Won-soon. *The National Security Law: Instrument of Political Suppression in South Korea*. Los Angeles: Korea NGOs' Network for the UN World Conference on Human Rights, et al., 1993.

Ridgway, Matthew. *The Korean War*. New York: Da Capo Press, 1967.

Saccone, Richard. *Koreans to Remember*. Seoul: Hollym Corp., 1993.

Sakong, Il. *Korea in the World Economy*. Washington, DC: Institute for International Economics, 1993.

Sands, William Franklin. *Undiplomatic Memories*. Seoul: Royal Asiatic Society, 1975.

Setton, Mark. *Chong Yagyong: Korea's Challenge to Orthodox Neo-Confucianism*. Albany: State University of New York Press, 1997.

Simmons, Robert R. *The Strained Alliance: Peking, Pyongyang, Moscow, and the Politics of the Korean War*. New York: Free Press, 1975.

Song, Byong-nak. *The Rise of the Korean Economy*. Hong Kong: Oxford University Press, 1990.

Tak, Jin, Kim, Gang-il and Pak, Hong-je. *Great Leader Kim Jong Il* (2 volumes). Tokyo: Sorinsha, 1985–6.

Thompson, Reginald. *Cry Korea*. London: MacDonald & Co., 1951.

Underwood, Lilias H. *Fifteen Years Among the Top-Knots*. First published 1904. Reprinted, Seoul: Royal Asiatic Society, 1977.

Weems, Clarence Norwood (editor). *Hulbert's History of Korea*. New York: Hillary House Publishers Ltd, 1962.

Winchester, Simon. *Korea: A Walk Through the Land of Miracles*. London: Grafton Books, 1988.

Yang, Sung-chul. *The North and South Korean Political Systems: A Comparative Analysis.* Boulder, Col: Westview Press, 1994.

Yi, Kyu-tae. *Modern Transformation of Korea.* Seoul: Sejong Publishing Co., 1970.

Yu, Chai-shin and Guisso, Richard (editors). *Shamanism: the Spirit World of Korea.* Berkeley: Asian Humanities Press, 1988.

Index